THE
WORLD
IN THE
TWENTIETH
CENTURY

THE
WORLD
IN THE
TWENTIETH
CENTURY

JEREMY BLACK

An imprint of **Pearson Education**

London • New York • Toronto • Sydney • Tokyo • Singapore • Hong Kong • Cape Town
New Delhi • Madrid • Paris • Amsterdam • Munich • Milan • Stockholm

PEARSON EDUCATION LIMITED

Head Office:
Edinburgh Gate
Harlow CM20 2JE
Tel: +44(0)1279 623623
Fax: +44(0)1279 431059

London Office:
128 Long Acre
London WC2E 9AN
Tel: +44(0)20 7447 2000
Fax: +44(0)20 7240 5771
Website: www.history-minds.com

First published in Great Britain in 2002
© Pearson Education, 2002

The right of Jeremy Black to be identified as Author of this Work has been asserted by him in accordance with the Copyright, Designs and Patents Act 1988.

ISBN 0 582 47284 9

British Library Cataloguing in Publication Data
A CIP catalogue record for this book can be obtained from the British Library

Library of Congress Cataloguing in Publication Data
A CIP catalogue record for this book can be obtained from the Library of Congress

10 9 8 7 6 5 4 3 2 1

Cover and text design by Lisa Glomberg
Picture research by Debbie Hughes
Set in 9/14 ITC Stone Serif Medium
Typeset by Fakenham Photosetting Limited, Fakenham, Norfolk
Printed and bound by Bookcraft, Midsomer Norton, Wiltshire, UK

The Publishers' policy is to use paper manufactured from sustainable forests

for
NICK AND SARA SMART

CONTENTS

PREFACE

Although this book was written in 2001, its genesis was longer, and therefore the debts I must acknowledge are many and varied. The big idea behind this book is to provide a clear, thematic account of the twentieth century from the perspective of the twenty-first, not a reprinted and slightly changed view from, say, 1985 or 1990. This book will be for people who want to know how today has arrived. They will not be wanting dry scholarship, or a slow narrative that separates the last 100 years into segments, many of which are far distant from today. Instead, the 1910s or 1920s are of interest to today's readers for how they relate to today. So, one key word is 'relevance'.

The second is 'global'. All too often, histories of the modern world focus on a world centred on Europe and North America. This can be seen not only in the coverage but also in the categorization and classification of developments. This book will be global in two ways: first, it will give due weight to other parts of the world, not least Africa, Latin America, Oceania and South Asia; and, secondly, it will focus on the relations between parts of the world and show how they provide much of the dynamic of the history of the modern world.

THEME

The book is not only thematic in approach, but also makes a determined attempt to avoid a political 'spine'. This can be seen with the space devoted to politics and also with its placing: at the end. Instead, pride of place and space are devoted to the human impact on the environment and its consequences. This is not some faddish product of early twenty-first-century environmentalism, but the consequence of the extent to which these issues are of central importance in the history of the last century, as will appear even clearer in the future.

Noteworthy features of the book include the emphasis on the role and resilience of religion, and the determination to give due weight to the Third World in the discussion of the very varied nature of political systems and developments across the century. There is also a full discussion of how economic shifts affected all the regions of the world, not least because these serve as an introduction to political pressures and developments.

The book records a series of major transformations. In 1900, when most of the world was under the direct control of Western powers, there was a powerful international system of free trade dominated by the leading imperial and commercial power, Britain. By the end of the century, this system had been re-created by Britain's successor, the USA. However, in place of a small number of Western and Westernized (Japan) states, the fall of the Western colonial empires, and later of the Soviet Union, was responsible for a world divided between a large number of independent states. This large number helped make it difficult to devise workable systems for international co-operation, although there were also important differences over the nature of any such co-operation.

In the meantime, free-trade capitalism, and the political values that accompanied it, had been challenged from the 1910s, and, more particularly, the late 1940s, by socialist systems that sought to introduce community ownership and state planning, because they were allegedly fairer and more efficient. Free-trade capitalism had also been challenged, especially in the 1930s, by authoritarian regimes that sought state control and autarky (national self-sufficiency) but without socialist rhetoric and policies, most prominently Nazi Germany.

Part of the history of the century is that of the failure of these attempts. It is as much a matter of economics as of politics and ideology, and this helps to link chapters 5 and 7, which are intended as mutually supporting. Such links between developments can, however, be found throughout the book. For example, disillusionment with centralized planning and big government towards the close of the century combined with widespread consumerism and democratization, to make it increasingly difficult to envisage winning mass popular support for ecologically motivated limitations on economic growth.

PURPOSES

Writing this book in the space allotted necessarily involves choices of what to include. There is no point pretending some Olympian detachment or Delphic omniscience.

These choices are personal. They reflect my views as a historian faced with the difficult tasks of trying to cover such a vast subject and of writing about a world that both
writer and reader have experienced in person. I hope my decisions on what to include
and how best to cover it prove as stimulating for the readers as they have done for the
writer, and that they can be seen as individual (as all history is), but not eccentric.

It is important for the reader to be aware that what is here, how it is treated and organized, and what is omitted reflect a process of choice. The past is viewed very differently
by commentators, and these differences should lead us to more searching questions
about what is being discussed and about the process of writing history. This is most
apparent and valuable when discussing the recent past. Reading any work of history
that deals with this period necessarily throws light on both subject and process.
Readers should consider how *they* would organize the book and approach writing
about the twentieth century as an active part of considering the period. This point is
stressed because this book is written in my conviction that a 'trade' book should not
talk down to the readers or treat them as a passive body that is there to be entertained.
I work on the basis that my readers are intelligent people like me who may not have
had the time to study the period, but who can be introduced to difficult topics, rather
than being restricted to the comforting pattern of a conventional approach and narrative. This is a challenging book, but history is no fairy story; or, looked at differently,
this book is high in protein, not fat or carbohydrate.

CHANGE

All periods of history centre on the interplay of change and continuity, an interest
that is sometimes dramatic but always as insistent as the rhythm of the seasons and
the course of generations. The last has been the century that, *so far*, has involved the
most striking changes and the greatest pressure of change. It is the modern age. This
process of change is the major theme of the book, and the book is written in thematic
chapters so that the separate narratives and patterns of change can best be considered.

The broadening of range that it is necessary to address when discussing the twentieth
century is at once part of the history covered in this book, as well as part of its method.
For example, during the century, it became less convincing to discuss social structure
in terms solely of class- or occupation-based criteria. Instead, it became increasingly
clear that issues of gender and ethnicity play a central role in social structure and,
furthermore, that they could not be discussed simply as adjuncts to class-based
analysis.

MODERNITY

'Modern' is a term that is worth considering. It is necessarily both subjective and transitory, and its application is obviously open to debate. This writer can recall the distinguished medievalist Walter Ullmann declare in a lecture in 1976 that Britain was still in the Middle Ages because the sovereign (Elizabeth II, Queen 1952–) was a hereditary monarch. Most commentators would have a less rigid view, but what is modern, and where do modern times start? With the creation of a global economy in the sixteenth century, or the cult of progress in the eighteenth-century Enlightenment, or the Industrial Revolution, which may itself be variously dated or defined? At the global level, none was as important as the creation in the twentieth century of an overwhelmingly urban and industrial society. This was the century that saw the major transformations in theoretical and applied science and technology in most fields, whether transport, the generation and distribution of power, medicine, contraception or agricultural yields.

It is difficult to define modernity, as what is modern to one generation generally (although not always) dates rapidly. The term 'modernity' tends to assume a process of modernization – becoming modern – and makes that the central theme and organiz-ing principle of study. This does violence to the variety of the past and the complexity of the processes of change. Furthermore, it can be misleading, as such an approach is inherently teleological (inevitably leading towards the present) and present-minded.

Instead, the question of how to define the modern can be approached in a different way. Modernity can be understood as a period of experience, that which is contem-poraneous with those who are alive, and, in addition, that which immediately pre-cedes this period and actively shaped it. This is the working definition adopted here. By focusing on a period of time – the twentieth century – it avoids the problem of adopting a thematic definition – of modern, modernity and modernization – that might in fact be partial, not to say partisan. Indeed, the political, economic, social and cultural history of the world in the twentieth century indicates that very different definitions of modern have been offered, and also shows the extent to which change has not been welcome to all.

This book will work if it makes you think – think not only about what is written here, but also about what you have experienced, and the world around you. If you disagree, think why. Look around and consider the significance of the changes you see. The historian is not a magician able to unlock the past, but a guide who stimulates you to see with your own eyes.

* * *

I would like to thank Kristofer Allerfeldt, Steven Fischer, Bill Gibson, Warwick Lightfoot and Nick Smart for their comments on all or part of an earlier draft. Heather MacCallum has proved an exemplary commissioning editor and Justin Dyer a first-rate copy editor. I have benefited from the opportunity to develop some of the arguments advanced in the book by invitations to give lectures to the University of Oxford Department of Continuing Education and as a Mellon Visiting Professor at Stillman College. It is a great pleasure to dedicate this book to two good friends and fellow scholars.

ILLUSTRATIONS

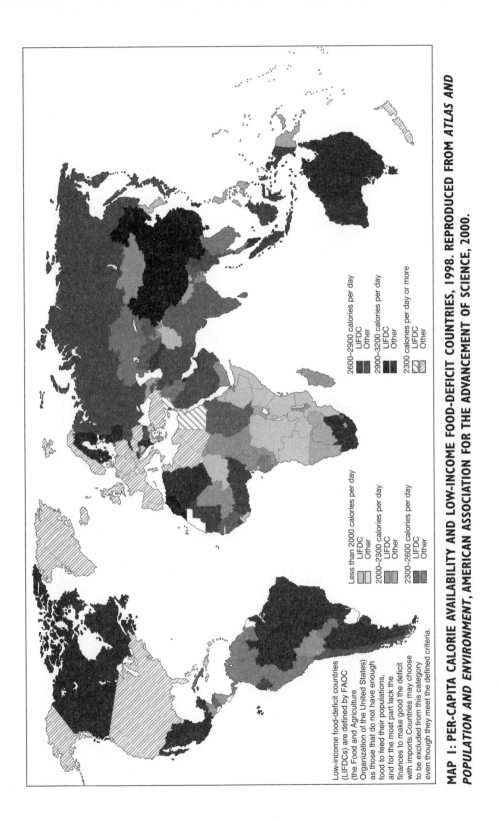

Low-income food-deficit countries
(LIFDCs) are defined by FAOC
(the Food and Agriculture
Organization of the United States)
as those that do not have enough
food to feed their populations,
and for the most part lack the
finances to make good the deficit
with imports. Countries may choose
to be excluded from this category
even though they meet the defined criteria.

Less than 2000 calories per day
LIFDC
Other

2000–2300 calories per day
LIFDC
Other

2300–2600 calories per day
LIFDC
Other

2600–2900 calories per day
LIFDC
Other

2900–3200 calories per day
LIFDC
Other

3300 calories per day or more
LIFDC
Other

MAP 1: PER-CAPITA CALORIE AVAILABILITY AND LOW-INCOME FOOD-DEFICIT COUNTRIES, 1998. REPRODUCED FROM *ATLAS AND POPULATION AND ENVIRONMENT*, AMERICAN ASSOCIATION FOR THE ADVANCEMENT OF SCIENCE, 2000.

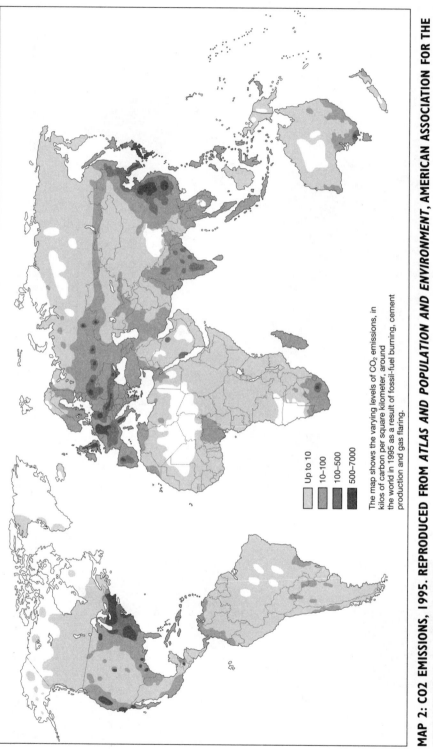

The map shows the varying levels of CO_2 emissions, in kilos of carbon per square kilometer, around the world in 1995 as a result of fossil-fuel burning, cement production and gas flaring.

Up to 10
10–100
100–500
500–7000

MAP 2: CO2 EMISSIONS, 1995. REPRODUCED FROM *ATLAS AND POPULATION AND ENVIRONMENT*, AMERICAN ASSOCIATION FOR THE ADVANCEMENT OF SCIENCE, 2000.

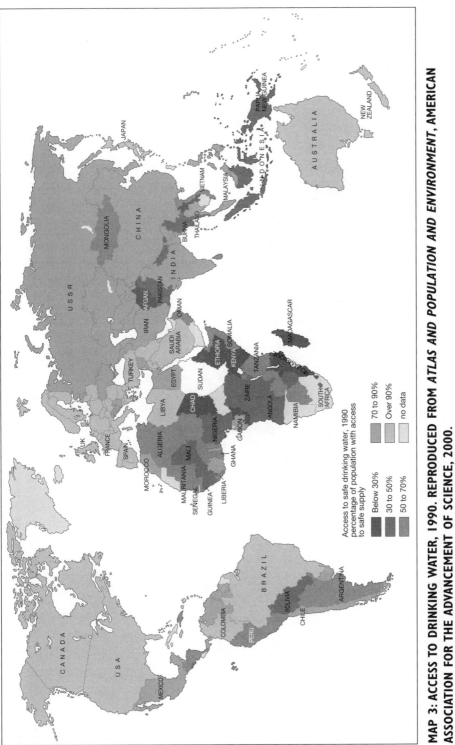

Access to safe drinking water, 1990
percentage of population with access
to safe supply

Below 30%	70 to 90%
30 to 50%	Over 90%
50 to 70%	no data

MAP 3: ACCESS TO DRINKING WATER, 1990. REPRODUCED FROM *ATLAS AND POPULATION AND ENVIRONMENT*, AMERICAN ASSOCIATION FOR THE ADVANCEMENT OF SCIENCE, 2000.

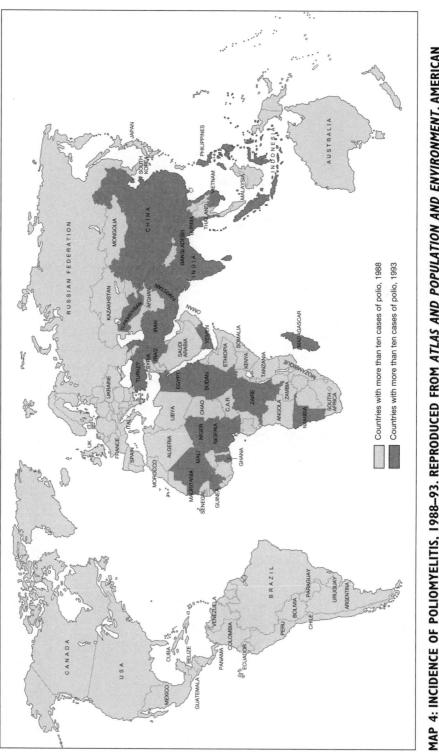

Countries with more than ten cases of polio, 1988

Countries with more than ten cases of polio, 1993

MAP 4: INCIDENCE OF POLIOMYELITIS, 1988–93. REPRODUCED FROM _ATLAS AND POPULATION AND ENVIRONMENT_, AMERICAN ASSOCIATION FOR THE ADVANCEMENT OF SCIENCE, 2000.

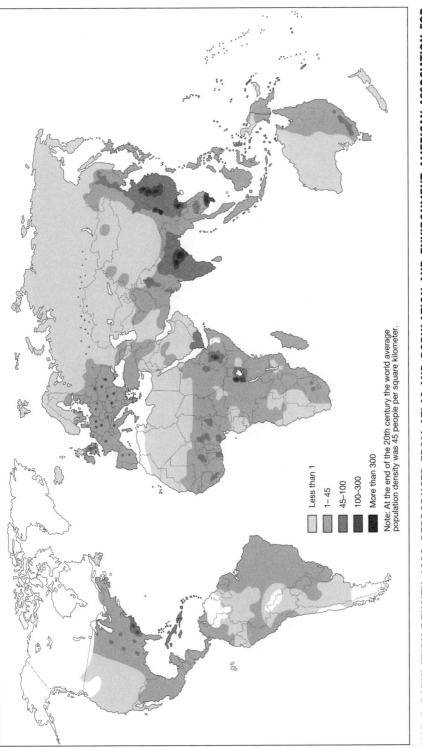

Less than 1
1– 45
45–100
100–300
More than 300

Note: At the end of the 20th century the world average population density was 45 people per square kilometer.

MAP 5: POPULATION DENSITY, 1998. REPRODUCED FROM *ATLAS AND POPULATION AND ENVIRONMENT*, AMERICAN ASSOCIATION FOR THE ADVANCEMENT OF SCIENCE, 2000.

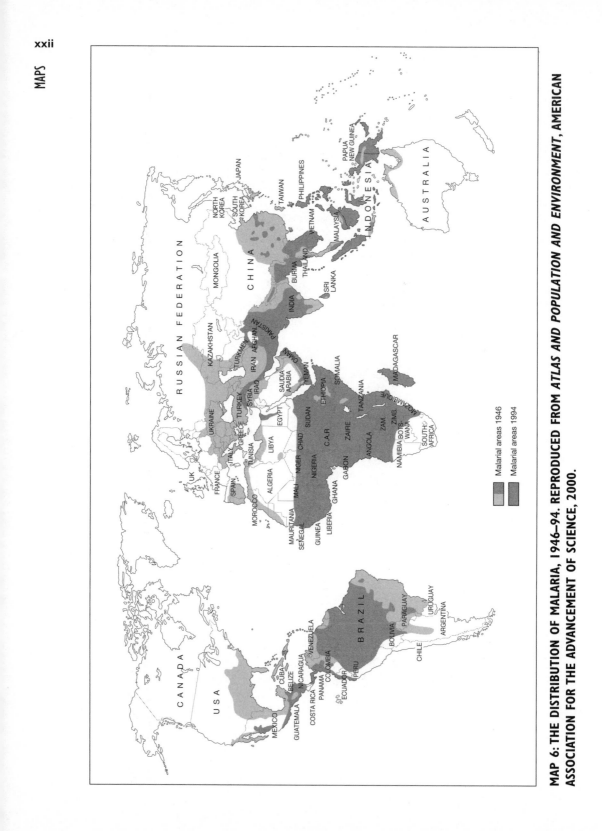

MAP 6: THE DISTRIBUTION OF MALARIA, 1946–94. REPRODUCED FROM *ATLAS AND POPULATION AND ENVIRONMENT*, AMERICAN ASSOCIATION FOR THE ADVANCEMENT OF SCIENCE, 2000.

INTRODUCTION:
WHOSE WORLD
HISTORY

L et us start with Sudan. If this seems an eccentric choice, then that is because the narrative and analysis of the history of the modern world has focused on Europe, the USA and the USSR. Insofar as attention has shifted further afield, the focus has been on East Asia, especially China and Japan. This is understandable, and these areas will receive due attention in this study. However, there is also here a determined attempt to engage with other regions. These were, and are, important in their own right. In addition, the attacks on New York and Washington in September 2001 serve as a harsh reminder of the interaction of very different parts of the world. Furthermore, a stress on regions such as Africa and South Asia reveals that a narrative and an analysis of world history set in terms of the familiar cast of topics have to be at least qualified.

At one level, this is a comment on the modern world from the twenty-first century. The classic themes – the two World Wars, the Depression, the onset of the Cold War and the beginnings of decolonization – have receded, so that they all

THE ATTACKS ON NEW YORK AND WASHINGTON IN SEPTEMBER 2001 SERVE AS A HARSH REMINDER OF THE INTERACTION OF VERY DIFFERENT PARTS OF THE WORLD.

occurred before the half-way point from 1900 to today, and therefore should play a less dominant role in the narrative than hitherto. More generally, these themes now seem less satisfactory as an account of the modern world, both as period and as process.

Thus to Sudan. In this brief introduction, there is only space to offer a few remarks about its history, but it is an appropriate subject because it reflects wider trends and shows how they impacted on the particularities of local circumstances. Discussion of Sudan also underlines the point that it is by no means apparent why the established cast of subjects for discussion should not be reshuffled or replaced to give greater weight not only to Sudan but also to other countries that are generally ignored. Many readers will of course disagree, and that is all to the good as the purpose of this book is to encourage reflection and debate.

THE CASE OF SUDAN

The history of Sudan, an area of nearly one million square miles, about five times the size of France, can be presented very much in accordance with the seminal political developments that any history of the globe in the twentieth century would focus on. This begins with European imperial conquest, in the case of Sudan by Britain. The defeat of the Mahdists at Omdurman (1898) was followed by the defeat of surviving Mahdist forces (1899). Independence was not regained until 1956, when it was part of the widespread decolonization of much of South Asia, Africa, Oceania and the West Indies from 1947.

In the meanwhile, colonial-era Sudan had been affected by the leading political events in the world. World War I (1914–18) led to security concerns that encouraged an expansion of British control, with the conquest of the territory of Darfur, while the war acted as a positive impact on the economy as food exports rose to meet wartime demand. At the same time, the war disrupted established economic patterns, leading to, and as a result of, both price and wage inflation.

The Great Depression of the 1930s not only hit the economy, with cotton exports falling badly, but also cut government revenue and expenditure, causing a measure of discontent. World War II (1939–45) saw further native politicization, while the war lapped Sudan, with an Italian occupation of a border region for several months and conflict in neighbouring Eritrea and Egypt.

Sudan also registered several of the other master-narratives of the modern age. It did so in accordance with existing social, cultural and ethnographical identities, but these were put under great pressure by the varied processes of change. The British drive to control the environment was explicitly seen as a way to transform economy and society. The attempt to use the Gezira plain for the cultivation of cotton began in 1900, and was pressed with the construction of an expensive irrigation scheme that was officially opened in 1926. This served to produce a cash crop designed to further the British imperial economy, and was therefore an example of the process by which distant regions were more intensively integrated into the global economy. Prior to irrigation, the Gezira instead had been used to grow grain for Khartoum.

Economic and political integration was further pressed forward by the extension of new communication systems. Major Sudanese rivers were affected by *sudd* (blockages of vegetation), but these were attacked by the British, a process helped after World War I by the use of mechanical dredgers. This was an aspect of the worldwide spread of advanced technology that was important to the global economy and to societies across the world. New port facilities were constructed on the Red Sea (Port Sudan) and the rivers, while the railway system, initially built to help British conquest, was greatly extended. Human control and technology were linked, with a common theme of economic development and the exploitation of resources in order to serve the interests of the dominant political group. This theme was to be repeated with oil exploration in the 1990s into the new century: oil revenues rose to over $1 billion in 2000, helping fund the dictatorial regime that had seized power in 1989.

Yet there were other aspects of Sudanese history that cannot be so readily subsumed into the customary themes of world history, focused, as they are, on the major powers. The drought and famine of the early 1980s, which were matched in some other parts of Africa, for example Ethiopia and Somalia, were a world away from the food surpluses of the 'First World'. They were also a reminder of recurrent patterns: Sudan had known a terrible famine in 1889–90. This serves to underline the extent to which the century did not necessarily witness the demise of earlier demographic and other circumstances.

Another recurrent pattern was found in the attempt of the Arabic-speaking Islamic tribes of the north of Sudan to control and exploit the southern tribes, which are varied, but mostly neither Muslim nor of Arab descent. Insofar as the White Nile has served as the thoroughfare of the country, it has been as an axis of exploitation, not of consensus. This was the case prior to British conquest and has again become so since independence. The resulting conflict, from 1956 to 1972, and then again from 1983, has inflicted terrible damage on society in the south, with large numbers of refugees. Southern separatism has been thwarted, but so also has been the attempt of successive

Khartoum-based governments to control the South and to wage a successful *jihad* (holy war). As I write, Sudan continues to be the site of one of the major 'forgotten wars' of recent decades. Yet there is no more reason to forget this war, both in terms of its impact on the Sudanese and because it tells us much about the recent history of the world, than there is to slight much of what is generally retold in the history of the 'First World'.

one

DOMINION OVER EVERY LIVING THING
CHALLENGING THE EARTH

If it is a cliché that every age brings change, not least in human relations with the natural environment, this has never been more the case than with the twentieth century. In both the short- and the long-term, the impact on the environment was the most potent aspect of human activity during the last century, not least because in transforming the context within which it lives and operates, humankind has not only affected all the other species that live on, above and in the Earth, but has also created a new, and troubling, sense of where human history will lead. To devote the first chapter to the environment and how we have changed it is to remind us that the Earth is the setting for everything that follows, and that future generations will look back on us as much, if not more, to consider these changes as for anything else. If you want to consider how you are shaping the world of 2050 or 2100, think about how you live, rather than how you vote.

IF YOU WANT TO CONSIDER HOW YOU ARE SHAPING THE WORLD OF 2050 OR 2100, THINK ABOUT HOW YOU LIVE, RATHER THAN HOW YOU VOTE.

KNOWLEDGE

The human impact on the environment will form the subject of this chapter, but it is necessary to start with the tremendous expansion in human knowledge of the Earth, for this increase in human capability acted as an enabler of exploitation and impact. It links scientific advance and economic drives to environmental pressures. In three major respects, there were new ways to understand the world, although they in no way exhausted the list of human ingenuity. The exploration of the land surface that had fired the imagination of the nineteenth century now sought new spheres.

It is easiest to concentrate on air and space, but it is also important to understand underwater knowledge. Knowledge of the oceans advanced greatly. Earlier, there had been important developments in the nineteenth century, not least with the invention of workable submarines and of diving apparatus. Furthermore, there had been extensive use of the underwater for communications. Telegraphy, the Internet of the Victorian age, had spanned the world as a result of the development of underwater cable-laying. This involved not only great expense but also the use of a learning cycle in order to improve methods. Thus, for example, it was discovered that, if laid taut, cables would eventually break under the weight of encrustation that built up on them. As a result, it was necessary to lay them loose.

The twentieth century brought major advances in underwater technology. The specifications of both submarines and diving equipment greatly improved during the century, and knowledge was applied. Within six days of the Normandy landings in 1944, an underwater petrol pipe was being laid from Britain to France. Submarines could remain underwater for longer, could carry heavier loads, and could resist greater pressure, and thus dive more deeply. Nuclear power was applied to power submarines, and, as a consequence, they were able to navigate under the ice of the Arctic Ocean: in 1958, the USS *Nautilus* travelled under the North Pole.

Increased capability led to a massive expansion in knowledge of the seabed, especially of the deeper waters that had been inaccessible in the nineteenth century. The oceans could be mapped as never before. Knowledge of the deep ocean also increased with the discovery (not that they needed to be discovered) of what seemed strange fish and plants, and, off South Africa in 1938, in a curious throwback, of *Latimeria chalumnae*, 'fossil fish', the coelacanth of the Palaeozoic era about eighty million years ago. As was frequently the case with the enhancement of human capability, much of the drive came from military competition, in particular concerns to improve submarine and anti-submarine effectiveness. Increasingly, there was also interest in the possibility of

exploiting mineral deposits on and under the ocean bed, and this became more insistent in the closing decades of the century, not least with the extraction of underwater
oil deposits, for example from the North Sea from 1975.

THE SPACE AGE

Air and space capability are better known. Manned flight preceded the twentieth century, with balloon technology steadily improving in the nineteenth. However, it was
the twentieth that saw the rapid development of heavier-than-air flight, and, subsequently, the space age. The rapid leap from one to the other, from the Wright
brothers in 1903 to the first intercontinental ballistic missile in 1957, clearly demonstrated the 'accelerated' nature of change in the twentieth century. The space age
greatly increased knowledge of the world and provided strikingly new images. The
American Apollo space missions, which led to the landing of man on the Moon in
1969, left as a legacy, photographs of the Earth as a whole: a potent image of one-
world.

Satellites also produced more detailed information of the Earth. From the 1970s,
NASA, the American National Aeronautics and Space Administration, used remote
sensing by Landsat imagery in order to generate satellite images of the Earth's surface
from electro-magnetic radiations outside the normal visual range; an enhancement of
human capability that was a common theme of the technology of the age. The use of
different wavelengths enabled viewers to see and therefore 'know' different aspects of
the world. Thus infra-red is especially valuable for vegetation surfaces and for water
resources.

Unmanned space missions were also sent to explore the solar system. Thanks to
recording and communications technology, these missions provided information on
planets such as Mars that humans have not yet reached. An unmanned probe reached
Venus in 1965, while two *Viking* probes, launched in 1975, landed instruments on
Mars in order to search for life. They were unsuccessful.

USING THE ENVIRONMENT

As influential commentators pointed out, knowledge was power. Knowledge served
two different but related ends: utilization and protection of the environment. An
understanding of the issues present in the latter helped to clarify the damaging extent
of utilization. The pressures of demographic and economic growth, the intensification of regional economies and the globalization of the world economy led to a

situation in which the search for, and utilization of, resources became ever more wide-spread, pressing and important. These developments were exacerbated by the exhaustion of established resources, such as fish, oil and water, and the possibilities of profitable exploitation in regions hitherto deemed inaccessible and unprofitable.

The 'development' of the western USA proved a good example of this process. Transforming the 'waterscape' through irrigation played a central role in the new engineered landscape of dams and irrigation canals that was designed to provide rapid gains similar to those resulting elsewhere from deforestation, but seen as superior and scientific. However, this proved more difficult to ensure than had been anticipated, and also had serious environmental consequences from the outset of the period. Thus, the overstocking of rangeland led to the serious degradation reported by the American Department of Agriculture in 1916: it estimated that the carrying capacity of public and private rangeland had dropped by 30 per cent since 1906. The pumping of groundwater led to rising soil salinity in the 1900s, and a declining water supply. In the Tulare Basin, the rate of depletion even led to land subsidence.

The engineering of water supplies in California had other unexpected consequences, including, in some areas, rising water levels following decades of flood irrigation. This led to salinity, and thus the need for more water to flush the land. High salinity poisoned plants' roots. The irrigation run-off led to the buildup of alkalis in sink areas, and these affected the wildlife that lived there. In particular, selenium, a toxic soil compound brought to the surface by agricultural practices, helped cause serious deformities in wildlife. Throughout California, natural waterways (and native grasses) had been replaced or subordinated, and, by the end of the twentieth century, river currents were controlled by computers.

ENVIRONMENTALISM

The commodification and use of natural resources had been linked to a reconceptualization of the world in which, in response to humanity's ability to transform it, the physical environment seemed less important. In the early decades of the twentieth century, there had been a strong belief in limiting the importance of environmental factors, for example terrain, on society and human development, and a concern about how to understand the flow of influence from physical to non-physical geography. In addition, it was argued that environmental influences best explained the different political trajectories of various ethnic groups: the processes by which they had become nations and states with particular characteristics and interests. Environmentalism made these processes appear natural and necessary. In *Die Erde und das Leben* (*The Earth and Life*, 1902), Friedrich Ratzel, the leading German political scientist, emphasized the role of environmental circumstances in affecting the process and progress of struggle between states. He presented international relations in the Darwinian terms of a struggle for survival, and saw states as organic (like living organisms), thus ignoring divisions within them. Furthermore, the culture of particular peoples was defined in terms of the integration of nature and society.

This belief in the role of the environment did not extend to care for nature or to any assumption that all humans had equal rights to their environment. Instead, a combination of the Darwinian belief in competition between species and a sense that civilizations could be ranked encouraged an ideology of expropriation. The Oxford academic Hereford George, in his *Relations of Geography and History* (1901), wrote of the Americans and Canadians:

> Before both alike the red men disappeared: they were incapable of assimilating civilization, and have in great measure died out. . . . The analogy is very close with many of the movements of pre-historic man, when newcomers expropriated the old inhabitants, driving them out or destroying them. . . . Civilized man works by different means, and with less definite intention to destroy; but the result is the same.

Environmental determinism, the view that human history was determined by environmental considerations, was increasingly replaced in the second quarter of the century by the idea of an interaction between humanity and environment, which, itself, could be presented in terms of the different abilities of particular peoples to achieve progress. In place of determinism, Lucien Febvre advanced what he termed *'possibilisme'*. The focus from the 1930s was now more clearly on human activity. Combined with technological advances, this led to a strong sense that humanity could mould the human environment and transform or transcend the limits of physical geography and environmental influence.

For example, roads, rather than natural features, particularly rivers and mountains, came increasingly to locate routes and boundaries, both in the mind and in maps. The world appeared as a terrain to shape, a commodity to be used.

THE WORLD APPEARED AS A TERRAIN TO SHAPE, A COMMODITY TO BE USED.

This approach was challenged from the 1950s by the proposition that the world was a biosphere operating in an organic fashion and using natural feedback mechanisms to sustain life. The globe was now presented as an environmental system affected by human activities such as atmospheric pollution, which affected the feedback mechanisms. The working of this system was increasingly clarified by the spread of environmental concern and knowledge. Thus, it became possible to track and dramatize the movement of air- or water-borne pollutants, for example air-borne sulphur dioxide from Britain to Scandinavia or the USA to eastern Canada, or of pollutants down the Rhine from Alsace and the Ruhr to the Netherlands and the North Sea. Books such as *Silent Spring* (1962) by the American ecologist Rachel Carson highlighted the environmental threat posed by pesticides, especially DDT.

A major shift of consciousness occurred in the 'First World', the term used to describe the affluent societies of Western Europe, North America and Australasia. For long, the expansion of the human imprint on the world had been seen as the march of progress, a necessary and beneficial march that linked the twentieth century to the beliefs in technological progress and providential destiny seen in the nineteenth. Thus, *The March of Civilization in Maps and Pictures* (1950) declared of the USA, 'its freedom-loving people have devoted their energies to developing the riches that Nature has so lavishly supplied', and most Americans saw this as their manifest destiny, and indeed the 'fruits of the Earth' as God-given to them. In January 1973, the London-based *Geographical Magazine* printed an article about the Trans-Amazonica Highway:

> One is moved with admiration at the manner and spirit of the Trans-Amazonica undertaking. Young Brazilians, bursting with optimism and trained and equipped with the most sophisticated paraphernalia of modern civilization, are in direct confrontation with the jungle. The road under construction in the Amazon basin will do much to bring about the taming of this great wilderness bastion.

Similar claims were made about other developmental projects of the period.

It was indicative that the second item just cited was about a project in the 'Third World', or 'developing world', terms frequently used to describe all of the world that was not in the 'First' or the 'Second' (the Soviet Union and Eastern Europe). By then such an unabashed description of a major development project in the 'First World' might have seemed dated in light of the rise in environmental consciousness. However, this consciousness was far from evenly spread, not least in the 'First World'. Outside the 'First World', governments eager for economic development generally paid little heed to environmental considerations, and this largely remains the case, although we know all too little about popular views.

Whatever the concerns of individual societies, the global environment became a more central theme in international consciousness and diplomacy. This was such that, in the 1990s, major efforts were made to achieve a negotiated reduction in the onslaught on the environment, not least in the face of rising concern about its impact. This concern could be seen in particular in anxi-

ONE OF THE MAJOR THEMES OF MODERN HISTORY OUGHT TO BE HOW WE HAVE GOT TO THIS STATE.

ety about global warming. One of the major themes of modern history ought to be how we have got to this state. Indeed, in its importance it dwarfs the familiar topics of global history, and it is appropriate that this chapter comes first.

ENVIRONMENTAL PRESSURES

It is very easy to attribute this pressure on the environment to the rise in the world's population (see the next chapter), and indeed that was of great importance. The clear implication is that this is all the fault of 'ordinary people' having lots of children and consuming goods; and/or that the inevitable nature of the rise in population, once the constraints of disease and famine had been reduced, if not removed, is environmental degradation. However, it is also necessary to look at how resources were used during the century. The pattern was very skewed. The more affluent regions of the world used their affluence in order to consume a greatly disproportionate share of global resources, and their affluence was, in part, measured by this consumption.

The net effect was that environmental pressure was strong in three particular areas: regions of affluence; regions where global economic pressures were readily able to extract resources in order to satisfy the regions of affluence; and regions trying to become affluent. As these categories covered much of the world's surface, it was scarcely surprising that environmental pressures were intense.

At the same time, it is worth noting the continued vulnerability of human society to environmental forces. This could be seen with diseases, not least new and newly vigorous ones (see the next chapter). Climatic factors were also important. Advanced technology made it easy to follow and even predict major storms such as cyclones and typhoons, but it remained impossible to prevent them. Thus, Madagascar and Mozambique were severely hit by cyclones in 2000. More generally, drought hit harvests across the course of the century, serving as a powerful reminder of the vulnerability of agriculture. Earthquakes, such as the one that hit Peru in 2001, and volcanoes were important examples of other aspects of continued vulnerability. They also pose the problem of assessment. In the latter decades of the century, the ability of international aid agencies rapidly to fly in large quantities of relief supplies was a powerful example of humanity's developing capability, but, at the same time, the devastation created by natural disasters was a comment on the limits of this capability.

There will be more focus on resources in chapter 2, but here the prime question is the impact of humankind on the physical environment over the last century. This impact was not new and, in some respects, human history entails the never-ceasing interaction of humanity and environment. More specifically, much that attracted attention in the twentieth century, for example deforestation or the hunting of whales, was both of long genesis and had also been pressed hard in the nineteenth century. It was then also that much of the world, for example Australasia and North America, was exposed to unprecedented human pressure. In many respects, the confidence in humankind's right to change the environment, and in human capacity to do so for good and profitable effect, that was to be seen throughout much of the twentieth century was a continuation of nineteenth-century attitudes.

Yet the extent of pressure on the environment was greater than ever before. This was not simply due to larger human numbers. Technology also helped in the exploitation of the environment. For example, the flexibility of motor transport and roads over railways increased the tempo of human action. Thanks to greater technological capability, the range and impact of extractive processes, such as mining, increased. Local environments were transformed, often dramatically so. Thus, phosphate mining made the Pacific island of Nauru all but uninhabitable.

SPECIES UNDER ATTACK

It is necessary to consider the human impact on other species that share the same physical environment. The relationship between humans and other species, both animals and plants, has always been dynamic, which is one way of saying that humans have destroyed them. In part, this has been the result of hunting and other aspects of deliberate extermination, but two other factors have been important: the introduction of alien species and habitat destruction, the last a process about which commentators became more aware and concerned in the last third of the century.

All three processes were accentuated in the twentieth century, in part because of the marked increase in human numbers, but also because of greater rates of human activity, for example of long-distance movement. Attempts to manipulate the environment by introducing animals or plants that use it to the greater benefit of humans frequently had a negative effect on other species, and, in the last third of the

century, this was increasingly seen as a challenge to human interests, not least due to a stress on the value of biodiversity. In the 1980s, about fifty species of the cichlid fish indigenous to Lake Victoria became extinct as a consequence of the introduction there in the 1960s of Nile perch.

This example is deliberately chosen as a reminder of the extent to which the assault on other species is not restricted to the well-known ones, such as the big apes, elephants and whales. Instead, there is a more widespread, and thus insistent, assault that threatens entire food chains. In addition, this is an assault in which large numbers are involved. I was urged to make this book more attractive by putting greater stress on 'heroes or villains, scientists, politicians, artists, writers: in fact the makers of the twentieth century'. In practice, these makers were largely anonymous: they were the large numbers who cut down the trees, ploughed the land, and fished out the seas.

HUMANS AND MARINE LIFE

Marine life in general was threatened by human activity. This was especially apparent with large marine animals such as whales – despite the protection attempted from 1946 by the International Whaling Commission, which sought to ensure sustainable whaling – and also with coral reef life (see p.22). Attempts to control whaling, which culminated in the 1986 moratorium on commercial whaling, exemplified the problems of obtaining international co-operation and enforcing international agreements, and also illustrated other trends of the period. These included the rising tide of public discussion, at least in the First World, and the role of NGOs (non-government organizations) in seeking to influence policy. Globalization, in the sense of the impact on particular communities of global pressures, also played a part, with pressure on traditional whaling communities (albeit their whalers employing modern technology) in Japan, Iceland and Norway to respond to global concerns. The core of the whaling issue was cultural, with some nations failing to join the sentiment that whales were other than large food sources.

There were also problems for fish species caught for human consumption. Heavily fished waters, such as the North Sea, witnessed a marked depletion in fish stocks, but that was also true of waters more distant from major areas of settlement. This became particularly pronounced from the 1980s as more countries entered long-distance deep-sea fishing and as the technology improved, with, for example, sonar devices, to detect shoals. Fishing thus became an aspect of the 'needle in the haystack' approach to environmental use: thanks to improved detection and exploitation technology, it became easier to find low-density or otherwise inaccessible resources, such as oil and mineral deposits. Knowledge was transformed into power and wealth.

Fish are therefore hunted, although that is apparently made more acceptable by referring to the 'harvesting' of the seas. The use of words is interesting. To refer to fish as 'hunted' would now suggest to most Western readers that there is an implication that this process is unacceptable (for the record I eat fish and meat), whereas 'harvested' appears far more acceptable, not least because it implies that something is being put back. This contrast itself is a revealing comment on modern Western attitudes, for it hardly needs pointing out that there is much Western criticism of the hunting of tigers in Asia for medicaments and of mammals, including apes, in Africa for meat. What these have in common with modern fishing techniques is that they challenge the ability of animal populations to reproduce, and thus threaten the biodiversity of the globe.

HUMANS AND ANIMALS

Hunting was not the sole issue. The change of animal habitat due to human action over the last century was certainly greater than that over any century in the previous two millennia. This hit all animals, although it was easier to chart the process for larger animals, especially big mammals, than, say, for amphibians, let alone insects, and it is likely that the impact on smaller animals has been underrated. Across the world, animals were affected. Habitats at a considerable distance from concentrations of human activity were altered. In 2000, it was suggested that industrial chemicals, evaporating in warm conditions and condensing when the air cooled, were responsible for the discovery that polar bears in the Arctic were acquiring hermaphrodite (male and female in the same animal) characteristics, a parallel to suggestions that chemical pollution was responsible for changes in human male sexual potency and characteristics.

Human knowledge of other animals expanded, and it became nearly impossible for them to hide. Hitherto unknown or remote species were 'discovered' due to the spread of human activity. These included, in 1901, the okapi and, in 1912, the Komodo dragon, which had been regarded as a superstitious invention until sighted by Westerners. This process was taken further in imaginative literature and popular journalism, with imaginary animals discovered and apparently recorded as a result of human activity, as in the American film *King Kong* (1933).

At the same time, it was clear that the human impact on the environment did have beneficial consequences for some animals. Global warming was held responsible for an increase in the badger population in Britain in the 1990s, and this process may have been more generally beneficial for animal life. At a more local level, wastewater emissions from power stations and factories raised water temperatures and led to greater animal and plant activity nearby.

The great expansion in population, man-made environments and products during the century, particularly in its second half, ensured that animals that benefited from contact with humans increased in numbers. In part, this was a matter of animals that humans wished to see, whether as farm animals or as pets. Demand for the latter spawned a major industry that recorded many of the processes discussed elsewhere in the book, including consumerism, fashions, growing trade, specialization and social changes: the rising importance of developing and satisfying the sensibilities of children in the First World was significant in the growth of the pet industry. Social and environmental trends also affected its composition: in the 1980s and 1990s, the trend from dogs to cats reflected the growing percentage of the Western population living in small dwellings, the decreased ability or willingness to take dogs for walks, which, in part, reflected other leisure options (such as the cult of the gym), and the greater role of women and female self-images in the choice of pets. However, pets involved only a very small percentage of humankind, almost exclusively in a few First World countries. Dogs continued to be eaten in Asia and Oceania throughout the period, while horses were eaten in some European countries, for example Belgium.

In large part, the animals that benefited from humanity were less welcome than pets. Rats, cockroaches and other wildlife benefited from the growth in the volume of rubbish produced by humans. The rise of rubbish, one of the themes of the century, owed much to the greater unwillingness to re-use material, but was also a product of rising affluence and of the transformation of material culture, including major changes in packaging. Animals such as foxes, squirrels, bears, boars, even elk, altered their activity patterns in order to exploit bins and other sites of rubbish accumulation and disposal. Indeed, foxes became increasingly urban. New crops or areas of agricultural production and monoculture attracted what were termed 'pests'. Bacteria found in human waste, such as faecal coliform, thrived as sewage levels increased.

THE CENTURY WITNESSED AN ACCELERATING RACE BETWEEN HUMANS AND OTHER ANIMALS FOR PROFIT FROM WHAT HUMANS SAW AS THEIR HABITAT

As a consequence, the century witnessed an accelerating race between humans and other animals for profit from what humans saw as their habitat, but which was also of course that of animals. In part, humans used animals of their own in this contest. The age-old remedy of employing cats against rats and mice continued. However, in general, the remedy was chemical, in both houses and fields. This dramatically increased the volume of chemicals in the world, especially those not 'contained' in manufacturing plant. The rhetoric of exterminating natural enemies became insistent, but the resulting 'war' on insects and other enemies had unwanted side-effects. In some cases, such as against rats, there were signs in the 1990s of increasingly limited success in this process, as rival animals developed immunity. There were other problems with chemical warfare. DDT was used, with good results, against mosquitoes in the long battle with malaria, but also had an effect on the animal and human population. For example, the use of DDT in Soviet cotton cultivation affected the fish in the Caspian Sea and then their predators: seals and humans. Malaria itself became more resistant to drugs. The chemical offensive was also employed against plants. Herbicides in particular played a major role in the 'agricultural revolution' by which crop yields were raised. This, however, led to a fall in biodiversity that threatened the value offered by the revolution.

CLIMATE CHANGE

The rate at which these and other changes occurred is not clear, particularly outside the First World. This does not, however, make them less important than other events, such as wars, that can be dated. Furthermore, the significance of what can be measured is unclear. For example, temperatures can be readily recorded, but the significance of the important rise since 1976 is debated. The trend was upwards: when periodic falls in temperature occurred after 1976, in every case they were to a higher level than the temperature in the mid-1970s. From 1975 until the end of the century, the Earth's surface temperature rose by about half a degree centigrade, reaching the highest figure for the last millennium and one apparently greater than in any period of human habitation. Global warming was also an accelerating process.

Aside from the impact on the world as a whole, these changes also ensured that climatic zones moved both geographically and in terms of the terrain (more northerly and higher regions became warmer). This was significant for desertification, while greater heat had an important consequence for water availability. Alongside shortages of fresh water on land came a rising sea-level as the warming oceans expanded when polar ice melted.

POLLUTION

Other changes that can be measured include carbon dioxide emissions and acid deposition, the former the result of burning forests or fossil fuels, the latter a consequence of sulphur and nitrogen production from industrial processes. Economic growth, greater affluence and increased numbers of people put pressure on the environment. 'Acid rain' damaged woodland and hit both rivers and lakes. Pollution spread widely. When caused by 'high-stack emissions', it had the capacity to affect distant environments, both in the countries where the pollution originated, particularly in the uplands, and in other countries also. The assault from pollution was also very varied. Lead emissions from traffic seriously affected air quality. The consumer society produced greater and greater quantities of rubbish, much of it non bio-degradable and some of it toxic. Environmental damage as a consequence of accidents was also important. This was true at sea, with, for example, the shipwreck of oil tankers, such as the *Yuyo Maru No. 10* off Japan (1974) and the *Exxon Valdez* off Alaska (1989), and on land with leaks from oil pipelines. In addition, noise and light pollution became more serious and widespread. The latter ensured that the view of the sky at night was increasingly affected, particularly in societies in the First World that had the affluence to use large amounts of lighting.

However, for the purposes of a history of the last century, there are serious difficulties in assessing environmental change, because relevant data series for the first half of the century, and, in many cases, for the first three-quarters, are limited. There were also major attempts to present misleading accounts of environmental circumstances. This was particularly the case from the 1960s as sensitivity to environmental issues increased. As a consequence, the communist bloc in particular disguised the severity of the resulting damage, for example the atmospheric pollution produced by the use of lignite (brown coal) in East Germany, or the impact of water extraction for irrigation in what was Soviet Central Asia on water levels in the Aral Sea, which indeed lost 75% of its volume between 1960 and 1989, creating a salt desert as the sea receded or the extent of pollution on rivers such as the Elbe, Yangtze, Yenisei and Volga. High-sulphur coal also caused serious problems in China, such that Lanzhou became the world's most polluted city at the close of the century, while, due to industrial production, Beijing was not far behind. Outside the communist bloc, there was also a lack of governmental interest in environmental damage, and/or a sense that it was an acceptable or necessary cost of economic development, as in Mexico City or Athens. These factors have been important for decades, but, earlier in the century, there was the additional factor of a lack of interest on the part of the colonial powers that controlled much of the world.

As a consequence, much of the environmental change over the last century can be discussed with some, if any, precision only for recent decades. Nevertheless, allowing for this, it is still possible to draw attention to earlier shifts. On the Indonesian island of Java, for example, the very rapid increase in population in the first four decades of the century far surpassed the rise in agricultural production, and this encouraged pressure on the environment, leading to very small landholdings, as well as to deforestation and soil exhaustion. The same process occurred in many other parts of the world.

For the last decades of the century, although soil erosion across large areas is difficult to measure, it is possible to use satellite data to note deforestation, a crucial change in terms of animal habitat that also affected the climate. Between 1970 and 1995, about 10% of the world's natural forests were lost. Between 1960 and 1990, about 450 million hectares of forest were lost in the developing world, although public concern about losses was strongest in the developed world, for example North America. In New Zealand, another First World country, schemes to cut the beech forests of the South Island in the 1970s led to fierce debate. In recent decades, the highest rates of tree loss have occurred in the tropics. This often involved attacks on indigenous people. For example, in 1999, para-military Chilean Special Forces police were deployed against Mapuche Indians who were in dispute with the powerful forestry industry. The impact of logging in some areas, for example Amazonia, received much public attention, but it was also a serious problem in many other regions. Thus, Japan's demands for tropical hardwoods hit hard in the islands of the south-west Pacific, such as New Caledonia and Vanuatu.

Whereas in temperate zones, such as Canada and Scandinavia, there was extensive new planting in order to provide a sustainable 'crop' of timber for 'harvesting' (instructive choices of words), in the tropics there was very little new planting. Instead, deforestation was a product of land hunger, as well as of a specific desire to exploit forest resources. The former was in large part the product of the population growth discussed later in the book, although it was also encouraged, for example in Brazil and Indonesia, as an aspect of what was termed 'development': agricultural land was seen as more productive and advanced than forest.

Poverty and commercial opportunism proved a potent mix in limiting sensitivity to the environmental consequences of forest clearance. The burning of forest in order to clear land for crops led in 1997 to a serious crisis in Indonesia, with huge fires causing a smog that hit air quality across much of the region. Humans suffered serious respiratory problems and animals lost their habitats. Illegal logging in the Indonesian national parks by commercial firms seeking hardwoods for export – local enablers of global pressures – also destroyed habitats. This hit the Asian great ape, the orang-utan, and its numbers halved in the 1990s. The net effect of such policies was a major change in the physical environment across the tropics, an important part of the more widespread assault on the environment.

Coral reefs were another natural environment that suffered serious damage from human action, with about 30% of those in the world destroyed during the century. All records of mass bleaching (loss of colour) occurred after 1979. Pollution from sewage, oil and other pollutants inflicted damage, as did rising temperatures and other forms of human interference, such as blast fishing. Reefs were particularly badly hit in the Indian Ocean, especially during 1997–8, when a rise in sea temperature proved fatal. Nearly all the reefs in the Maldives, the Chagos Archipelago and the Seychelles died. The degradation and destruction of reefs had serious effects not only on tourism but also on the food chain, as reefs were crucial breeding grounds for fish. Reefs also protected islands from coastal erosion, and their loss accentuated the problems caused by rising sea-levels.

Anxiety about environmental pressures led to pressure for what was termed 'sustainable development'. This proved a nebulous concept, difficult to define and enforce, and one that was contested by local communities anxious for jobs, companies keen to maximize revenues and governments determined on development.

ENVIRONMENTAL DIPLOMACY

Concern about global warming led in 1992 to the earth summit at Rio de Janeiro, which agreed the Framework Convention on Climate Change, and, in 1997, to the Kyoto Protocol, under which the major industrialized states agreed to reduce their emissions on greenhouse gases to an average of about 5 per cent below their 1990 levels. However, it proved difficult to reach agreement on how to enforce the agreement, and in 2001 the USA, whose emissions rose greatly in the 1990s, rejected the Kyoto treaty. The reluctance of the world's leading economy to tackle the issue was matched by an important growth in pollution by industrializing countries in the developing world, particularly China and India, although their emissions of tons of carbon per person in 1997 were considerably less than a fifth of those of the US figure. At the same time, the movement of environmental issues to a prominent role in international diplomacy was a major development that mirrored the comparable change in the position of human rights.

CONCLUSIONS

The debate over global warming reflected the nature of modern culture and politics in advanced societies. There was an emphasis on a secular process of cause and effect, on policymaking informed by scientific knowledge and controversy, and on widespread public debate. Yet, at the same time, neither policy-making informed by scientific knowledge nor secular processes of cause and debate were a reality for many governments nor were they for large numbers of individuals. Instead, traditional notions of cause and effect, focused on providence or luck, remained powerful. They encouraged widespread interest in using religious or occult means to understand fate, for both individuals and communities.

Other consequences of development are considered in terms of the interaction of resources and pressures in chapter 2, but the overriding point is that the commodification of the environment was pressed more intensively over the last century than ever before. This is the most potent consequence of the changes generally summarized as globalization.

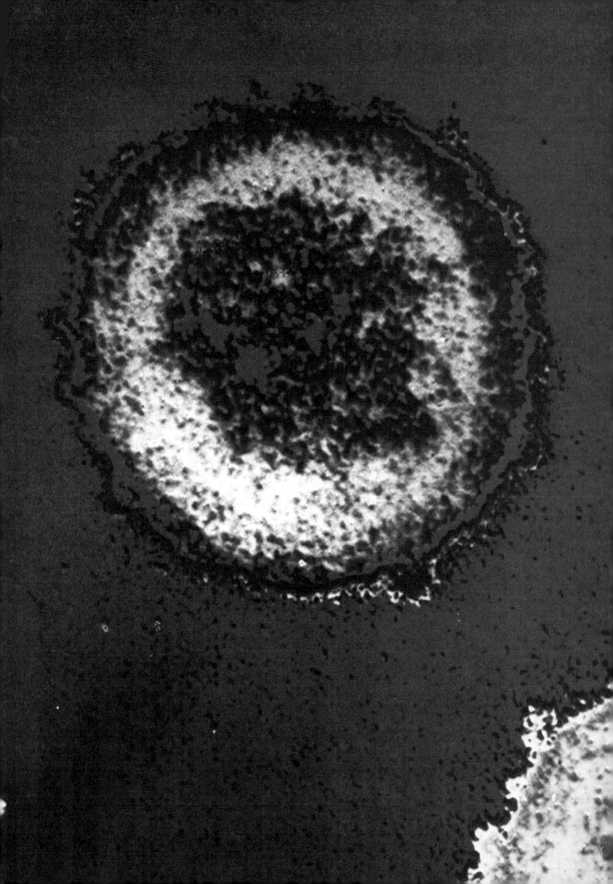

two

THE CROWDED WORLD
RESOURCES AND PRESSURES

FAR MORE PEOPLE

The massive rise in world population over the last century has acted as a major engine of growth and has continually tested the always difficult relationship between resources and demands. Figures for global population are approximate, but the following can be given: 425 million (1500), 1,000 million (one billion; about 1804), 1,600 million (1900), 2,000 million (1927), 3,000 million (1960), 6,000 million (1999). This rise, the driving narrative of modern world history, becomes even more striking if individual countries are considered. The population of China, the world's most populous country, rose from 582 million in 1953 to over one billion in 1982 and to 1.26 billion in 2001, and of India, the second most populous, from 300 million in 1947 to 1.03 billion in 2001.

If the rise in population was the motor of world change, it is important to consider why it has occurred. As with much change over the last century, it is a shift that has been most pronounced in recent decades: more in the second half of the century than in the first half, and most of all in the last quarter-century. However, the total rise in population is not the same as the increase in growth rates. Having risen from about 1 per cent per annum, in the 1920s and 1930s, to 2.04 per cent per annum in the late 1960s, a major leap, these rates have since declined, although they are still higher than they were in the 1930s.

A rise in the number of babies being born has combined with increasing life expectancy, ensuring that, as the numbers of those in the childbearing cohort have risen throughout the century, so the impact on the world's population has been accentuated. At the same time, as so often, the aggregate change can be broken down to note great variations by country, as well as considerable variations by ethnic and religious group.

Over the last half-century, growth rate has been lowest in Europe. This has been particularly pronounced in Eastern Europe, for example Hungary and Russia, but has also been the case in Western Europe, not least in countries, such as Italy, formerly noted for high birth rates. The population of the European Union, 375 million in 1998, rose only to 376 million in 1999, leading to concern there about the future availability of labour. Furthermore, if immigrant groups are subtracted, the low growth rates in countries such as Britain and Italy were even clearer. Indeed, without immigrants, the populations of Germany, Italy and Spain all fell in the late 1990s. The Russian population in the 1990s was hit by decreasing average life expectancy (due to a rise in the death rate for both infants and adults), as well as by a low birth rate and emigration. Male life expectancy in Russia fell from 64.2 in 1989 to 57.6 in 1994, only recovering to 60.9 in 1997. This was an abrupt comment on the disruption attending and following the collapse of communism. Psychological stress in Russia fed through into high rates of acute alcoholism. Also affected by the problems of transition from communism, Ukraine and Latvia saw major falls in population in the 1990s.

Conversely, birth rates have been higher in most of the rest of the world. This is particularly true in the Islamic countries of northern Africa and the Middle East, but is also the case with many Latin American countries. Growth rates over the century as a whole are difficult to assess due to limitations in the data for its first half, and there is uncertainty for some countries subsequently, but, nevertheless, it appears that there was a major shift in the distribution of the world's population. The percentage of the world's population living in Europe (including Russia) fell most dramatically. The percentage living in North America fell in the twentieth century due to greater growth elsewhere, although the total population in North America has risen greatly, thanks in part to immigration into the USA. The population of the USA, in millions, rose from 76 (1900) to 106 (1920), 132 (1940), 179 (1960), 223 (1980) and 274 million (2000). In California alone, the population in millions rose from 5.7 (1930) to 15.8

(1960) and 32.4 (1996). Nevertheless, restrictions on immigration from the 1920s and the impact of the economic crisis of the 1930s was such that in 1930–50 the American population increased by only 14 per cent, its lowest rate till then.

Conversely, the percentage of the world's population living in Asia and Latin America rose greatly. This was also the case in Africa despite the severity of famines and, more recently, the impact of disease in the shape of AIDS (Acquired Immune Deficiency Syndrome) in some countries, especially Botswana and Zimbabwe. The population of Nigeria, Africa's most populous country, grew by 2.8 per cent in 1999 alone.

To return to the causes of population increase, across the world, fertility rates did not fall at the same rate as life expectancy improved. It proved far easier to cut death rates than to persuade people to reduce their families. The fall in death rates was due to improvements in health and to the availability of adequate supplies of food and clean water. Infant mortality fell dramatically in the developed world in the early decades of the century: in terms of deaths per 1,000 live births between 1890 and 1930, there was a percentage decline of 67 in Germany, 55 in France, 44 in Italy and 55 in the USA, although only for the 'white' population. As marital fertility dropped as well in these countries (by 59, 32, 24 and 44 per cent, respectively), parental care could be focused on fewer children. There were also important changes in public health, for example, thanks to the pasteurization of milk. In the Canadian city of Toronto, chlorination of the water began in 1910 and was completed in 1912 (an instance of the rapid implementation of public health and engineering projects), pasteurization became compulsory in 1914, and water filtration was completed in 1917. Both typhoid and infant diarrhoea and enteritis fell dramatically in Toronto in that period.

THE BATTLE AGAINST DISEASE

The pace and impact of medical changes was greater in the twentieth century than ever before. In his novel *When the Sleeper Awakes* (1899), H.G. Wells felt able to look forward 200 years to a world in which disease had been vanquished and there was enough food. Indeed, as general medical knowledge increased enormously, the ability to identify and treat disease increased exponentially. These improvements touched the lives of billions and altered the condition of the world's population, and are arguably far more important than the details of political manoeuvres that tend to play such a major role in historical accounts.

MEDICAL IMPROVEMENTS ARE ARGUABLY FAR MORE IMPORTANT THAN THE DETAILS OF POLITICAL MANOEUVRES THAT TEND TO PLAY SUCH A MAJOR ROLE IN HISTORICAL ACCOUNTS.

Previously fatal illnesses or debilitating diseases and conditions were overcome as a result of new discoveries and their dissemination. The impact of diabetes, for example, was greatly lessened by the discovery of insulin in 1922. Its use, from the mid-1920s, enabled young diabetics to live. In the interwar years (the period between World War I [1914–18] and II [1939–45]), other medical advances included the use of gamma globulin against measles, the first sulphonamide drugs (effective pre-antibiotic anti-bacterial agents) and improved blood transfusion techniques. In 1928, Alexander Fleming accidentally discovered a mould that could destroy bacteria – this was penicillin. It was eventually isolated and produced as a drug, leading the antibiotics revolution that began in the 1940s. Antibiotics were of enormous benefit for dealing with bacterial infections, helping fight septicaemia, pneumonia, meningitis, endo-carditis, post-operative infections and venereal diseases. From the 1950s, an antibiotic developed in the USA, streptomycin, helped overcome tuberculosis. However, some strains of bacteria developed resistance to penicillin, leading to the production of semi-synthetic penicillins – the first, methicillin – in 1960.

Antibiotics were not alone. Common childhood diseases that caused high mortality and high morbidity in children, such as measles, whooping cough and diphtheria, were hit by immunization programmes that were part of a widespread attempt to improve public health by securing the health and welfare of children. A vaccine against polio developed by the American epidemiologist Jonas Salk was first widely administered in 1956. Population screening was pushed furthest in affluent countries with state medical systems. Thus, in Britain, from the 1970s, there was the introduc-tion of limited population screening for the early detection and treatment of diseases such as breast and cervical cancer.

The range of surgical treatment greatly increased during the twentieth century. The two World Wars, especially the Second, saw a major improvement in surgical tech-niques, with, for example, the development of plastic surgery using pig skin grafts. This was one aspect of how war, ironically, could lead to improvements in people's lives.

Another dramatic branch of surgery, transplants, had been tried in the nineteenth century, and a successful technique for corneal transplants had been developed. Further attempts were made in the twentieth century, for example with renal (kidney) transplants. However, although the technical skills were present, the basis of rejection was not understood until the 1930s, while, in addition, patients were too ill for the operation. These problems were overcome from the 1940s. Renal transplants became possible as patients could be kept alive on dialysis and thanks to antibiotics. The first kidney transplant was carried out, in Chicago, in 1950.

More generally, a major increase in anaesthetic skills, due to greater knowledge and the introduction of increasingly sophisticated drugs, meant that complex surgical operations could be performed. Once-serious operations, such as appendectomies, became routine and minor. There were also major advances in the treatment of the heart, and bypass and transplant surgery were completely developed after World War II. Between the 1950s and the 1980s, the transplantation of human organs was transformed from an experimental, and often fatal, procedure into a routine and highly successful operation. This was one aspect of the growth of specialized surgery. In the 1950s and 1960s, open heart surgery became possible and major drugs for coronary heart disease were introduced. In 1967, the world's first human heart transplant was performed in Cape Town by Christiaan Barnard. The first heart–lung transplant followed in 1971. Medical technology developed in numerous directions, whether artificial hip and then knee joints, heart pacemakers, invented in 1926, but developed in the 1950s, or the use, from the 1980s, of anti-viral agents for the treatment of viral infections: antibiotics had been useless against them.

There was also a revolution in the knowledge and treatment of mental illness, which was found to affect an appreciable proportion of the population. The twentieth century brought recognition of the importance of psychological and mental processes. Diagnosis and treatment both changed. The development from the 1940s of safe and effective drugs helped with major psychoses and depression, dramatically improving the cure rate. Psycho-pharmacology developed in parallel with psychotherapy. Tranquillizers, however, can be over-prescribed, and become addictive, and this was a particular problem from the 1950s.

Although these, and other, developments had a major impact on individual and collective experience and in decreasing anxiety, not all illnesses were, or are, in retreat. This is a difficult problem to assess, in part because of reporting issues that may give a misleading impression of the prevalence of illnesses. A more thorough collection of statistics as the century progressed led to a more comprehensive coverage of health problems.

There is evidence of a deterioration in some areas of health in recent decades. Changes in lifestyle were responsible for the spread of some diseases. A lack of exercise stemming from sedentary lifestyles and an increase in food consumption led to a rise in diabetes and heart disease. Pollution is another issue, with pressure on the environment also affecting humans. Possibly as a result of increasing car exhaust emissions and general pollution, respiratory diseases such as asthma, and subsequent mortality, definitely rose, and this was combated by asthma clinics, nurses and drugs. This was part of a major rise in the incidence and prevalence of increasingly diverse and dangerous allergic reactions in the developed world, a rise not only over the century but especially in its later decades. In addition, eye irritation as a response to particles in the air became more serious, not least in industrializing China and India, while allergies and food intolerances were more frequently reported.

The massive increase in the movement, treatment and burial of hazardous waste in the last quarter of the century also led to concern about possible health implications. Pollutants were linked to declining sperm counts and to hormonal changes, specifically the acquisition of female characteristics by men. Global warming, a consequence of pollution, has been blamed for the spread of some illnesses.

Other problems were not related to pollution. Increased use of 'recreational' narcotic drugs from the 1960s led to much physical and psychological damage, a large amount of which became apparent decades later. Narcotic drugs also led to many deaths. The frequency of sexually transmitted diseases rose in some countries, while AIDS developed as a new killer in the 1980s (it was first recognized as an infection in 1981), and by 2001 had killed about 22 million people. Infection with HIV, the crucial prelude to AIDS, was far more widespread. By the end of the century, the HIV immunodeficiency virus had infected nearly sixty million people, and the rates of adult prevalence were over 20 per cent across most of southern Africa. In 2001, South Africa's Medical Research Council estimated that 40 per cent of all deaths among the sexually active between 15 and 49 were due to AIDS and that if the disease continued to rage unchecked it would kill up to seven million people in South Africa by 2010, leading to a fall in average life expectancy from 54 to 41.

A lack of willingness on the part of some governments to disclose accurate figures suggests that there may have been under-reporting in, for example, South Asia. This was certainly the case in China, as was openly admitted in 2001. The origin of AIDS was (and remains) a matter of considerable controversy that in part throws light on cultural assumptions, not least doubts about science. Thus, it was widely argued that AIDS arose as a result of failed medical policies, specifically the contamination of oral polio vaccines used in Africa. This appears unfounded and it is likely that AIDS derived from the consumption of diseased primates. More particularly, chimpanzee and monkey viruses probably spread to humans as a result of the expansion of human settlement into parts of Africa, which increased contact between the species.

So far no cure has been found for the disease, although expensive anti-viral strategies are available to those who can afford them. AIDS punctured the confident belief and expectation that medical science can cure all ills, a belief that had developed with the antibiotics revolution. The spread of AIDS threw into sharper focus not only the issue of

AIDS PUNCTURED THE CONFIDENT BELIEF AND EXPECTATION THAT MEDICAL SCIENCE CAN CURE ALL ILLS.

human ability to understand disease but also the extent to which the response to diseases reflected social and cultural assumptions about personal conduct and the nature of society. Many states proved resistant to acknowledging the presence of risk practices such as prostitution and homosexual sex. Traditional views on risk were found wanting, with, for example, unprotected sex becoming a major hazard. This also tested conventional assumptions about propriety. Thus a willingness to discuss sex, and an ability to understand disease, were both far too rare in regions such as sub-Saharan Africa that were affected by AIDS. In contrast, in Europe and the USA, there was a greater openness to public education, which led to a far higher use of condoms. This reflected a range of factors, including culture, affluence and education. As drug users sharing needles was another form of HIV transmission, the epidemic also focused attention on different attitudes to drug use.

Food as well as sex gave rise to concern. In the 1990s, anxiety about the conditions in which animals were kept and the food chain operated was related to worries about the impact on humans, specifically of bovine spongiform encephalopathy (BSE) and a new variant of Creutzfeldt–Jakob disease.

Previously unknown diseases that were recognized in the last third of the century included Lassa fever, Eboli and Green Monkey virus diseases, Legionnaire's disease and Lyme disease. These reflected the impact of previously unknown bacteria and viruses.

The rise of some illnesses cannot be explained with reference to only one factor. For example, tuberculosis, which had become less serious from the 1950s, made a comeback in Britain in 1987, partly due to refugees and immigrants from countries where it was more common, but also due to homelessness and the appearance of drug-resistant strains of the disease. In Russia, social stress and governmental deficiencies contributed to serious problems in public health in the 1990s, including the spread of drug-resistant tuberculosis and of venereal disease. More generally, the rise in global travel has aided the spread of disease for centuries, and this became more insistent in the twentieth century as the speed and frequency of travel increased. This can be seen as a factor, for example, in the spread of a virulent form of influenza in 1918–19, which killed about 27 million people, and of AIDS in the last two decades of the century, and probably in the arrival of West Nile virus close to the major international airports in New York in 1999.

As another example of the interaction of social trends with medical developments, it is possible that children who were bottle-fed, a practice that developed in Western countries immediately after World War II, did not receive important vitamins and minerals to boost their immune system. It has also been suggested that, psychologically, they missed the important human bonding that comes from breast-feeding, leaving them more detached and susceptible to questioning authority and to independence. This has in turn been related to the 'protest generation' of the 1960s. Such suggestions may be far-fetched, but it is possible that bottle-feeding changed society in ways that are difficult to measure.

Although some illnesses are rising, the general picture remains one of an increase of average life expectancy across most of the world for both men and women. This was true of all age-groups, but the fall of infant mortality was most important. In large part, the demographic history of the world over the last century reflects the timing and impact of this fall. This fall in infant mortality was linked to a change in the causes of death. Whereas infections were a major cause of death for the entire population in the first half of the century, by the 1990s they were less significant, especially, but not only, in affluent countries. Instead, infections increasingly only killed people who were suffering from associated disorders and who were at the extremes of life. Instead, later-onset diseases, especially heart disease and cancers, became far more important as causes of death. In 1999, circulatory disease, including heart disease, was responsible for 30.3 per cent of deaths in the USA and 43 per cent in England and Wales, with cancers being responsible for 23 per cent and 24 per cent, respectively.

In the developing world, the major shift in improved health care occurred in the second half of the century. This was in part driven by the improved repertoire of drugs already discussed, as well as by others that combated tropical diseases, such as ivermectin against river blindness (caused by a parasite). Other factors were also important. Public health improved as a result of a better and more widespread understanding of disease control, of policies to ensure better access to health care, not least child immunization programmes, and thanks to better nutrition. The dramatic increase in food production in countries such as India and China in the 'green revolution' (see chapter 5) lessened the impact of famine in the second half of the century. Thus there was no recurrence in India of the famine of 1943–4, which killed about 1.5 million people in Bengal, while the death of about twenty million people in China in 1959–61 was due largely to government agrarian policy, specifically Mao Zedong's Great Leap

Forward policy, rather than to inherent crises in postwar Chinese agriculture. Global immunization programmes, organized by the World Health Organization (WHO, established in 1948), were directed at diseases such as measles and tuberculosis, although, in some countries, they were affected by political turmoil or governmental lack of interest. Nevertheless, in 1948–66 the WHO was responsible for 180 million vaccinations against tuberculosis. In addition, in the developing world, there was some success in improving the public infrastructure that is so important to health, not least by providing clean water, although, across much of the world, this was always incomplete and also was hit by demand from a rising population.

CHANGING DEMOGRAPHY

The strains upon public health will be returned to, but the key point here is that there was a major change in life expectancy in most developing countries from the 1950s that was largely due to the fall in infant mortality. Major falls in infant mortality in China and India were particularly important for global numbers. By 1999, life expectancy had risen to 70 in China and 63 in India, where, in comparison with China, poverty was more widespread and health expenditure low. The change in life expectancy in the developing countries led to an unprecedented rise in the global population and an important shift in its distribution. Even if the situation of rapid population growth soon stabilizes, these changes are unlikely to be reversed, and they constitute the central narrative in the global history of the last fifty years.

CHANGES IN LIFE EXPECTANCY CONSTITUTE THE CENTRAL NARRATIVE IN THE GLOBAL HISTORY OF THE LAST FIFTY YEARS.

There are indeed signs over recent years that the demographic situation is changing, and this ensures that accounts of global history produced twenty or even ten years ago that predicted continuing massive rises in population can now be seen as dated. The same of course will be true of this work, as one of the crucial lessons of the last century is that demographic trends were far from constant and that it is necessary to guard against exponential projections from recent developments. Over the last three decades, and especially since the 1980s, there have been major falls in fertility rates in a number of states, including China (from 6.1 in 1965–70 to 2.47 in 1985–90), Bangladesh, Japan, Iran and Kenya. These are states from different culture areas, and they suggest the need for caution before asserting that high fertility rates are an inevitable consequence of particular cultures, such as Islam, or indeed of poverty. Instead, it appears to be important to provide information and support for effective family planning. Furthermore, female education, female health and the assertion of women's rights can all contribute to a fall in fertility rates: they are not really separable from effective family planning. A fall in infant and child mortality is also a necessary prerequisite for effective family planning, as it gives parents confidence that the children they do have will grow to maturity.

Variations in fertility rates between neighbouring or similar countries, such as Iraq and Iran, or Malawi and Kenya, highlight the role of governmental policies and other circumstances particular to individual states. A striking contrast is that between China, where birth control policies have been followed with some consistency, and India, where the situation is very different. In China, birth control was pushed after the 1953 census had revealed the large size of the population, only to be abandoned during both the Great Leap Forward (1958–61) and the Cultural Revolution (1966–9). However, in the 1970s, families with more than three children suffered penalties and in 1979 this became harsher when a 'one-child family' policy was introduced. Aside from benefits for those who restricted the size of their families, a range of penalties included compulsory abortion and sterilization. Birth rates fell substantially.

In contrast, the rapid rise of its population will ensure that India becomes the world's most populous state, on current projections, between 2045 and 2050; but it also absorbs India's resources and leads to a seriously degraded environment as a result of population pressures. There was some improvement in the 1990s, with the annual average rate of population growth falling from 2.1 per cent in the 1980s to 1.9 per cent in the 1990s, largely due to falls in Indian states where female literacy was highest. Conversely, in others, such as Bihar, high birth rates contributed to severe pressures on living standards. A reminder of the extent of variety, whereas life expectancy rose in India, in neighbouring Myanmar (Burma), life expectancy fell in the 1990s as infections spread (and exacerbated malnutrition) and the government mounted an inadequate response. Malaria and anthrax were particular problems there.

The consequences of high population growth included unemployment and under-employment. Owing, for example, to the growth of Iran's population by 3.5 per cent per annum in the 1980s, a growth that led to the birth of eighteen million people, the economy by 2001 required one million new jobs a year, a serious challenge.

At the close of the century, infant mortality (per 1,000 live births) had fallen to 38 in China, 31 in Thailand and 45 in Indonesia, which, with about 200 million people, was one of the most populous countries in the world, but was 70 in India, 90 in Ivory Coast and 112 in Nigeria. This contrast was related to a number of factors, including very different rates of access to clean water (89 per cent in Thailand, 50 per cent in Nigeria).

In Nigeria, high child mortality continued to encourage large families. More generally, aggregate national rates concealed major variations, including the experience of the poor. Malnutrition was an aspect of the latter across most of the world. It affected physical growth: for example, in Madagascar in the 1990s, that of half of all children under three.

Allowing for these important variations, the overall effect has been a fall, first, in population growth rates from the early 1970s and, secondly, in annual additions to the world's population from the late 1980s. If these trends continue, they will lead to the world population peaking in about 2050, but it is very difficult to gauge how fertility rates will change. Cultural assumptions, resources and government policies all play a role. The 1999 United Nations Population Fund Study suggested a rise in the world population from 6 billion in 1999 to 8.9 billion in 2050.

IF TRENDS CONTINUE, THEY WILL LEAD TO THE WORLD POPULATION PEAKING IN ABOUT 2050.

Fertility shifts had a major impact on population composition as well as numbers. The percentage of the population aged over 60 rose in developed countries as life expectancy increased and fertility dropped. In Britain, where life expectancy for men rose from 58.4 in 1931 to 74 in 1996, and from 62.4 for women to 79, so the percentage of those aged over 60 rose to 20 in 1997. The percentage of the elderly was higher in developed than in developing countries: 16 per cent of the Japanese population was aged 65 or more in 1998, and the percentage was even higher in Italy, although, owing to higher fertility rates, the American population was younger.

The rise in the elderly increased dependency ratios in Western societies, although medical advances ensured that much of the elderly population was not physically dependent until close to death. The increase in dependency represented an important new labour demand, not least because much of it was no longer handled within extended families. The resulting demand for support helped greatly in the expansion of the service component of employment in the second half of the century, and also placed major pressures on public (governmental) provision of social welfare.

In developing countries, lower infant and child mortality ensured a totally different age profile, with only 5 per cent of the Brazilian population being 65 or older in 1998; although, if the lower fertility rates of recent decades can be sustained, the number of the elderly in developing countries will rise greatly. This will shift the balance between the generations, and between those in work and the rest, a shift that has already occurred in the developed countries.

DEMANDS FOR FOOD

More people has meant much more pressure on the environment, although it is equally important to focus on the issue of average per capita (each person) consumption, for rising living standards also pressed hard on resource availability. Indeed, belief in a likely future fall in population growth, and in the more recent decline in growth rates, presupposed a rise in per capita demand, as it asserted a virtuous linkage of falling population and economic growth. More generally, economic growth was a cause of instability, because, despite technological improvements in productive efficiency, the growth posed major demands upon available resources. Space is one of the fundamental resources and has been hit hard by rising numbers and changing lifestyles, a subject we will return to in the next chapter. Food, water and non-renewable energy have also been prime topics of concern.

Food is a renewable resource, although soil availability and quality can be degraded. Food production is one of the many areas of human activity that has changed greatly over the last century, and this change has been crucial to human history; again, to hammer home the point, far more so than the political developments that usually dominate discussion. An unprecedented rise in the global population meant an unprecedented rise in the demand for food. This rise was generally met, and severe failures in food provision, in the form of famine, were the consequence of war, foolish agrarian policies in command economies, such as China 1959–61, or extreme environmental conditions, particularly drought, rather than any long-term mismatch of production and consumption.

At the same time, variations in calorific consumption remained large and, in some cases, became larger. In particular the high consumption in developed countries, where obesity became a more serious problem and slimming an important health issue and fad, was not matched elsewhere. The situation was particularly bleak over much of sub-Saharan Africa, as well as in large parts of South Asia and in parts of Latin America, although, within these areas, there were important social differences, with the affluent enjoying a standard of consumption that contrasted greatly with the non-affluent. The latter were more prone to disease, although, in the developed world, the processing of food led to problems with the rise in the consumption of saturated fats.

Africa had a particularly high rate of population increase and this led to a marked fall in land availability: from 0.5 hectares of cultivated land per person in 1965 to 0.28 in 1995. This pressure of rising numbers on local farmland was disguised by the widespread urbanization of much of the developing world, which stemmed from large-scale migration but was, nevertheless, a ratio that was crucial for food availability and environmental pressures.

In North America, in contrast, food production rose and more than matched rising population, so that both the USA and Canada were major food exporters. Agricultural settlement spread across the Canadian Prairies, with much of Saskatchewan and Alberta settled in the 1900s and 1910s. The prairie was rapidly converted to crops, with the introduction of Marquis wheat in 1910 proving particularly important. It lessened vulnerability to early frost and offered a high yield. Irrigation helped open up southern Alberta to wheat cultivation. The spread of railways in the 1900s and the development of grain elevators in the 1900s and 1910s were also important to the growth of Canadian grain exports.

Growth in agricultural production in much of the world was concentrated in the second half of the century. Thanks to the 'green revolution', especially the widespread distribution of improved crop strains, the widespread use of chemical fertilizers and pesticides, mechanization and, in part, increased use of irrigation water, the figure for the average amount of grain available per person rose from 135 kilos in 1961 to 161 in 1989. For example, in Brazil, mechanization led to an increase in agricultural production in the last decades of the century. It also led to a social and geographical switch away from small family farms and towards agribusinesses with large farms, particularly in the *cerrado* region of the interior south of Amazonia. Large fields were more amenable to mechanization, and crop strains and layouts that could be readily harvested by machine were developed. The social cost in Brazil, however, was a crisis in traditional farming that involved impoverishment and a movement from the land.

There was a particularly important increase in grain yields in Asia; maybe a dull remark but one that summarizes a formidable effort and the application of impressive expertise. There had been no comparable increase in agricultural productivity earlier in the century in India and China and, combined with a rural politics that left the peasantry with only a portion of their crop, this had contributed greatly to rural immiseration, and a lack of local capital and incentive for agricultural improvement. The Chinese government did not enforce the 1930 land law that limited rent to three-eighths of the main crop and other agrarian reforms in the first half of the century also had only limited impact. There was no major shift in agricultural technique or organization in China or India until the 'green revolution' after World War II.

The environmental consequences of the 'green revolution' were very serious. The monoculture that came from an emphasis on a few high-yield strains lessened biodiversity and provided a food source for particular pests, while the nature of agricultural practice led to soil erosion and depletion. The latter further encouraged the application of unprecedented levels of fertilizer, particularly over the last three decades. This had many environmental consequences, some of which were directly harmful for humans. Thus, fertilizers and pesticides increasingly affected the crops that were consumed. There was also a major impact on water resources as fertilizers ran off into rivers with ground water, or were transferred into the water system through leaching into the soil or evaporation. Concentrations of pollutants were accentuated by decreases in water supply. The widespread application of nitrogenous fertilizers also had an effect on global warming as nitrogen evaporated from soils. Similarly, pesticides evaporated, entered the atmosphere and distilled out in colder air zones, with poisonous consequences for local animal and human populations. Pesticides had a more direct impact on the health of the agricultural workforce. The aerial 'topdressing' of fertilizers from crop-dusting aircraft, which became increasingly common in Australasia and the USA from the 1950s, spread fertilizers widely.

Over the last fifty years, it became increasingly possible to chart the degradation of cropland. The organic matter in soil was widely degraded, while cultivated land left without a protective cover of vegetation suffered from the erosion of soil by wind and water. This was a widespread problem in both the developed and the developing world. Thus, the southern central USA in the 1930s and southern Russia in the 1960s were badly affected by wind erosion, although these were only the more conspicuous examples of a widespread process. As a consequence, across the world, large amounts of cropland ceased to be fertile, and much of it fell out of cultivation.

As population pressure and land-hunger drove people to cultivate unpromising terrain, for example heavily sloping land, which is particularly prone to erosion once vegetation has been removed, so the problem was accentuated. Human action greatly increased the impact of natural erosion. Thus, cutting the trees on the mountain slopes of the Himalayas increased the amount of soil washed into the Bay of Bengal, probably the biggest movement of soil during the century. This was not solely a problem in the developing world. For example, the deforestation that contributed to the Esk valley floods in New Zealand in 1938 had not been sufficiently reversed to prevent a serious recurrence in 1988.

Soil loss was also a major problem in Africa, with wind and water erosion hitting hard across the continent. Population pressure and its impact on farming practices led to a degrading of marginal farmland, especially in Namibia, Ethiopia and along the Sahel belt south of the Sahara, and each of these suffered desertification. Aside from the strain on both environment and living standards, there were also resulting political pressures and conflicts over land, for example between Ethiopia and Somalia. More generally, across the world, it remained unclear whether growth in food production could be maintained. Hungry regions exported their hunger, by importing food if wealthy, or exporting migrants if poor.

HUNGRY REGIONS EXPORTED THEIR HUNGER, BY IMPORTING FOOD IF WEALTHY, OR EXPORTING MIGRANTS IF POOR.

Cereal crops were not the sole source of food. Meat and fish were also important, and their production changed greatly over the last century, with, again, the major shift occurring in the last half-century. Rising incomes, first, in developed countries and then in developing countries, led to greater demand for meat and fish, and this consumerist pressure accentuated the impact of population growth. Growing demand for meat led to a major shift in the pattern of meat consumption. The yield of meat per acre became a more important consideration, and this led to a move away from beef cattle, which were generally fed on pasture, to animals that could be fed more intensively from feedlots throughout the year, especially pigs and chickens. The latter led to what was termed 'factory farming' in the second half of the century, with land ceasing to be the main factor of production in agriculture as animals were kept, in high-density, in buildings throughout the year. This challenged ruralist conceptions about the relationship between agriculture and land, led to concern about food safety, and greatly increased the problems posed by animal waste. In his futuristic novel warning about the cult of change, *Brave New World* (1932), Aldous Huxley prophetically noted: 'From the grounds of the Internal and External Secretion Trust came the lowing of those thousands of cattle which provided, with their hormones and their milk, the raw materials for the great factory at Farnham Royal.'

FISHING

Fishing changed greatly from the 1950s, with a shift from a focus on inshore fishing to an emphasis on deep-sea activity. This brought all the world's waters within the scope of fishing, and they were then fished intensively by large 'factory ships', that themselves consumed substantial quantities of energy and were equipped with sophisticated finding devices. These industrial fleets hit fish stocks and helped to wreck local fishing, for example off the coast of West Africa. Many fishing fleets refused to use nets that permitted smaller (younger) fish to swim on in order to restock the species.

The failure of any global system of fish stock protection led to serious inroads into the ability of fish populations to maintain their numbers. The North Atlantic was particularly heavily fished, with the squid there fished out in the 1980s and the Grand Banks cod fishery off Newfoundland closed in 1993. In the Pacific, over-fishing hit the major catches, such as the California sardine in mid-century, the anchoveta in the 1970s and the chub mackerel in the 1980s. Demand in the Far East for shark fin hit shark populations across the world, again for example, off West Africa. In largely or partly inland waters, such as the Black, Mediterranean and North Seas, over-fishing and pollution combined to hit fish stocks. Owing to over-fishing, catches of sturgeon in the Caspian Sea fell dramatically in the 1980s and 1990s. Fish scarcity led to major price rises, as well as to cultural responses about fish consumption. For example, once common, salmon and oysters became luxury products, and, at the turn of the twenty-first century, cod seemed about to follow.

At the same time as natural resources were dangerously depleted, an effort was made to produce a man-made solution. Fish farms became more important in the last quarter of the century and, by 1998, produced more than a quarter of the fish consumed. Although generally associated with Europe, particularly for salmon, and the USA, especially for catfish, the world's largest fish-farmer was China, particularly for the production of carp.

Fish-farming fitted a modern tendency to make the most intensive use possible of all land and water that could be utilized. This posed a problem as such use itself consumed resources, not least fishmeal. Furthermore, the direct environmental consequences could be harmful. Alongside benign images of Scottish lochs exploited with little alteration for the fish-farming of salmon there were coastlines transformed into shrimp ponds, for example in Indonesia, leading to a loss of biodiversity and an accumulation of toxins. This led to an equivalent of the slash and burn approach to agriculture, with shrimp ponds being abandoned as new ones were established.

ALONGSIDE BENIGN IMAGES OF SCOTTISH LOCHS EXPLOITED WITH LITTLE ALTERATION FOR THE FISH-FARMING OF SALMON THERE WERE COASTLINES TRANSFORMED INTO SHRIMP PONDS.

THE DEMAND FOR WATER

Water was another resource that was placed under great pressure. This was true both of developed and of developing countries. In the former, the increased demand for water reflected consumerist pressures. The extensive use of hosepipes for washing cars and watering gardens, and the use of water for more toilets, baths and showers, and for machines such as washing machines and dishwashers, became increasingly normative. Industrial and agricultural use also posed problems. Intensive agriculture increased the need for water. For example, the traditional means of growing olives was replaced by more tightly packed trees, which increased water demands (as well as soil erosion and desertification). Across much of the developing world, irrigation was the major demand on water supplies. This was true, for example, of China, India, Egypt, Brazil and Argentina; although irrigation was also very important for Japan and, to a lesser extent, the USA, where irrigation contributed to the growing water crisis in the American West. Across the world, irrigation reflected the mismatch between water needs and local resources.

The spread of irrigation in the second half of the century indicated the growth of this problem. Large-scale irrigation projects based on dams, such as the Ming Tombs dam, played a major role in the Chinese Great Leap Forward of 1958, but this far-ranging government plan failed to raise food production, in part due to poorly conceived irrigation schemes. In the 1990s, Colonel Qaddafi of Libya backed the ambitious Great Man-Made River scheme to pump water from Saharan aquifers to the coastal cities where the bulk of the population lived, but the project not only hit underground water levels in the Sahara but also lost water due to the corrosion of the pipes.

Water use led to the growing extraction of water from rivers, so that the volume reaching the sea declined, for example for the Colorado, the Rio Grande, and the Nile, causing river levels to drop. In the Nile delta this led to an increase in salination as the falling volume of river water was less able to keep the salt water of the Mediterranean at bay.

Rising water consumption also led to the depletion of natural aquifers, and to the rationing of demand. The depletion of aquifers was a serious problem in much of the world: for example in India, where the major expansion of rice cultivation in the Punjab from the 1960s led to a serious fall in the water table. In Australia, the use of irrigation for cotton and rice in the Murray–Darling basin, the most productive agricultural zone, affected water supplies, leading to the movement of salt to the surface and to major losses of cultivable land in the 1990s. Deforestation contributed to the crisis by removing water-retaining vegetation. The Cochabamba valley, central to Bolivia's agriculture, was affected by increased demand, leading to a rapid fall in the water table, water shortages in the 1990s and popular disturbances in 2000. Rationing of water use across the world was in part ensured by rising prices, but there were also more specific limitations. Thus in Britain, hosepipe bans in 1990 affected twenty million customers. Greater demands for water also exacerbated droughts, such as that of 1995 in Britain.

In both the developed and the developing world, demand for water led to the drowning of valleys for reservoirs. Thus, in Britain, Newcastle was provided with water from the Catcleugh Reservoir in Redesdale completed in 1905, and from the Kielder Reservoir on the North Tyne, completed in 1982. Dam-construction and related water transfer schemes were the supply-side solutions that found most favour in response to rising demand for water over the last century. They corresponded to the enthusiasm for the onward march of medical science seen from the antibiotics revolution. Artificial water-delivery systems were a product of ideology and politics. They developed out of specific historical circumstances, and were not natural or immutable. Los Angeles, a megalopolis built in the middle of a desert, symbolized the determination to locate human activities without reference to resources. Dams were seen as sources of controlled water flow both for water consumption and for the hydro-electric power that was presented as a safe alternative to nuclear power in replacing fossil fuels. Across the world, dams became symbols for, and examples of, humankind's ability to control its future. This was true of such major projects as the dams in the Tennessee River valley and across the west of the USA, the Snowy Mountains scheme in Australia, the Aswan dam in Egypt, the Cabora Bassa dam in Mozambique and the Three Gorges dam on the Yangtze in China, humankind's latest greatest engineering undertaking.

LOS ANGELES, A MEGALOPOLIS BUILT IN THE MIDDLE OF A DESERT, SYMBOLIZED THE DETERMINATION TO LOCATE HUMAN ACTIVITIES WITHOUT REFERENCE TO RESOURCES.

As with other aspects of human activity, disadvantages became apparent soon after schemes were completed. Aside from the cost and human disruption of dam projects, there were also problems for fluvial systems, with fertile silt trapped behind dams instead of moving downstream, a major problem in the Nile valley. In the 1980s and 1990s, there was increased concern about the impact of dams and the limitations of supply-side solutions to the water issue. Thus, there was widespread criticism of the Three Gorges project. In New Zealand, where rivers had been dammed for hydro-electric power, there was criticism of new schemes from the 1970s. For example, under the Tongariro power project, approved in 1958, about 97% of the flow of the headwaters of the Whanganui was diverted for hydro-electric power, but, in response to public concern about river levels, minimum flow levels for the river were set in 1983. Across the world, from the 1980s, demand-side policies led to an emphasis on more effective water use for domestic, industrial and agricultural purposes.

There was also greater concern about the contamination of water. Industrial, agricultural and domestic wastes all posed a problem, and helped lead to the spread of water-related diseases. In some areas, there were improvements. In the developed countries, greater concern about the environment from the 1960s, and an increased understanding of the processes and effects of pollution and of possible solutions, led to marked changes. The toxicity of rivers decreased, permitting the return to them of species of fish and shore wildlife. Concentrations of heavy metal pollutants declined. The large-scale adoption of detergents after 1945 affected water quality, but, once the problem was recognized, the industry itself went a long way to resolving it. In place of discharging untreated sewage into rivers and seas, developed countries increasingly first processed it in treatment works. However, the pollution of rivers in the developed world continued, for example of cyanide-laden sludge into the Danube in 2000, while sea pollution remained a major problem, with heavy metals, oil and domestic sewage all having a major impact. Sea pollution also became an issue in tourism as beaches were affected.

The situation was far less benign in developing countries. There, measures to maintain, let alone improve, water quality were infrequent, and population growth, irrigation and industrial use pressed on increasingly inadequate supplies. The provision of clean water did not keep pace with urbanization. In Iran, water shortages in the 1980s and 1990s led to pumping of well water from steadily lower levels. The problem encouraged an angry politics of water in areas of shortage such as the Middle East, exacerbating tension between Israeli and Palestinian settlements on the West Bank of the Jordan, while also leading to Syrian and Iraqi concern about Turkish dam projects on the rivers Tigris and Euphrates. In the tropics, in contrast, clean water, rather than water availability, was the major problem, particularly in rural areas.

DEMANDS FOR ENERGY

Throughout the world, there was also growing pressure on fossil fuels during the century, a product of growing demand and of supply-side problems. Rising energy needs reflected the enormous growth in both per capita and aggregate (total) energy consumption in response to shifts in economic activity, social processes and living arrangements. The range of energy uses increased. Thus, oil-based additives became important in agriculture, while the spread of agricultural machinery increased demand for oil. In the 1990s, the greater use of computers and the Internet pushed up demands for electricity.

The global consumption of commercial energy rose at a greater rate than the rise in population, especially in the second half of the century. This led to a range of concerns, focusing, first, on the availability and cost of energy, and, secondly, on the environmental consequences of increased use. The world's energy profile changed greatly during the century. At the outset, coal was the major energy source in developed countries, and wood elsewhere. Dung was also important, a reminder of the persistence of traditional, organic sources of fuel. During the century, the role of wood (and dung) as energy sources decreased, although they remained important, especially in Asia and Africa. There was also a major shift in the prime source of fuel for industrial and domestic use. Global coal consumption rose, in large part as countries that had not hitherto had much industrialization experienced greatly increased energy demand, particularly China. While production developed in some areas, not least parts of China, nevertheless, the relative role of coal fell.

In its place, oil and natural gas became important energy sources, so that, by 1998, oil provided about 40 per cent of the world's energy consumption (excluding wood and dung), compared to 26 per cent for coal and 24 per cent for natural gas. Reliance on oil was a result of government and corporate policies and consumer options within the context of pricing policies and technological availability, not an immutable historical need. Furthermore, this trend became more pronounced as the century passed. The rise of oil and natural gas can be further clarified to note that the ratio of gas production increased from the 1960s, as techniques for using and transporting it were developed. In the case of both oil and natural gas, there were also important developments in both engineering and information technology that aided utilization. For example, it became feasible to drill to greater depths, while the ability to understand how best to exploit oil and gas fields grew.

The availability of energy was a major problem for countries that consumed more than they produced, particularly Japan and much of Western Europe, and for people who could not afford to meet their needs for fuel for cooking, heating and lighting. Nuclear power became important in some states, such as France and Japan (Japan had 51 nuclear reactors by 2001), but that led to environmental concerns. In 2001, electricity shortages in Brazil and California, the political consequences of a dramatic rise in the price of oil in Zimbabwe, and concern about the political stability of the Middle East underlined the problems of energy supply.

In the second half of the century, there was also great concern about the impact of energy use on the environment. Climate warming has a number of causes, but fossil-fuel emissions of greenhouse gases were perhaps the most important. The emission rate of the most important greenhouse gas, carbon dioxide (CO_2), rose throughout the twentieth century, to reach six billion tons of carbon annually by 2000. The highest per capita emissions were in the USA, in large part due to the strength of the car culture there. In 1990, 158 million tons of CO_2 was dispersed into the environment above Britain alone. Other emissions were also damaging. A combination of cars and the petrochemical industry led to the Houston conurbation in Texas sending skywards 200,000 tons of nitrogen oxide annually by the late 1990s.

THE STRUGGLE FOR RESOURCES

The relationship between resources and pressures has not only been a general theme of relevance for our understanding of the environment, but has also affected the lives of individuals, communities and nations. Furthermore, this relationship had an important role for what is defined, more narrowly, as the political history of the world. This history can in part be understood in terms of a struggle to obtain, or direct, the use of resources, and those themes can be seen both in relations between states and in their internal history. Thus, the dominance of the USA was in part linked to its central role in the exploitation of the oil industry, first as a major source of production and refining and, secondly, because American oil companies played a crucial role in the development of oil resources elsewhere, particularly in Saudi Arabia, which became the leading producer, and also in controlling the oil trade. America's opponents in World War II – Germany and Japan – lacked such resources. Conversely, one reason why the Soviet Union, despite its economic inefficiencies, was able to mount a sustained challenge to the USA in the Cold War (1945–89) was because it was one of the world's biggest producers of oil and natural gas and, in particular, developed the production of the latter during this period. The importance of countries during the century frequently rested on the availability of oil. Thus, in Iraq, where oil was discovered in large quantities in 1927, it provided nearly 20 per cent of government revenues in 1931–2 and 65 per cent by 1954. By the close of 1975, Iraq's annual oil income was about $8 billion and, like other oil powers, it was possible to spend heavily on arms. Iraq's attacks on Iran in 1980 and, particularly, Kuwait in 1990 were primarily motivated by a determination to seize oilfields, and oil wealth enabled Iran and Iraq to continue fighting until 1988. Sub-Saharan Africa's leading producer of oil, Nigeria, received about $280 billion in oil revenues in the last three decades of the century.

Periods of conflict – hot or cold – obviously saw an emphasis on resource availability and use as the means to pursue the struggle and enhance capability. Resource issues were also of importance during peacetime. They provided an important subject for international relations, but were even more important as a goal for domestic politics. At the simplest level, these politics provided a means to shift the distribution of resources, which can be a benign way of referring to the seizure of the goods and livelihood of others. Thus, communist regimes, most prominently the Soviet Union and

China, pushed through 'land reform' both in order to pursue agricultural productivity and to create a new social politics in which groups judged reactionary, particularly landowners, were dispossessed and collectivities regarded as progressive – the poor peasantry – were rewarded, although only on the terms of the state. The history of these countries can, in part, be written around the issue of control of the land, with the important caveat that when this became less significant with the movement of large numbers to urban areas, that itself was partly due to the inability of the land to provide the desired livelihood.

DOMESTIC POLITICS PROVIDED A MEANS TO SHIFT THE DISTRIBUTION OF RESOURCES, WHICH CAN BE A BENIGN WAY OF REFERRING TO THE SEIZURE OF THE GOODS AND LIVELIHOOD OF OTHERS.

Clearly, politics involved more than the pursuit of resources. To take land reform, this operated very differently depending on the context. Thus, land reform in Japan in the late 1940s was imposed by the American occupying power, and, as in Mexico after the 1910 revolution and India following independence in 1947, in order to create a buoyant peasantry of individual proprietors (at least in theory), not in pursuit of the collective ownership seen in communist countries. However, in these countries, and elsewhere, the long-term effect of a large number of individual proprietors was an inefficient system that found it difficult to compete with larger and better-capitalized farms that could invest in new methods and machinery; although the encouragement of a large number of peasant proprietors was socially more stable than the consolidation of holdings into large farms, as the latter led to greater numbers leaving the land. Furthermore, where labour was cheap, the intensive agriculture seen with large numbers of peasant proprietors could support large numbers on the land; although this was challenged by population rises beyond the land's capacity to provide sufficient food.

In China, land was redistributed from landlords to poor peasants under the 1950 Agrarian Reform Law, but collectivization was pushed hard in 1954-6 and peasants lost their private plots in the Great Leap Forward. The resulting loss of incentive contributed to the fall in production. Private plots were restored in 1959 and, alongside an investment in fertilizers and machinery, this led to a rise in agricultural output in the early 1960s, a process taken further from 1979 when the use of private plots was encouraged.

CONCLUSIONS

Much of the history of the century can be written around the struggle for resources in the face of competing demands and pressures. Aside from resources of a conventional type, such as land and water, there were also disputes over resources of a more 'modern' type, such as quotas in educational opportunities, housing and government jobs, and the allocation of economic subsidies. They provided the lightning rod for regional, ethnic, religious and class tensions, for example in Pakistan in the 1990s. We will return to other aspects of politics, but it is important to remember the relationship between resources and pressures, on the one hand, and the social and political histories of the period, on the other.

three

CONCRETE AND STEEL
THE HUMAN ENVIRONMENT

While the natural environment was pressed hard, its human counterpart was extended and remoulded during the century. More humans and their altered expectations ensured that the human environment, both urban and rural, changed considerably. The main development was the march of urbanization, such that human life and experience were increasingly framed in urban terms. However, just as urbanization became most intense, the cultural icon of rural life grew in attraction, particularly in the USA and Britain. The definition of urban varies, but, however defined, it is clear that one of the major changes of the last century was the rise in the percentage of the world's population who lived in urban areas, a change that was more marked in the second half of the century.

URBANIZATION

Furthermore, the urban experience was increasingly that of cities rather than towns, and, more particularly, of large cities. As a consequence, the direct experience of the countryside became relatively less common. The shift to cities was worldwide. In 1900, large urban areas were concentrated in Europe and North America, with the largest being, in order of population, London, New York, Paris, Berlin, Chicago and Vienna. By that date all the major American cities had been founded. During the century, the urban areas in Europe and North America increased, and there was also a marked shift from rural to urban in the location of the population. This was even true of areas that were already heavily urbanized, such as England and Scotland. By the early 1970s, only 2.5 per cent of the UK's workforce was employed in agriculture. However, this shift was more pronounced in areas that were not already heavily urbanized. Thus, there was a significant move from the land in France and Germany in the third quarter of the century as agricultural mechanization gathered pace and as opportunities beckoned in areas of industrial expansion.

The same process occurred in developing countries, but there much of the shift occurred later: in the last quarter of the century. This was particularly the case in China. In addition, the rapid rise in population in these countries put pressure on agrarian society, particularly on the availability of land, and encouraged migration to the cities, where much of the growth in population anyway occurred. Poor harvests provided specific incentives to this migration. More generally, rural life was often grindingly poor, and migration was encouraged by the availability of jobs in towns, as well as their role in expanding horizons and as centres of news, consumption, excitement and real, or apparent, social mobility.

By the end of the twentieth century, the largest cities in the world were mostly in the developing world. They included Bombay (India), Lagos (Nigeria), São Paulo (Brazil), Dhaka (Bangladesh), Karachi (Pakistan), Mexico City and Shanghai (China). Lagos's growth reflected the shift of the population of Nigeria, the most populous country in Africa, towards the towns: the urban proportion of Nigeria's population rose from a fifth in 1963 to over a third in 1991. The same process was seen throughout the developing world. In the 1980s, the widespread droughts that affected the Sahel belt in Africa led, for example, to much of the population of Mauritania abandoning nomadic herding and becoming city-dwellers, especially in the capital, Nouakchott. In some states, such as Angola, this process was accentuated by the disruptions of war.

The major cities in the developed world did not enjoy comparable growth in the second half of the twentieth century, although, in part, this reflected the nature of institutions. Urban governmental areas were not expanded to take note of the spread of urban areas based on cities such as London, Paris and Washington, and the traditional core of such cities frequently lost population as people moved to lower-density housing in the suburbs. Furthermore, the cities of the developed world were affected by its lower population growth rate compared to the developing world.

Nevertheless, immigrants to the developed world tended to concentrate on the major cities, and this helped them to grow. Thus, in the 1950s, Jamaicans moved to London, while the Puerto Rican population of New York rose from 187,000 to 613,000.

Across the world, the rate of growth of big cities was greater than that of smaller urban settlements. As a result, the urban hierarchy became more pronounced. Urban ranking and hierarchization were related to the increased interaction between cities made possible by improved communications. Linked to this, in many countries what had formerly been cities or towns lost status and were treated, respectively, as towns and villages if they failed to keep pace with the new population sizes now expected of them.

THE QUALITY OF URBAN LIFE

Several of the leading cities in the developing world were long-established as major centres, for example Beijing and Mexico City, but none were prepared for the rapid growth they experienced. There were insufficient jobs to prevent a major increase in unemployment and under-employment. The urban infrastructure proved particularly deficient on a number of counts, including water supply, public health, housing and transport, although communist states provided housing in cities and sought to meet infrastructure needs. The quality was often poor, as a visit to Ulan Bator, the capital of Mongolia, or other former communist cities today will show, but provision for the poor was better than in cities in Africa or Latin America.

Across the developing world, the percentage of the population with access to safe drinking water and sanitation was greater in urban than rural areas, but, even so, many urban areas lacked clean water. This encouraged epidemics of communicable diseases, such as diarrhoea. Health provision was particularly poor for recent migrants into towns and cities, many of whom lived in the more marginal residential districts, especially squatter camps. The percentage of the population who lived in such accommodation reflected the inability of urban regions to meet demands for affordable housing. Conditions in slums were such that many of the changes discussed elsewhere in this book were of limited impact. Housing without lighting, let alone electricity, offered scant prospect of access to modern technology or communications.

Such urban areas proved very difficult to police, and state authority in them was frequently limited. Instead,

HOUSING WITHOUT LIGHTING, LET ALONE ELECTRICITY, OFFERED SCANT PROSPECT OF ACCESS TO MODERN TECHNOLOGY OR COMMUNICATIONS.

gangs competed with each other, and with the police, to dominate large tracts of cities such as Karachi in Pakistan and São Paulo in Brazil. This led to high rates of urban violence. In Greater São Paulo, the number of murders rose above 6,000 in 1994 and above 8,000 in 1998 and, even more, 1999 – with the rate of murders per 100,000 passing 40 in 1994 and 50 in 1999. Murder rates climbed in many cities, for example Johannesburg in South Africa in the 1990s. The counterpart of gang warfare was the widespread pillaging carried out by corrupt officials. This was concentrated in the urban environment, where opportunities were greater. Corruption influenced not only the effectiveness of government, including in autocratic regimes such as communist China, but also the living circumstances of the people.

HOUSING

The extent of longer-established slums reflected not only the nature of the housing stock, but also the degree to which the housing needs of much of the world's population could only be met in that fashion. There were cities that did not face these problems, but they were 'artificial' creations unrelated to economic prospects. The most prominent were capital cities built to serve as symbols of national unity, such as Canberra, which became the seat of the Australian government in 1927, Brasilia, built in Brazil from 1957, Abuja, in Nigeria, from the 1980s, and Putrajaya, in Malaysia, from the 1990s.

It has been argued that developing countries experienced strains of urbanization comparable to those of areas that urbanized earlier, such as Britain and parts of the USA. There, in the late nineteenth century, poor urban sanitation, housing and nutrition were blamed for the physical weakness of much of the population, there was terrible overcrowding, and much of the urban environment was polluted.

It is therefore instructive to consider the subsequent process of amelioration in these countries, although it is worth bearing in mind that they also faced major problems in creating an infrastructure to match massive urban expansion, and many continue to face major problems in providing adequate public services, including law and order, clean water and care for the destitute. In greatly expanding cities, such as Los Angeles and Houston, each of which, by the 1990s, had economies larger than most countries in the world, far-flung water and sewage services had to be established as the suburbs spread over great distances.

In the twentieth century, housing in the developed countries involved urban regeneration, as crowded inner-city slums were torn down, and also extensive building on 'green field' sites, especially the expansion of suburbia. This reflected the pressure of rising numbers and the desire for a life away from factory chimneys. After World War II ended in 1945, there was a resumption of slum clearances, as well as new building to replace wartime devastation, and, in many countries, people were moved into new public housing. In Toronto, for example, Cabbagetown was demolished and the Housing Authority, created in 1947, built Regent Park North, a scheme characterized by low-density multiple housing.

As with the antibiotics and green revolutions, these were important aspects of a modernity that had been foreshadowed in earlier hopes and planning. It is also necessary to have a view on these changes: while it is important to consider how best to place the changes that occurred, altering views are indeed part of the history of the century. The suburbia of the 1930s and the new building that followed 1945 reflected contemporary aspirations, but their effects became controversial. Suburbia became sprawl in the eyes of critics who decried the space built over and the heavy reliance on the car in suburban culture.

This concern encouraged higher-density housing after 1945, although not for those who could still afford space. Alongside architectural and planning fashions, developments in construction technology and high land prices, this contributed to the high-rise development seen across the developed world. Pre-fabricated methods of construction ensured that multi-storey blocks of flats and office buildings could be built rapidly and inexpensively.

Extolled at the time, and illustrated alongside castles and cathedrals in guidebooks and promotional films of the 1960s, municipal multi-storey flats (projects in the USA) were subsequently attacked, particularly in Britain, as being of poor quality, ugly, out of keeping with the urban fabric, discouraging to community feeling and, thus, breeders of alienation and crime. The extent to which this was the fault of planning is a matter of controversy. The failure of many new estates of concrete inner-city tower blocks designed as entire communities, with elevated walkways called streets in the sky, may have been because of an absence of social cohesion on them that reflected far more than poor planning.

THE FAILURE OF MANY NEW ESTATES OF CONCRETE INNER-CITY TOWER BLOCKS DESIGNED AS ENTIRE COMMUNITIES MAY HAVE BEEN BECAUSE OF AN ABSENCE OF SOCIAL COHESION IN THEM THAT REFLECTED FAR MORE THAN POOR PLANNING.

It is also difficult to recover the attitudes of the 1950s. The buildings of the time, many of which were fairly generous with space, should be distinguished from the system-built tower blocks of the 1960s. Many of the new houses provided people with their first bathrooms and inside toilets, and, for the people involved, this was a more important development than the political narrative that usually dominates books of this type. There is considerable evidence to suggest that the problems of poorly built estates were much more apparent from the 1960s, and that earlier developments were often better built and more popular.

Municipal building ensured that a large percentage of the population in the developed world lived in publicly provided housing. This became more the case in Europe during the first three-quarters of the century as private rental housing declined, in part as a consequence of changes in tax policy and investment but, more generally, because private landlords could not meet the demands for new housing. Public provision also rose in the USA, but the private rental sector remained more important there than in Europe. Throughout the developed world, the number of urban-dwellers owning their own homes rose, but this remained very much a class matter, with the poor, most of the working class and much of the middle class unable to join in this process, although the social configuration of housing varied greatly by country.

Housing standards and specifications improved across the developed world during the century, and houses came to be integrated into wider networks, with the widespread provision of electricity, gas and telephone supplies and links. None of this was true for much of the housing in the developing world. Instead, urbanization there saw a borrowing of international forms of construction, but with only a limited ability to ensure adequate provision and necessary standards.

In China, where there was a major attempt under the communists, from the 1950s, to provide housing for town-dwellers, system-built blocks of flats were thrown up, as in the West, and this remains the case today. Older townscapes, especially the Beijing neighbourhoods known as *Hutongs*, which, with their narrow alleyways and courtyards, did not lend themselves to the scrutiny of government and the streamlined clarity of planners, were destroyed without consultation. The destruction underlined the extent to which new townscapes were not simply about housing people. They also represented political and economic power and cultural assumptions. At least in China, there was a major effort to provide housing. In contrast, in much of the developing world, the state made little or no effort to meet demands for housing, nor even to regulate its quality.

A NEW WORLD OF COMMUNICATIONS

Across the world, changes in transport were even more dramatic than those in housing. They were a product of the shift from natural parameters to a human environment largely shaped by societal pressures that resulted from urbanization, and also helped to drive this shift forward. As a greater percentage of the world's population lived in urban areas, where their environment was the product of human action, so also, thanks to technological developments, they were exposed to new or unfamiliar means of interaction. The unfamiliarity is an important corrective to the habitual focus simply on new inventions, because the key change across much of the world was the exposure of large numbers to already established technologies. This was true, for example, of rail, electricity, car and telephone, all of which were actually nineteenth-century technologies. If the Panama Canal, opened in 1914, provided a new American-dominated route between the Atlantic and the Pacific, the British-dominated Suez Canal, opened in 1869, had done likewise between the Mediterranean and the Red Sea (and thus the Indian Ocean). Other earlier technologies continued to spread. Thus, the impact of steam-power on industry and transport spread greatly in the developing world in the early decades of the twentieth century. Steam-powered boats, mills and other machines helped render uneconomic earlier techniques dependent on human, animal, water and wind power, or wood burning. This had major consequences for economic production, organization, the nature of work and the sense that change could, and would, transform life.

Much of the world's population had never seen a train by 1900, and that was even more the case with cars and telephones. Even within the developed countries, where new technology had been rapidly adopted, its use was still for long restricted for reasons of cost. The spread of electricity into industry and, even more, rural areas took many decades. In Britain, private car ownership rose from 0.13 million in 1914, but was still only at 2.26 million in 1950. Only 42 per cent of British households had a telephone in 1972. Thus the personal transport and communications revolution was very much a twentieth-century development, and, again, like so much else, one focused on the second half of the century.

CARS

In the first half of the twentieth century, the two major areas of car manufacture and ownership were the USA and Europe, and figures for the rest of the world, especially East and South Asia, remained low. The situation changed greatly in the second half of the century. As with many other examples of change, this was a case of an

intensification of trends in the developed world, and a transformation in the developing world. Again, as in other cases, it is necessary to distinguish among countries and social groups in the latter. For example, there was little by way of the car revolution in Ethiopia, and in other poor countries, such as Chad, Eritrea, Mali and Somalia, all in Africa, rates of car ownership remained very low.

Nevertheless, the general picture in the developing world was one of a spread in car manufacturing and a marked increase in ownership. From the 1960s, first Japan and later Brazil and South Korea developed important manufacturing capacity and, by the end of the century, production growth was greater in Asia, including in Iran, Malaysia and India, than in any other continent. Within Europe, there was a significant increase in Spain, West Germany, France, Italy and Sweden. On Easter Island in the Pacific, there was only one car (a jeep) in 1956, but over 3,000, equal to the island's population, in 2000.

As cars were traded widely, this rise in production helped to drive a worldwide increase in ownership, so that, by 1990, there were nearly 600 million cars in the world. Within the developed world, the rise in ownership was rapid. In Britain, private car ownership rose from 3.53 million in 1955 to 20.7 million in 1992. The rate of ownership also rose. In Britain, car ownership rose from 224 per 1,000 people in 1971 to 380 per 1,000 in 1994. Two-car families became more common.

Whereas in much of the developed world, there was a crucial rise in car ownership during the 1950s as wartime austerity and controls ended, and with the car industry helping to drive economic growth, in the developing world the relevant period came later. Thus, in China, there was an important shift in the 1990s, and that was also a period of major road construction there.

The net effect was that, although large numbers of town- (and rural-) dwellers continued to rely on non-motorised transport, principally bicycles and their own feet (often for very long journeys), the urban environment throughout the world changed in response to the car, while the car also became one of the distinctive features of the human imprint. Cars, and the roads they used, took up much space, and there was also a major impact on the environment in terms of pollution. 'The sound of horns and motors', referred to in T.S. Eliot's poem *The Waste Land* (1922), became more insistent. Furthermore, social life was altered, as the car affected a wide range of activities, for example courtship rituals, and also led to the development of particular cultures, as well as an

THE CAR BECAME ONE OF THE DISTINCTIVE FEATURES OF THE HUMAN IMPRINT.

international mass culture (or at least a mass culture). New roads led to new smells and sounds, and affected the visual context of life, both in towns and in the countryside. Roads created new demands for road signs, lamp posts, manhole covers and traffic lights, and led to new boundaries and commands. The role of government was extended with car-related construction, licences, offences and funding.

In towns, thanks to the intensity of use, major routes became obstacles, as high streets were turned into through routes. Neighbourhoods that were not thus bisected were still affected by the car. Side streets became 'rat runs' – quick shortcuts linking busier roads – and the sides of all roads filled up with parked cars.

Cars altered the urban environment. Greater personal mobility for the bulk, but by no means all, of the population in the developed world, especially from the 1960s, enabled, and was a necessary consequence of, lower-density housing and a declining role for public transport. This was linked to changes in employment patterns and urban structures. In place of factories or mines that had large labour forces, most modern industrial concerns were capital-intensive and employed less labour. They were often located away from the central areas of cities on flat and relatively open sites with good road links. This was true of business, science and shopping 'parks'. Related changes in location were also of great importance in such areas as education, health, shopping and retirement. Cars also affected the development of leisure. 'Days out' and the Sunday afternoon drive changed the nature of leisure and especially of 'the day of rest'. In rural areas, cars halted the decline of villages by permitting commuting from them and providing day-excursion economies.

In developed countries, cars were an equalizing mechanism, making work and leisure more accessible. Great mobility for most, but not for all, of the population, however, exacerbated social stratification. Car ownership brought a sense, maybe an illusion, of freedom, and an access to opportunities and options for many, but not all. The division of the population into communities defined by differing levels of wealth, expectations, opportunity and age was scarcely novel, but, thanks to changes in transport, it became more pronounced during the century; and an obvious aspect of what was termed the 'underclass', in both town and countryside, was their relative lack of mobility.

The car replaced rail services as the major force in the development of suburbia, although rail links remained of importance in the first half of the twentieth century in metropolitan areas such as London. Suburbia was already well established at the beginning of the century, and it was explicitly contrasted with both rural life and that of the densely packed city centres. Rickie, the protagonist of E.M. Forster's novel *The Longest Journey* (1907), 'had taken his first walk on asphalt. He had seen civilization as a row of semi-detached villas, and society as a state in which men do not know the men who live next door. He had himself become part of the grey monotony that surrounds all cities. There was no necessity for this – it was only rather convenient to his father.'

After 1945, although rail systems expanded in metropolitan areas such as London, Paris, San Francisco, Tokyo and Washington, the expansion of cities owed more to roads. For example, in Auckland, the leading city in New Zealand, the outer suburbs grew markedly and the green belt designated in the 1949 Development Plan was extensively breached in the 1950s. Whereas earlier suburbs had relied on trams, and a 1950 plan had recommended the expansion of suburban rail services, the 1955 Master Transportation Plan, instead, called for a series of urban motorways, and roads served as the basis for what became an urban sprawl. American metropolitan areas also grew rapidly in size. In New Zealand, as in the USA, this was linked to an emphasis on private home ownership rather than on public provision of housing and transport services. However, by the end of the century there was an attempt in Auckland and many other cities to develop light rail transport and to decrease dependence on the car.

The reshaping of the urban environment in the developed world reflected not only the role of roads within urban areas, but also the development of road links between towns. These altered the nodality and ranking of urban centres, but also provided a different shaping for towns to that offered by rail. Rail systems had a limited number of routes and access points, but road transport was far more flexible in routes, access and services. Instead of encouraging a focus of the urban environment on the major rail station(s) in the centre, roads encouraged a move to the periphery.

Long-distance, multi-lane roads, designed to provide effective high-speed routes, were pioneered in Germany from 1934, and taken up after World War II. The most important was the development of the American interstate highway system from the 1950s. This replaced long-distance passenger rail services and offered a free national network, in contrast to the turnpikes that had been built in individual American states. The first British motorway was opened in 1958. The Trans-Canada Highway followed four years later, although the development of highways was slower there than in the USA. Road transport proved more flexible than rail for freight as well as passengers, although this was helped by taxation policies that ensured that road users did not pay the full cost of the road system. By 2000, there were about seven million trucks (lorries) in the USA. The bridges and tunnels that formed part of ambitious new transport links helped to remould geography by providing new physical links, for example, in the

1990s, the Channel (rail) tunnel between Britain and France (opened 1994) and the Storebaelt Bridge between Denmark and Sweden (opened 1998).

In the developing world, long-distance road links were also built, although the network was far less intensive than in Europe and North America, and the standard of maintenance tended to be lower. Nevertheless, as in the developed world, road links helped to create economic opportunity and to lead to a reordering of urban functions and rankings. Lorries proved particularly important for freight movements in the developing world as rail links were often poor. By 2000, Mexico had about 375,000 lorries.

Car technology was also a cause of high rates of pollution. At the end of the century developments in fuel cell technology opened the prospect of a cleaner technology, but, in the meanwhile, there was a toll from air pollution and other damaging effects of road travel and traffic congestion. This was true both of cities in the developing world, such as Bangkok, Manila and Mexico City, and also of those in the developed world, such as Los Angeles.

More generally, urban expansion moulded countries, not least by affecting the countryside, both nearby and at a distance, as well as rural interests. They found space, water and other rural resources used for the benefit of the cities. For example, the Los Angeles (or Owens valley) Aqueduct carried water 233 miles to Los Angeles from the eastern Sierras. In Los Angeles itself, the architect William Mulholland was hailed as a civic hero. However, in California's 'Little Civil War' over water rights, ranchers in the Owens Valley blew up the aqueduct and seized its principal diversion works in 1924. When, three years later, the bombing of the aqueduct was resumed, the City of Los Angeles sent train-loads of guards armed with machine-guns, and this show of force proved effective. The needs of expanding cities denuded water resources in the west of the USA and elsewhere in the world.

CONCLUSIONS

Much of the history of the century was a history of cities or, at least, was enacted in them. The human environment was also increasingly focused on cities on a scale that alienated or frightened many, and that left large numbers of their population feeling anonymous. An ambivalent response to urban life and the city was central to the sensibility and culture of much of the developed world in the twentieth century.

MUCH OF THE HISTORY OF THE CENTURY WAS A HISTORY OF CITIES OR, AT LEAST, WAS ENACTED IN THEM.

four

THE SHIFTING KALEIDOSCOPE
SOCIAL CHANGE

INTRODUCTION

It is unclear how best to describe people. Are they primarily motivated by their economic position, ethnic group, parental background, personal assumptions or peer-group pressures? How much does any one of these flow from the others? Do terms like 'class' mean much for the bulk of the population, and, if so, what? Do they merely describe a situation, or do they also explain it? This chapter has to introduce the reader to concepts and methodology, because the way in which social change is discussed throws considerable light on the actual processes of social formation and interaction. The variety of approaches employed in the study of social structures and attitudes in part reflect the ambiguous nature of social categories and the difficulty of assessing the complexity of modern society.

DO TERMS LIKE 'CLASS' MERELY DESCRIBE A SITUATION, OR DO THEY ALSO EXPLAIN IT?

CLASS

Class-based analyses of society were the most important in the twentieth century. A class is essentially a large group of people who share a similar social and economic position. Much of the basis of class analysis derived from Marxism. Karl Marx claimed in the *Communist Manifesto* (1848) that 'the history of all hitherto existing societies is the history of class struggle'. Although his analysis was influential among many commentators who were not strictly Marxists and, indeed, among many who rejected Marxism, the Marxist analysis was particularly important in communist states (primarily Russia from 1917 and China from 1949), where it provided the theoretical underpinning of public ideology, and hence was of major importance.

In Marx's analysis, class was linked to economic power, which was defined by the individual's relationship to the means of production, society being presented as an engine for the production of goods and for the distribution of tasks and benefits directed by the dominant class. Society was divided between two self-conscious groups: the proletariat or 'workers', who lived off the sale of their labour power, and the bourgeoisie or property owners, who bought that labour power. These groups were assumed to be in a conflict to benefit from, and control, the fruits of labour power, and society itself was the sphere for this conflict and was shaped by it.

Non-Marxist analyses were less dominated by the notion of conflict and keener to present social structures as more complex, although Marx himself was explicit about complexity in his historical works. Income and status (in part market position) differences between occupational groups dominated such analyses. They centred on a difference between the 'middle class' – white-collar (non-manual) workers – and the 'working' class – 'blue-collar' (manual) workers. These differences were further refined by consumer analysts, concerned to dissect society for marketing purposes, and by government surveys.

However, the classification of society in terms of jobs was weakened by its social assumptions, not least a focus on male, not female, occupations. There was also a problem if the particular characteristics of youth society were ignored. A stress on the distinctive lifestyles of youth, and particularly on youth independence, underlines the more general fluidity of social life. In addition, to be 'working' or 'middle' class meant very different things at different stages of life, and this challenged notions of class coherence, let alone unity. Furthermore, at the 'micro' level, families increasingly contained individuals who were in different social groups. It was also clear that attitudes towards social mobility varied greatly, both between individuals and within social groups.

There were other problems with class-based analyses of social structures. Class issues were of little, if any, relevance to most of tribal humankind for most of the century, while social shifts in the developed world in recent decades led to an emphasis on the irrelevance of traditional classes. Nevertheless, there is a danger in ignoring the persistence of class differences in the developed world. Furthermore, class acted (and acts) as an important prism for refracting views and identities. It was particularly important in the first four decades of the century.

Despite this, social structure was not as rigid as much of the discussion might suggest: there was much fluidity in the concept of social status; notions of social organization, hierarchy and dynamics all varied; and the position of individuals and groups, and the cohesion of the latter, involved and reflected much besides social status. This challenged class consciousness and the discussion of society in terms of class. Both religion and ethnicity were very important to this situation and process.

ETHNICITY

Thanks to large-scale migration, the ethnic composition of countries changed greatly. Migration affected not only neighbouring states, but also more distant countries. Australia, which had developed during the century as a country largely inhabited by European immigrants, with Greeks and Italians being added to the earlier British emphasis, received large numbers of refugees from Vietnam and China after the 'White Australia' policy was ditched in 1966, although this more liberal policy towards refugees aroused criticism, especially in the 1990s. In spite of efforts in the first quarter of the century to check the influx of immigrants, the USA became increasingly Asian and Latino during the century, particularly in the last quarter, although most immigrants wanted to learn English. By 2000, thanks to immigration, nearly three million of France's sixty million residents were of North African origin, with another about 415,000 residents from Turkey and the Middle East, and 250,000 from sub-Saharan Africa.

Migration often contributed to a sense of greater ethnic consciousness and division within countries, rather than to a sense of national identity transforming different ethnic legacies. Both processes could be seen in the USA. Furthermore, across the world, government steps to end religious or ethnic discrimination towards both immigrants and long-established minorities (sometimes the indigenous population) frequently had only limited effect. The newly independent Indian state abolished Untouchability, replacing it with the concept of scheduled castes who were allocated a quota of places in education and government employment. However, discrimination remained strong in India and neighbouring countries. As a similar example, Amerindians in Latin America suffered discrimination, if not worse, during the century. Their fate was poverty, not social mobility, although government-sanctioned policies of extermination or assimilation as a result of state action became increasingly rare after 1945.

Aside from this treatment of groups that were in effect excluded from the dominant community, perceptions of ethnicity and race frequently provided the key element in the detailed cartography and dynamics of communities, leading to patterns of settlement, occupation, education and sociability, and to the different success of particular groups. Despite attempts by autocratic governments to fix these relationships, as with white-dictated apartheid (separate development) in South Africa from 1948 until the early 1990s, they were constantly dynamic, and were also a cause of tension and disputes, which served to test strengths and boundaries. For example, the major difference between the wages of white and Chinese seamen led to a widespread successful strike in China in 1922 that was important to the process of worker politicization.

On the whole, social identities and interests were defined on the national scale, and not with reference to those doing similar jobs in other states. Attempts to develop international working-class solidarity had only limited success. Within many countries, especially in the USA, the model of economic advance, a strong governmental and public ideology developed that pressed for a focus on shared national concerns, and not on racial, religious or linguistic differences. Many regimes, however, preferred, as with the anti-Semitism of Nazi Germany (1933–45), to pursue national concerns by demonizing groups they disliked within the countries they governed. Furthermore, a focus on shared national concerns could co-exist, as in the USA, with a form of caste system defined by attitudes to colour. Thus, in the American territory of Hawaii in the first half of the century, Whites dominated, Hawaiians were at the bottom of the heap and mixed-race people occupied an intermediate position. Across much of the world, similar social practices became increasingly unacceptable in the second half of the century when equality of opportunity, controversially if apparently necessary through positive discrimination, became a more important goal, certainly in the USA.

At the same time, the complexities of racial identity were increasingly understood, at least among those open to scientific advances: no race possesses a discrete package of genetic characteristics; there are more genetic variations within, than between, races; and the genes responsible for morphological features, such as skin colour, are atypical. Races were constructed as much as described. Bi-racial marriages and unions helped to underline the very fluidity of the situation: unless entrenched through endogamy (marriage within the clan), demographic developments undermined classification in terms of race. At the same time, rates **RACES WERE CONSTRUCTED AS MUCH AS DESCRIBED.** of intermarriage varied. Thus, for example, they were higher in Hawaii than in New Zealand, and this contributed to the Westernization of the native population of Hawaii.

Migration was often crudely presented in almost entirely negative terms, and the language was indicative: with a 'flood' of economic migrants seeking to 'sponge' off a welfare system and this 'provoking' racial tension. However, aside from enormous advantages to individual migrants, and the provision of new labour and skills to host countries, there was also the social and cultural enrichment of multiculturalism.

CLASSIFYING SOCIETY

In place of an account of society that presents human identities and choices as determined, or at least heavily influenced by, social 'structures', particularly class, it is possible to emphasize the role of human agency (activities). The resulting stress on the role of human decisions, and on concepts and ideologies, in social formation and attitudes led to a less clear-cut and more complex, not to say indistinct or 'messy', situation, particularly if the individual, rather than the collective, was seen as the basic unit of decision-making. Patterns of social behaviour became less apparent and processes of causation less easy to define. The growing emphasis on self-identification as a major source of social location in the second half of the century necessarily limited both broad-brush approaches and 'realist' analyses based on measurable criteria, whether related to the means of production, income or other factors.

Social location through self-identification involved a number of factors, including not only age, religion and ethnicity, but also lifestyle. Here it is important to pause and to note that much of the classification and discussion of social structure presupposes an urban, industrial and Western society, but that, at the global level, it is the move towards such a situation, at least in part, that was the major factor in social history over the last century. The structures and assumptions of the primarily rural and agrarian societies that comprised much of the world's population in 1900 were different to those of the far more urban societies of today, but rural society also changed over the century. There were two constants, however: inequality and diversity.

Social groups faced very different circumstances and opportunities across the world during the century, but, in addition, there was a marked diversity in social changes, particularly in the developing world. In part, this diversity reflected distinctive old-established characteristics, such as religion, but more recent political events also played a major role. Thus, in China, the communist revolution of 1949 was followed by an unprecedented degree of collectivization and state direction. This built on the traditional power of the Chinese state, but gave it a very radical dimension at the level of individuals. The situation was very different in the other most populous Asian countries – India, Indonesia and Japan: there, the state did not seek to transform society and culture to any comparable degree.

COMMUNIST SOCIETIES

Communist states used public ownership of industry and land (nationalization and collectivization) to justify a marked degree of control over the people. If socialist labour was the social duty of all, then the state, as the representative of the community, had to ensure that everybody was able and willing to fulfil his or her duty. The contempt displayed towards other arrangements and existing (pre-communist) lifestyles was shown in *Virgin Soil Upturned* (1932), a novel by the communist Mikhail Sholokhov (1905–84), who rose to be a Deputy to the Supreme Soviet, and was awarded the Nobel Prize for Literature in 1965:

> The 'dead season' in agriculture, the period between the spring sowing and the haymaking, was first abolished in 1930. In former years, when the peasants lived in the traditional way, those two months were not called the 'dead season' for nothing. When they had finished their sowing the farmers leisurely made ready for haymaking … Not a soul was to be met in the lifeless street at noonday. The cossacks were either out on journeys, or resting in their huts or their cool cellars, or idly wielding axes. And the sleepy women were comfortably settled in a cool spot, catching their fleas. An emptiness and drowsy peace reigned in the villages.
>
> But the very first year the collective farm existed the 'dead season' was violated. Hardly had the grain begun to shoot when weeding began … demonstration of good management, which would put the entire village in movement.

The reality was not only economic mismanagement and widespread poverty, but also a degree of harsh policing, presented as class struggle against reactionary forces, including in the Don region Sholokhov described. In communist states, surveillance, internment camps and large black economies existed alongside supposedly full employment and comprehensive social security. The demands of the community, that is, the state, extended to private life, as opinions were policed and attempts made to mould gender and generational relations by, for example, encouraging women into factories, or to have, or not have, children (Romania and China, respectively).

The Russian novelist Alexander Solzhenitsyn (1918–), who himself had been in prison camps (1945–53) for making critical remarks about the Soviet dictator Joseph Stalin, set novels such as *Cancer Ward* (1968) and *The First Circle* (1968), which won the Nobel Prize in 1970, in the dehumanizing institutions of the Soviet police state. In the latter novel, Solzhenitsyn captured the uncertainty of transferred prisoners and the cruelty and harshness of their treatment: 'will they stop his correspondence for years on end, so that his family thinks he is dead? . . . Will he die of dysentery in his cattle truck? Or die of hunger because the train does not stop for six days and no rations are issued?'

SOCIAL CONTROL

Tensions between collectivization and individual ownership, and between national-ization and free enterprise, were as important to social structures and assumptions as they were to political and economic history. Like much else, these tensions reflected problems and opportunities. The former included how best to structure society, a question that most governments considered an issue for their explicit attention, in what was a widespread expansion of state claims to power and roles. Governments grasped the opportunity of using the resources of society in order to obtain political goals, both international and domestic. Thus, across much of the world, society was presented as a subject of, and enabler for, government. At the extreme, this encour-aged action against groups judged unwelcome, such as Armenians under the Ottoman (Turkish) empire and Jews under Nazi Germany.

Although generally far less extreme, such authoritarianism was widely displayed; and aspects of it could be seen in countries such as the USA that lacked a rhetoric of state control. Furthermore, decolonization (see chapter 9) greatly increased the number of countries in which governments had to decide how best to define the relationship between society and the state. In addition, in the mid-twentieth century, the long-established governmental policing of public morals and popular culture was accentu-ated. This was because fears of political and social subversion and the disruptive consequences of individualism influenced attitudes to practices that were not in the accepted social mainstream, and because the emphasis on collective effort and pro-vision led to a hostile attitude towards those who did not accept norms.

The growing statism of societies where governmental powers were extended, or at least more comprehensively institutionalized, ensured that it was national

ACROSS MUCH OF THE WORLD IN THE FIRST TWO THIRDS OF THE CENTURY, ABORTION, SUICIDE, HOMOSEXUALITY AND PROSTITUTION WERE CRIMINAL OFFENCES.

government, rather than local authorities and communities, that set codes and criminalized habits judged unacceptable, such as drug-taking. Across much of the world in the first two thirds of the century, abortion, suicide, homosexuality and prostitution were criminal offences, and consenting adults therefore had no privacy. Restrictive divorce laws affected marriage, child care and sexuality. Censorship affected what could be read, seen and listened to. Leisure activities such as drinking and gambling were regulated, and alcohol consumption was prohibited in the USA from 1919 until 1933. Such restrictions made criminals out of the large numbers who broke them. Corporal punishment (beating) remained common in schools. Those judged mental defectives were incarcerated and in some countries, for example Sweden, the USA, Germany and China, sterilized in pursuit of eugenicist assumptions about how best to improve the population. Young men were brought under the sway of the state through conscription, which continued in Britain and the USA after World War II. The ability of government to inflict capital punishment – execution – contributed to the sense of powerful states with moral codes that they were determined to enforce.

That was not the same, however, as unchanging views. During the century, especially from the 1960s, there were to be major changes in social norms and governmental regulation. These can be presented in terms of an overthrow of conservative norms and state regulation by a more liberal society, but that is too partial a view. First, it presupposes a situation in which change only occurs through conflict, when, in fact, a degree of interaction is more common. Secondly, this view ignores the extent to which 'conservative' societies and states are not without a capacity for change. Third, and more significant on the global scale, much of the pressure for social change came from radical governments, rather than from 'society'. Thus in Britain, capital punishment (hanging for murder) was abolished in 1965 despite considerable public support for its continuance.

GENDER

All these points can be illustrated from the perspective of gender. At the outset of the century, there were few areas where women had the right to vote. The first American state to grant women the vote was Wyoming in 1869, and the first country to give women universal suffrage was New Zealand in 1893. However, across much of the world, successive extensions of the franchise in the nineteenth century were restricted to men. Modern standards of equality were a long way off, even in countries that considered themselves progressive. The notion of 'separate spheres' was well established at the beginning of the century: women's special role was defined as that of home and family. This was employed to justify the exclusion of women from other spheres and served to stigmatize the large number of women who had to work. Furthermore, the concept of 'separate spheres' did not do justice to the complexities of gender relationships. The pervasive and distorting impact of male concepts was to be described in a number of works, especially the influential *The Second Sex* (1949) by the French existentialist writer Simone de Beauvoir (1908–86).

In some parts of the world, gender relationships at the beginning of the century were affected by the declining influence of religion and the rise of scientists to become the new authorities. Older ideas of the intellectual superiority of men over women were given new authority by claims that the greater brain size of men proved the point. Medicine presented women as normally unstable, and natural differences between men and women were stressed in order to make women appear unsuitable for public positions. In addition, the public ideologies, for example of race and empire, that helped shape the dominant constructions of masculinity did not award women a commanding role.

Much of the female population worked in non-household tasks, but, in agriculture and industry, women were generally given the worse jobs and denied access to the new technologies. Definitions of skills, which affected pay, were controlled by men and favoured them; skilled women were poorly recognized. Trade unions (essentially male organizations) co-operated with management to this end.

The subsequent history of women's rights can be divided into three overlapping periods. Until the late 1940s, the major changes occurred in the developed world, but, from then, the developing world became more important. From the 1960s, important social changes in the developed world combined with a self-conscious women's movement to produce, for at least some women, a gender revolution. In the first period, the two World Wars had a major impact in encouraging the expansion of the right to vote and in leading to more women entering the labour force, although it would be wrong to associate changes simply with the wars. Thus, the franchise spread both early in the century (women gaining the vote in Norway in 1913) and in countries that did not play a role in the World Wars. In Britain, female employment rose in World War I (1914–18), and new roles, many in industry, were performed by women. In Russia, women were enfranchised by the 1917 revolution, and in the USA in 1920, after the passing of the 19th Amendment.

However, the subsequent electoral position of women was constrained by a variety of factors, including ethnicity, class and political assumptions. Thus, although women of European origin in Kenya gained the vote in 1919, this was not extended to black women. Similarly, Australian Aboriginal, Canadian Native American and South African non-white women did not receive the vote. Social criteria included a restriction of enfranchisement in Bolivia to literate women until 1952, and in Britain the decision in 1918 to extend the vote to women, but only if 30 and over, and as long as they were householders, wives of householders, occupants of property worth £5 annually, or graduates of British universities. For men, in contrast, the age was 21 and there were no longer any socio-economic restrictions on the franchise. Younger men in the forces could vote. It has been suggested that war work gained women the vote in Britain, but women workers were mostly property-less and under 30. It is possible that 'mature' women were given the vote as a way to lessen the potentially radical impact of universal male suffrage.

FEMALE ENFRANCHISEMENT HAD ONLY A LIMITED IMPACT ON POLITICS.

Female enfranchisement had only a limited impact on politics. The election of women to national assemblies and their appointment to senior governmental positions was uncommon before the second half of the century. Women did not constitute a united bloc of voters with a shared interest and sense of identity. Instead, having won the vote, women's movements lost a measure of unity. Aside from the customary divisions that affected men – on social, ethnic, religious and ideological lines – there were also specific differences between, for example, housewives and employed women, married and unmarried, older and younger, feminist and non-feminists, and these categories as often clashed as coincided.

Enfranchisement did not ensure equality. Instead, women continued to suffer discrimination in most fields, including the jobs they were expected to do, and the tasks allocated to them. At the same time, across the developed world, there was a measure of liberalization in the treatment of women in the first four decades of the century. New opportunities were related to increased mobility and independence. This included a decline in control and influence over young women by their elders, male and female. As a consequence, there was a new sexual climate. Chaperonage became less comprehensive and effective, and styles of courtship became freer, a shift recorded both in literature and in public surveys. The percentage of illegitimate births rose. Furthermore, there was a greater interest in the informed public discussion of sex, with an emphasis on mutual desire as its basis. Although the notion of a 'home front' in World War I was in part an affirmation of established gender concepts and roles, with women seen as nurturers, social mores become more fluid. At the very least, Victorian codes were challenged. In some Western countries, divorce law was liberalized in the interwar years.

CULTURAL DEVELOPMENTS

These changes can be related, however tenuously, to cultural and intellectual developments in the early decades of the century. Modernism, a cultural tendency that aimed to make a break with the past and to find new forms and means of expression, was important, especially in Europe and the USA, although what was 'modern' was very much a relative concept. It was a characteristic of a range of international artistic movements that challenged traditional forms and assumptions and, instead, preferred an experimental moulding of form in order to shake the reader, viewer or listener from established patterns of response. Modernism was a reaction against the positivism, liberalism and realistic representational culture that had been so important for most of the nineteenth century. In part, it drew for inspiration on the new social sciences and their challenge to established assumptions, for example on Sigmund Freud's *The Interpretation of Dreams* (1900) and Sir James Frazer's classic of anthropology, *The Golden Bough* (1890-1915), which presented religions as social constructs that recorded evolutionary development. The sense of collapse engendered by World War I contributed to the general questioning of cultural norms and assumptions.

In literature, modernism's distinctive characteristics included the use of the technique of the stream of consciousness and a fascination with myth, both characteristics of the novel *Ulysses* (1922) by James Joyce (1882-1941), in which Dublin life ironically counterpointed Homer's classic the *Odyssey*. Free verse was used to throw together very different voices and fractured ideas in the influential poem *The Waste Land* (1922) by T.S. Eliot (1888-1965). Other major modernist writings included *La Coscienza di Zeno* (*The Confessions of Zeno*, 1924) by Italo Svevo (1861-1928), which was heavily Freudian, and the novels of Virginia Woolf (1882-1941), for example *To the Lighthouse* (1927), which displayed an experimental and fluid structure and lyrical use of language. Woolf rejected what she presented as 'materialist' writing and, instead, sought a new aesthetic sensibility. In her essay 'Mr Bennett and Mrs Brown' (1924), she distinguished between what she considered the false 'realism' of surface description and a 'modernism' that searched for true realism. In place of narrative, Woolf advocated a view of life as a 'luminous halo'. In music, the Austrian composer Arnold Schoenberg (1874-1951) offered atonal and serial compositions. In painting, Cubism, Expressionism, Vorticism, Surrealism and Dadaism assailed Realism. In the

Dada Manifesto of 1918, Tristan Tzara (1896–1963) declared 'Let each man proclaim: there is a great negative work of destruction to be accomplished. We must sweep and clean.' Some modernist writers, such as H.G. Wells, Aldous Huxley and George Orwell, consciously explored the future as a way of commenting on the present.

This was an international movement: Tzara was born in Romania, but lived in France; Eliot was born in the USA, but settled in England; and Svevo was the pseudonym of Ettore Schmitz, who was born in Trieste and educated in Bavaria.

There was also a reaction against classical literature in China. In the 1910s, there were calls for a new, more accessible style, although this cannot be readily placed alongside European and American modernism, not least because of interest in China in a realism to replace the earlier, more allusive timbre of the literature.

The impact of modernism on popular taste in Europe, the USA and elsewhere should not be exaggerated. Work by painters such as the Spanish Surrealist Salvador Dali (1904–89) and his compatriot Pablo Picasso (1881–1973) or architects such as Le Corbusier (pseudonym of the Swiss architect Charles Jeanneret, 1887–1965) and the German Walter Gropius (1893–1969) had only a limited appeal. Older styles, such as revived classicism in architecture and conventional approaches in music and art, had a stronger impact. Furthermore, the new music that had greatest public appeal was jazz. Some jazz figures, such as Duke Ellington (1899–1974), felt able to argue that jazz was as valid and accomplished as classical music. Jazz had an international appeal and American bands helped spread it in Europe, Ellington doing so in 1933. There was also an important ethnic dimension as jazz's appeal in part rested on its origins among African Americans.

The 'middle-' and 'low-brow' writers despised by the modernists enjoyed greater sales. They benefited from the rising disposable income of the interwar years, especially the 1920s, from the ready availability of inexpensive books, and from increased leisure. Women readers were of growing importance. The great range of work not conforming to modernist fashion did not seek to be radical, but there was a widespread willingness to present women as more independent emotionally and, often, more engaged in gainful employment than had been the case prior to World War I. Similarly, much of the cinema, a mass medium that developed greatly in the interwar period, revolved around sexuality, and presented women who were not defined by matrimony and motherhood.

THE 'MIDDLE-' AND 'LOW-BROW' WRITERS DESPISED BY THE MODERNISTS ENJOYED GREATER SALES.

In World War II (1939–45), the process of greater independence for women was pushed forward. Far more women were employed, frequently away from home. Many women also benefited from less constrained personal life: partners were absent, large numbers of unmarried young women left home for war work, for example as secretaries in the expanded American federal bureaucracy in Washington, and attitudes were less rigid. At the same time, the war brought terrible suffering to many women. Aside from the large number who suffered pain, sorrow and hardship from the loss of relatives, there was also much pain inflicted directly on women. Civilians were directly targeted by air attack, and in addition large numbers of women were raped, especially as Soviet forces conquered Eastern Europe in 1944–5, while the Japanese military used a system of enforced prostitution, particularly of Korean women.

A dramatic shift in the position of women after World War II occurred in the developing world, although there had been earlier changes there. Colonial governments had introduced a measure of Westernization, including the prohibition of some practices deemed unacceptable, there had also been some changes in Latin America, and, in addition, traditional societies that were attempting to modernize, especially Turkey under Kemal Atatürk, President 1923–38, rejected past practices such as polygamy. Women were granted the vote there, and in Japan and Thailand. Nevertheless, women were still very much second-class citizens in the developing world in the interwar period. Their position varied in accordance with cultural norms and economic circumstances, and, at the detailed level, relationships between individuals were crucial, but a major opening to opportunity, education outside the household, was routinely not offered to girls.

The pace of change stepped up after 1945. In China, the communist revolution saw a determined rejection of social and other customs, including, for example, changes to the language to make education and literacy easier: new, easier versions of the characters were introduced. In the case of women, this led, in 1950, to a Marriage Law, which promised them greater freedom, including the right to choose a partner freely and equal rights in divorce, child custody and property. The impact of this law was lessened by the strength of traditional patriarchalism and by the male-dominated character of Chinese communism, but, in 1980, the legal rights of women were confirmed in a new Marriage Law, although its raising of the age of marriage (for men to 22 and for women to 20) was a reminder of the extent to which the Chinese state saw it appropriate to dictate to its citizens.

More generally, across much of the developing world, decolonization was followed by at least formal democracy and the vote was extended to women. In addition, the extensive changes of the period, especially urbanization, led to a measure of social fluidity that gave women more opportunities (and responsibilities). Development policies included a concern with universal education, and female education was increasingly seen as important.

To a certain extent, this and other aspects of female circumstances were mediated through often diverse cultural assumptions. Thus, there was a greater willingness in Latin American than in Islamic countries to encourage secondary education for girls. In Saudi Arabia throughout the century, women were banned from driving. Female emancipation was one of the goals of the 'White Revolution' launched by Mohammed Reza Pahlavi, the Shah of Iran, in 1962, but it helped increase hostility to his policies. In 2000, Mohammed VI of Morocco's plans to extend women's rights with a 'national action plan', including equal rights of inheritance and the allocation of a third of parliamentary seats to women, led to virulent Islamic protests. Much of the Islamic world witnessed such opposition in the last three decades of the century, and in some Islamic countries such beliefs affected or determined state policy. In 2000, the Sudanese government banned women from working in the capital in public places where they might meet men.

At the same time, it is important to avoid cultural determinism. Some Islamic countries, for example Egypt and Syria, proved more receptive to secondary education for girls than others, for example, Pakistan or Mali. Moreover, Egyptian women gained the vote in 1956, whereas this right was not exercised until 2001 in Bahrain. However, in Egypt, at the end of the twentieth century, women were still not free to travel without their husband's permission. The World Bank's World Development Report reported that, in Egypt in 1998, 58 per cent of women aged 15 or over could not read and write; whereas for men the percentage was 35. The comparable figures for Niger were 93 and 78, and for Burkina Faso (formerly Upper Volta) 87 and 68. More generally, there was still a widespread preference for males, seen, for example, in the infanticide of female babies in non-Islamic countries such as China and India, particularly under the Chinese one child per household policy. Contrasting literacy rates also suggested very different cultural assumptions about the role and value of men and women.

INDIVIDUALISM AND SOCIAL CHANGE FROM THE 1960S

In the developed world from the 1960s, there was a major social shift that had important implications for women. This was a period in which fashions, in clothes and popular music, stressed novelty and in which there was an emphasis on the individual and his or her ability to construct their particular world. Songs and films featured sexual independence. Hedonism focused on free will, self-fulfilment and consumerism, the last the motor of economic growth. The net effect was a more multifaceted public construction of individual identities, and more fluid societies. The stress on the individual did not lend itself to a classification of identity, interest and activity in terms of traditional social categories, especially class; or to any simple explanation of cultural, intellectual and artistic developments in terms of comprehensive themes. One cultural consequence of this, which continued a trend seen earlier in the century, was the creation of artistic works that deliberately drew on different forms and transcended boundaries as an aspect of an attempt to discard established disciplinary classifications and conventions.

Youth culture, feminism, drugs and sexual liberation were international themes, as, more generally, was anti-authoritarianism and the questioning of authority. Although particularly true of the West, they also affected the developing world. Despite its 1979 Islamic revolution, by 2000 there were over two million drug addicts in Iran as well as high divorce rates. Divorce also rose in countries with very different cultures, for example Thailand. Novel gender and youth expectations and roles commanded attention across the world.

There was also legislative action, although the rate and extent varied. Divorce and abortion remained illegal in some countries as a result of the role of religion and traditional social concepts in their culture. Both remained illegal in Chile. In general, however, abortion and same-sex acts between consenting adults were legalized, divorce was liberalized and there were moves against the death penalty, censorship, conscription and racial discrimination.

These changes reflected not simply long-established liberal causes but also a more specific rejection of conventional social and cultural assumptions. In part, this arose from a challenging of earlier norms. Radical intellectual influences contributed to a sense of flux and also to established norms and values being seen as simply passing conventions. Structuralism, a movement that looked to the anthropologist Claude Lévi-Strauss (1908–) and the French literary critic Roland Barthes (1915–80), treated language as a set of conventions that were themselves of limited value as guides to any underlying reality. Although links (like definitions) were far from clear-cut, this looked towards the Postmodernism that became influential in the 1980s. Existentialism, a European post-World-War II nihilistic philosophical movement closely associated with Martin Heidegger (1889–1976) and Jean-Paul Sartre (1905–80), stressed the vulnerability of the individual in a hostile world and the emptiness of choice. Works affected by these ideas, such as the novels of Albert Camus (1913–60), for example *L'Étranger* (The Stranger) (1942), and the plays of Sartre, had an impact. So also did the non-realist 'theatre of the absurd' associated with the works of Samuel Beckett (1906–89) and Eugène Ionesco (1912–94), such as *Les Chaises* (The Chairs) (1952).

However, in terms of lifestyles, American popular culture had far more of an impact. Encouraged by the role of American films and television programmes, and of American-derived products in consumer society, the mystique of America as a land of wealth and excitement grew greatly in the 1950s, particularly in Western Europe, Latin America and Japan. The Disney theme parks in California (1955) and Florida (1971) were followed by others in Tokyo (1983) and Paris (1992). All were very popular and received more visits than famous 'high cultural' tourist sites. On 15 May 1950, the cover of the American news-weekly magazine *Time* showed a globe with facial features eagerly drinking from a bottle of Coca-Cola. American culture offered a seductive worldwide model. It seemed fresh, vital, optimistic and democratic, certainly compared to the war-scarred and exhausted societies of Europe. Its cultures weakened or discredited by defeat, collaboration or exhaustion, much of Western European society, especially that of West Germany, was reshaped in response to American influences and consumerism, which were associated with prosperity, youth, fashion and glamour. American culture also replaced European models elsewhere, particularly in Canada, Australia and Latin America. American culture thrived on the new consumerism and was particularly attuned to the worlds of television, the car and suburbia, which were increasingly influential from the 1950s.

> **AMERICAN CULTURE SEEMED FRESH, VITAL, OPTIMISTIC AND DEMOCRATIC, CERTAINLY COMPARED TO THE WAR-SCARRED AND EXHAUSTED SOCIETIES OF EUROPE.**

More than consumerism was involved. There was also a content that was more democratic, accessible and populist than that elsewhere. This can be seen by comparing American films and television with their European counterparts, or by considering the ability of American composers such as Gershwin, Copland, Ives, Barber and Bernstein to create a musical language that spanned classical and popular idioms, and drew heavily on the latter. George Gershwin's symphonic jazz work *Rhapsody in Blue* (1923) was a great success and influenced later composers. In works like *Billy the Kid* (1938), *Rodeo* (1942) and *Appalachian Spring* (1944), Aaron Copland (1900–90) celebrated American culture and sought to create an 'American Style', rather than

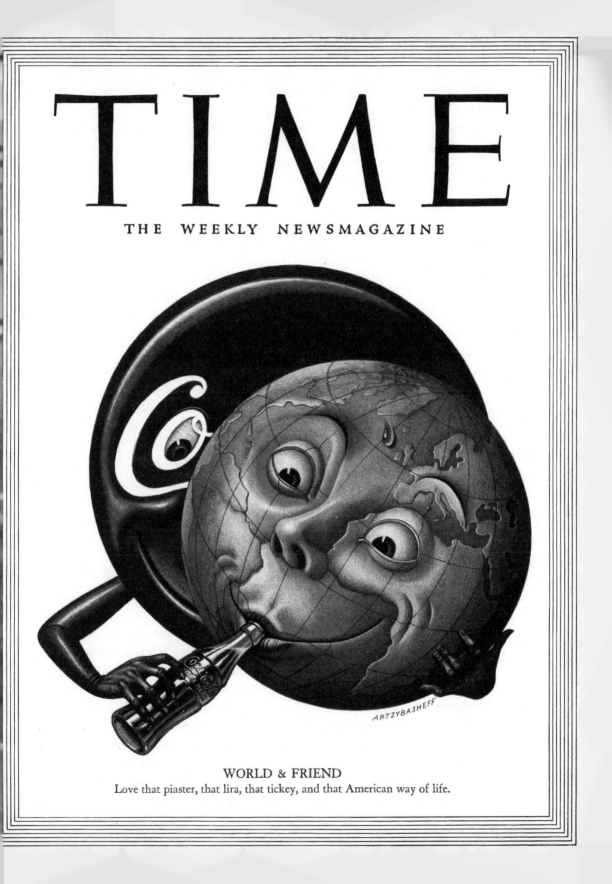

TIME

THE WEEKLY NEWSMAGAZINE

WORLD & FRIEND
Love that piaster, that lira, that tickey, and that American way of life.

looking to customary European models; Bernstein (1918–90) did the same in his musicals *On the Town* (1944) and *West Side Story* (1957). Gershwin, Copland and Bernstein also reflected the vitality of European immigrants in America. American popular music, in the form of rock'n' roll in the 1950s, had a particular impact in developing Western youth culture.

Social and cultural changes hit earlier taboos. The women's liberation movement was diverse, as can be seen by contrasting texts such as Betty Friedan's *Feminine Mystique* (1963) and Kate Millett's *Sexual Politics* (1970); but conventional assumptions and practices, including nuclear families, the authoritarian position of men within households and female sexual subservience, were all criticized, and there was a stress on 'consciousness raising' for women. Demands for the recognition of an independent sexuality included an assertion of women's rights to enjoy sex, to have it before marriage without incurring criticism, and to control contraception and, thus, their own fertility. The introduction and rapid spread of the oral contraceptive pill from the late 1950s helped this process by making it easier to separate sexuality from reproduction. Furthermore, later developments in contraception increased female control. These included the 'morning-after pill' and, from the 1990s, an injectable contraceptive that needed to be taken only once every three months.

Shifting attitudes were not simply dependent on technology. There was also a readiness to embrace privately, and even publicly, what had hitherto been regarded publicly, and generally privately, as promiscuity, as well as greater interest in sexual experimentation. Cohabitation before, and instead of, marriage also became more common and ensured that more children were born outside marriage: in the USA, the percentage rose from 18 in 1980 to 33 in 1999.

In another major reaction to earlier trends, divorce became more common. The rate doubled in the USA between 1958 and 1976, and, by 2000, two-fifths of first marriages there were likely to end in divorce. Partly as a consequence, the percentage of American households that were occupied by the 'nuclear family' – two parents and their children – fell from 45 in 1960 to 23.5 in 2000, a fundamental social shift, not least because of assumptions about what constituted normal behaviour. In the USA, the number of children in single-parent families increased each year from 1960 until 1995, before showing a slight decline. Divorce also became more common in Europe. Rising divorce figures challenged male norms about family structure and led to an increasing number of families headed by women who were not widowed. This important social shift helped to ensure that the position of women played a greater role in debates about social issues. They could no longer be treated as an adjunct of their husbands. As another aspect of female power, women played the crucial role in asserting and extending rights to abortion. In 1973, the American Supreme Court decided that they had such a right as part of the right to privacy. Women's health also became a significant issue in the West, leading to screening for cervical and breast cancer, Well-Women clinics and elective caesarian deliveries as a common method of childbirth.

There was also pressure for more radical or 'separatist' feminist options, including an affirmation of lesbianism. Aside from demands for legal changes and changes in the language to avoid male stereotyping, feminism led to pressure for lifestyles and social arrangements that put women's needs and expectations in a more central position. Jobs and lifestyle became more important as aspirations for women, complementing, rather than replacing, home and family. These changes were faithfully recorded, and encouraged, in the soap operas that put family life on American and other television screens. The genesis of the term 'soap opera' reflected the interaction of the consumer culture and capitalism, for the programmes were first sponsored by companies seeking to advertise to a female audience.

The number of married women entering the job market escalated from the 1960s, and more women returned to work after having children. By 1980, 52 per cent of Americans aged 16 or over were in the labour force, and in the 1990s the percentage rose to 67. The range of female activities expanded. The growth in the commercial and financial sectors provided women with many opportunities, while the decline in personal service (employment in domestic work) ensured a working environment that involved less subordination. The legal position of women was improved. Equal rights were enshrined in institutional practices as well as legal codes. The New Zealand government was not alone when, in 1960, it agreed to introduce 'equal pay for equal work' in the public sector. Women also came to play a more prominent role in politics and government and several countries had female heads of government, including India (1966–77, 1980–4), Sri Lanka (1960–5, 1970–7), Israel (1969–74), Britain (1979–90) and Indonesia (2000–).

Changes in the position of women cannot be separated from other social shifts. Female identity and experience shifted within social, economic and political contexts that themselves altered. These contexts were not primarily structured by gender issues. For example, the economic shift from manufacturing to service industries that was marked in the last quarter of the century created more opportunities for salaried work for women. At the same time, the condition of many women, especially, but

FEMALE IDENTITY AND EXPERIENCE SHIFTED WITHIN SOCIAL, ECONOMIC AND POLITICAL CONTEXTS THAT THEMSELVES ALTERED.

not only, in the developing world remained defined by poverty. Furthermore, the nature of some female work was often scarcely compatible with the hopes of feminism, most obviously in the case of prostitution.

MALE IMAGES

Gender was also an issue for men. In the developed world, decolonization and the widespread end of conscription affected notions of masculinity and also gendered constructions of citizenship. Less emphasis was placed on what had been seen as masculine values, and some of these were questioned, indeed mocked. This was part of a process of change in the images of masculinity. The decline of manual work and the growing importance of women workers also contributed to the same sense of changing, indeed, in some contexts, imperilled, masculinity.

Different attitudes to homosexuality contributed powerfully to this sense. The gay rights movement presented homosexuality, which had hitherto been treated in many countries as a crime, as normal and as deserving equal treatment with heterosexuality. Pushed from the 1970s, this movement led to legal and social changes in some countries, for example in Western Europe, where Bertrand Delanoe, a self-proclaimed homosexual, was elected mayor of Paris in 2001. However, pressure for homosexual rights had only a limited impact across much of the world, including most of the Islamic world, but also in many non-Islamic countries.

A very different male culture continued to be dominant in Latin America. Traditional notions of virility and patriarchalism remained powerful throughout the century. Further north, in the USA, these notions were contested, but the strength of established assumptions was shown by the continued role of gun culture. Personal ownership of guns remained higher in the USA than elsewhere in the developed world, and this contrast became particularly marked as ownership of guns declined and was increasingly made illegal in Europe. At the same time, gun ownership in the USA recorded social change with the growing rate of female ownership in the latter decades of the century.

CONSUMERISM

Societies were also shaped by expenditure patterns. The economic growth that characterized much of the century ensured that, particularly in the developed world after World War II, most of the population was left with more disposable wealth, and also with more leisure on which to spend it. American living standards were on average 82 per cent higher in 1973 than in 1948. During that period, median American family income rose on average by 3 per cent per annum, while output per hour in the American business sector rose by more than 3 per cent per annum. Across the West, staples – food, housing, heating – absorbed a smaller percentage of the average budget, and this was further encouraged by the rise in labour participation rates that stemmed in large part from a higher percentage of married female workers. Equally inflation, which was continuous after World War II, contributed to a pervasive sense of change in expenditure, income and value.

The ability of people to define themselves through spending accentuated the role of the money economy which had itself increased with mass urbanization. Fashion, cost and respectability helped determine choice, as captured by F. Scott Fitzgerald's description of unfashionable New York cabarets in his novel *The Beautiful and Damned* (1922):

> ... the little troubled men who are pictured in the comics as 'the Consumer' or 'the Public'. They have made sure that the place has three qualifications: it is cheap; it imitates with a sort of shoddy and mechanical wistfulness the glittering antics of the great cafés in the theatre district; and ... it is a place where they can 'take a nice girl' ... There on Sunday nights gather the credulous, sentimental, underpaid, overworked people with hyphenated occupations: book-keepers, ticket-sellers, office-managers, salesmen, and, most of all, clerks – clerks of the express, of the mail, of the grocery, of the brokerage, of the bank.

Consumer demand reflected the primacy of personal choice over public policy. Thus, despite health warnings, taxation and restrictions, by 2000, world spending on alcohol was about $252 billion and on tobacco about $204 billion.

YOUTH CULTURE

Consumer choice, and the need to shape and cater for it, combined to ensure a whole range of social shifts. One of the most striking was the emergence of the youth consumer, and the development of cultural and consumer fashions that reflected the dynamism and volatility of this section of the market. There was a widespread wish, and ability, of youth to create an adolescent identity – not to be younger copies of their elders – and to reject the opinions of their parents. Pop culture, which reflected a desire to focus the aspirations of youth on young adults, rather than on parents, was an important manifestation of this shift once the 'generation gap' (itself an instructive concept) began to emerge in the 1950s. As with so much else in the West,

Hollywood exploited and developed this trend, with actors such as James Dean (1931–55) and films such as *Rebel Without a Cause* (1955) and *The Wild One* (1953). It is possible that youth culture reflected the more liberal postwar approach to raising children associated in particular with Benjamin Spock (1905–98), an American doctor whose book *The Common Sense Book of Baby and Child Care* (1946) was very influential. Before his death, Spock made a public apology, as he had come to believe that allowing children's intrinsic desires to develop, as he had earlier argued, only increased their egocentrism, leading to a decline in necessary discipline and the rejection of inherited values.

The newly energized, demanding and distinctive youth culture of the 1960s drew on new technology, and the mass production of modern industrial society yet again provided the goods for popular culture. Artificial fabrics were employed more actively, leading to the use of modern plastic, such as PVC (polyvinyl chloride). Fashions changed rapidly, reflecting the mass market of modern consumer society and the concern of youth culture with novelty. The dominant theme was fashion appeal, not durability, nor other utilitarian goals (although the ubiquitous jeans were durable). Consumerism had become the utilitarian end. From the 1960s, massive open-air concerts focused the potent combination of youth culture and pop music. 'Pop', in turn, spawned 'subcultures' such as punk and 'heavy' rock.

CONSUMERISM HAD BECOME THE UTILITARIAN END.

The widespread willingness to try different foods, to holiday in different places, to move away from parental religious beliefs, to go on to higher education, or to purchase property were all part of the same process, as were subcultures of youth violence. The willingness and determination of the young to redefine themselves, frequently in opposition to their parents, greatly affected society and was also a means by which social change occurred. The rise in higher and further education, particularly in the second half of the century, was especially important in furthering social, geographical and ideological mobility.

Youth demand fuelled the drug culture that became more important from the 1960s, especially from the 'Summer of Love' in 1967. This had a number of important effects, both in providing and in consuming areas. In the former, for example Colombia, the world's leading producer of coca leaf for cocaine, the drug trade destabilized entire societies, leading to the corruption of politics and business, and to high levels of crime and social breakdown. In the latter, particularly the USA and Western Europe, drug use remained illegal and thus an appreciable portion of the population were familiarized to breaking the law. The inability of governments to suppress the trade was a powerful demonstration of the difficulty of policing society and influencing social habits. By 2000, world retail sales of illegal drugs were about $150 billion, of which about $60 billion was sold in the USA.

A more specific rejection of authority occurred in the USA in the 1960s. Opposition to American involvement in the Vietnam War rose because of the duration of the conflict and because the goals seemed ill defined, but it focused on hostility to the conscription necessary to sustain the large-scale American military presence. In 1965–73, about two million Americans were drafted. Anti-war sentiment contributed to a widespread critique of American society.

SOCIAL TRENDS IN THE LATE TWENTIETH CENTURY

Not only the young experienced and furthered social change across the world. In addition, for most of those in work in the developed world in the last third of the century, workers' rights became more prominent and leisure became more important. People had more time free from work and more money to enjoy it. As a consequence, a whole range of activities became more common, and this contributed to the consumer economy. Retirement also became a more common option as a result of greater longevity, statutory rights and pension provisions, although, as the experience of ageing became more widespread, so the resulting problems both for the elderly and for others became more pressing.

These changes affected communist as well as capitalist societies, but, with the fall of the Soviet Union and the communist regimes in Eastern Europe in 1989–91, the former lost their capacity to serve as an alternative model. Surviving communist societies were all in the developing world. Several openly endorsed capitalist practices. This was particularly true of China, but also, for example, of Vietnam, which opened itself to inward Western investment in the late 1980s. Nevertheless, significant differences in the relationship between the state and the citizen remained. The willingness of states such as China and Singapore to use capital punishment was not matched in Western Europe. The USA still used the death penalty, but many of the individual American states did not and on the whole in the USA by the last quarter of the century there was a concern with the legal right of defendants that was completely different to that in many Asian and African countries employing the death penalty. Firmly interpreted Islamic jurisprudence (*sharia*) prevailed in a number of Muslim countries, such as Afghanistan and Saudi Arabia. The latter used the Koran as its constitution throughout the century.

By the 1990s, the basic lineaments of societies in the developed world were defined by a prosperity that encompassed the majority. These societies were capitalist, consumerist, individualist, mobile, predominantly urban, property-owning, secular (apart from the USA, although it has no official religion) democracies, although they had responded differently to the full implications of the costs of financing social welfare. Across the West, rates of house and share ownership were far higher than in the 1930s, let alone the 1900s. This represented the growth not only of prosperity, but also of one that was widely shared.

Compared with earlier in the century, societies had become more homogeneous. This was a consequence of globalism, specifically consumerism, American culture and the English language, and, at the national level, the impact on regional practices of national broadcasting, state education and employment and nationwide companies, trade unions, products and pastimes. The adoption of Western dress and footwear by men and women for work and leisure was a powerful image of uniformity. In some countries, such as Turkey from the 1920s and Thailand in the 1930s, this was actively encouraged by governments as a sign of modernization, but, in general, the process reflected consumer pressures, urbanization and the shift to mass-production and mass-retail. The world's biggest companies by revenue in 2000 reflected the impact of the USA and of car culture: Exxon, Mobil, Wal-Mart Stores, General Motors and Ford Motors.

Identity across much of the world was defined in terms of the always shifting relationship of Western and indigenous cultures. Thus, in his *Omeros* (1990), the West Indian poet and playwright Derek Walcott (1930–), who won the Nobel Prize for Literature in 1992, provided a poem that used the idea of Homer's *Iliad* to probe and celebrate the interaction of Walcott's real and spiritual life in the West Indies, Africa, Europe and the USA. Across many cultures, other writers, for example the Anglo-Indian novelist Salman Rushdie (1947–), had to confront the tensions in their own lives that arose from the interplay of Western and other cultures.

No other country matched the USA for the growth and impact of its film and television industries. They spread potent images of American society and material culture and influenced style and consumption around the world. This was true of all types of film. American cartoon characters such as Mickey Mouse, devised by Walt Disney in 1928, were recognizable around the world.

Other cultures produced film and television but with far less impact outside their boundaries. This was true of the Soviet Union and also of India, the world's most active alternative to the USA in the film industry in the last three decades of the century. Bollywood, the Indian film capital in and near Mumbai (Bombay), was consciously named as an alternative to Hollywood, and, by the late 1990s, produced more than 800 films a year, of which over 200 were exported in 1999. However, although the ethos of Indian films accorded with those of many societies, especially in Asia and the Middle East, the international market was limited as a result of the dominant position of Hollywood.

External images had a potent impact. The destabilizing sense of a better world elsewhere that West German television brought to East Germany in the 1980s was repeated throughout the world. In 1963, 'Boney' Fuller, who had earlier been an influential British military strategist and military thinker, had seen propagating an attractive image of the West as the way to win the Cold War with the Soviet Union,

'PICTURE THE WORLD AS CONSISTING OF THREE BILLION BUYERS AND TWO GREAT DEPARTMENT STORES COMPETING FOR THEIR PATRONAGE.'

Picture the world as consisting of three billion buyers and two great department stores competing for their patronage. Then pose the question: which of the two is the more likely to gain control of the world market and eventually bankrupt the other? The answer is, the one which best supplies human needs and popular demands ... the Western problem is not a defensive (passive) one: to defend its way of life and preserve it as it is. Instead, it is an offensive (active) one: to improve its way of life, and render it so attractive that the Soviet way of life will go bankrupt, and Karl Marx – if anything is left of him – will wither away.

Television also challenged other orders. Extreme supporters of apartheid in South Africa tried to prevent the introduction of 'the devil's box' or television. It was not surprising that Islamic fundamentalists sought to prevent or limit the spread of information about Western life, nor that the Western model was perceived as a threat by them. Television was banned by the Taleban regime in Afghanistan.

Television spread the influence of particular languages, notably English, Spanish and Mandarin Chinese, and the Internet had the same effect for English, although the role of the language stemmed primarily from American, not British, influence and power in the second half of the century. This anglophone hegemony caused disquiet in some countries, for example France, where there were governmental attempts to stem the use of English words. Established national practices and assumptions were also challenged by other changes. Immigration undermined national stereotypes. So also did challenges to earlier patterns of racial discrimination, not least those seen as members of ethnic minorities were allowed to take a major role in popular culture and sport. From mid-century, black players began to appear in major league games in the USA.

Although there was less overall 'poverty' in 2001 than in 1900, it still existed in the developed and, even more, the developing world. In the former, what was called the residuum in the late nineteenth century became, a century later, the underclass, with state systems of support unable to mitigate the full extent of unemployment and homelessness, and with beggars a common sight in many Western cities, although not to the same extent as in the developing world. There, although poverty was a relative concept, it remained widespread, and state support for the poor continued to be inadequate. The number of people living in what the World Bank defined as extreme poverty – on less than one dollar daily – remained above a billion in the closing decades of the century. Although the percentages of the world's population these represented fell from 28 in 1987 to 24 in 1998, there were still 1.2 billion such people in both years. By 1999, 95 per cent of the rise in the global population was occurring in 'developing countries'. Poverty proved intractable, particularly in Africa and South Asia. By 2000, half of the population of sub-Saharan Africa lived on only 65 cents a day or less; although poverty is relative: in much of the world, 65 cents a day was bearable if there was no cash economy. High rates of poverty in India in the closing decades of the century can be traced to the absence of radical social reform after independence, but other factors, including rapid population growth and poor economic management, were also important. Across the world, the poor also became increasingly conscious of their relative deprivation, and this encouraged discontent and crime, for example in China in the 1990s, when inequality greatly increased and tested assumptions in what the government still presented as a 'socialist culture'.

BY 2000, HALF OF THE POPULATION OF SUB-SAHARAN AFRICA LIVED ON ONLY 65 CENTS A DAY OR LESS.

Furthermore, there was a political 'impoverishment', in that the means to press for significant change peacefully within political systems were often absent. In rural areas, this frequently led to a violent response against landlords. Thus, in the impoverished Indian state of Bihar in the 1990s, the private militias of landlords, especially the Ranbir Sena, competed with Maoist Naxalite guerrillas. The relationship between poverty (and other social indicators) and politics was amply demonstrated in transitions from communism, as (often inefficient) systems of public provision were replaced by a freer market that left many unprovided for. As a result, in the 1990s, poverty increased alongside economic growth in Eastern Europe, particularly in countries such as Moldova, Belarus and Ukraine that enjoyed only limited growth. Public health also deteriorated in these countries. Similar problems affected other societies that rejected communism in the 1990s. In Mongolia, poverty and family break-up increased markedly. Thus, whereas there were 300 street children in Mongolia in 1992, by 2000 there were 4,000, with many of those in the capital, Ulan Bator, living in manholes at considerable risk to their health.

CONCLUSIONS

Aside from poverty, there was also a persistent variety in social practices and views that challenged any simplistic presentation of social identity. There was also in the 1980s and 1990s a widespread reaction against the earlier positivism of much analysis of social structures, which minimized the role of human agency in favour of a structuralist interpretation in which human choices were determined, or at least heavily influenced, by parameters. By contrast, an emphasis on humans as the crucial element in change, patterns, concepts and ideologies and on the role of human decisions led to a less clear-cut and more 'messy' situation, especially if the individual, rather than the collective, was seen as the basic unit of decision-making. Patterns became less apparent, and processes of causation less easy to define or to agree upon.

These variations could be aggregated at the national level to permit an understanding of major contrasts between particular societies. However, there were also important social differences within countries thanks to the increased unwillingness of generations to heed the precepts and follow the practices of their predecessors. This was especially pronounced in societies where freedom of expression was widespread. Thus, in the USA, alongside the emphasis on a tolerant classless society bound together by common values came an emphasis on contrasts. Aside from overlapping differences in terms of ethnicity, religion, religious conviction, regionalism, housing type and wealth, there were important cultural divides in the USA, as also in Western Europe, not least between the individualism and tolerance associated with the 1960s and the more family-oriented and socially conservative perspective linked to the 1950s. Such cultural clashes could also be found elsewhere, for example in the response to the communist legacy in the Soviet Union.

Alongside the stress on variety, it is also appropriate to emphasize common themes in developments across the world, however much they have been only unevenly realized. These include the greater independence of women and youth, the strains upon both nuclear and extended families caused by individualism and other socio-cultural changes, and the impact of external models. At the close of the century, the USA continued to produce goods and services in a very exciting way, and to serve as a model for behaviour, not least through the impact of consumer culture.

"I recommend a Lucky in place of a sweet

—when your figure must be considered"

Elsie de Wolfe

Elsie de Wolfe,
Noted Interior
Decorator

The modern common sense way—reach for a Lucky instead of a fattening sweet. Everyone is doing it— men keep healthy and fit, women retain a trim figure.

Lucky Strike, the finest tobaccos, skilfully blended, then toasted to develop a flavor which is a delightful alternative for that craving for fattening sweets.

Toasting frees Lucky Strike from impurities. 20,679 physicians recognize this when they say Luckies are less irritating than other cigarettes. Athletes, who must keep fit, testify that Luckies do not harm their wind nor physical condition. That's why Luckies have always been the favorite of those men who want to keep in tip-top shape and realize the danger of overweight. That's why folks say:—"It's good to smoke Luckies."

A reasonable proportion of sugar in the diet is recommended, but the authorities are overwhelming that too many fattening sweets are harmful and that too many such are eaten by the American people. So, for moderation's sake we say:—

"REACH FOR A LUCKY INSTEAD OF A SWEET."

Elsie de Wolfe,
Noted Interior
Decorator

Reach for a Lucky instead of a sweet.

Coast to coast radio hook-up every Saturday night through the National Broadcasting Company's network. The Lucky Strike Dance Orchestra in "The Tunes that made Broadway, Broadway."

"It's toasted"

No Throat Irritation-No Cough.

five

ECONOMIC WORLDS

What an extraordinary episode in the economic progress of man that age was which came to an end in August, 1914. ... life offered, at a low cost and with the least trouble, conveniences, comforts, and amenities beyond the compass of the richest and most powerful monarchs of other ages. The inhabitant of London could order by telephone, sipping his morning tea in bed, the various products of the whole earth ... he could at the same moment and by the same means adventure his wealth in the natural resources and new enterprises of any quarter of the world. ... But, most important of all, he regarded this state of affairs as normal, certain, and permanent, except in the direction of further improvement, and any deviation from it as aberrant, scandalous, and avoidable.

John Maynard Keynes, *The Economic Consequences of the Peace* (1919)

INTRODUCTION

The economic history of the world is no mere adjunct to other themes, but, instead, a topic of crucial importance that requires treatment in a separate chapter if it is to receive sufficient attention. This chapter adopts a particular approach: alongside discussion of developments in the leading economic sector, there is also full consideration of other parts of the world. That is because their economic circumstances were fundamental to the course of political events. As this book also seeks to show the multiple character and impact of links between the various parts of the world, it is especially important to focus on economic factors, as these provided the content and dynamic of many of these links.

1900–1914

Globalization, a theme of much writing about the contemporary world economy, was also a characteristic of the situation at the outset of the period. The global economy was characterized by free trade and international capital flows. In the late nineteenth century, international trade dramatically increased. It was largely financed by international investment, which came mainly from Western Europe, with Britain, Germany and France the most important providers. The USA was a major recipient of investment income. There were also important transfers of technology, particularly from Britain, France, Germany and the USA. Furthermore, these countries organized the world economy, controlling trade, currency payments, insurance and shipping. Improvements in communications and financial infrastructure increased the efficiency of the global economic system and led to a convergence of prices. Widespread migration helped wages to converge.

GLOBALIZATION, A THEME OF MUCH WRITING ABOUT THE CONTEMPORARY WORLD ECONOMY, WAS ALSO A CHARACTERISTIC OF THE SITUATION AT THE OUTSET OF THE PERIOD.

Britain played the central role in this system. It was also the centre of the communication system, not only of shipping but also of telegraph routes. The pound sterling was the international reserve currency in a global financial system that relied on a fixed exchange rate regime and a gold standard for most significant currencies. In 1913, a third of Britain's wealth was invested abroad and 14.7 per cent of Britain's gross national product (GNP) was exported (Germany's percentage was 12.2).

A major form of economic exchange was of manufactured products from Western Europe and the USA for raw materials from the rest of the world, for example tin from Malaya, palm oil from Nigeria, rubber from Brazil and Malaya, copper and timber from Canada, and nickel and phosphate from the French Pacific colonies of New Caledonia and Tahiti respectively. There was also important trade in manufactured products between the major industrial powers, and they also produced raw materials, especially iron and coal, the latter the major energy source. Britain was the major exporter of coal. In addition to trades focused on imperial metropoles, major trade links also developed within imperial systems. For example, the export of rice from Burma to India, both of which were British-ruled, led to a substantial expansion in the acreage under rice in Burma, with important environmental consequences in the Irrawaddy delta.

A powerful sense of Western superiority, and of the extent to which conquest would mean a new order in which economics played a role, is captured in this account of a meeting in January 1902 between Sir Ralph Moore, British High Commissioner, and a 'big palaver of chiefs' in south-eastern Nigeria at the town of Iboum, recently devastated in the British conquest.

> He told them that we had come to help them in order that they might learn how to help themselves – we came for the good of the black man but that they would be subjects of the Great White King – not his slaves. While war lasts they must obey the order of any white man in the country. When war is over equal justice to all. The one thing to end the war was absolute submission, the handing over of all juh-juh priests and guns. He also compared a threepenny bit which he held up in his hand to the size of a native 'rod' of same value. He held out two pounds ten shillings – the value of 200 rods and showed the ease with which large amounts could be carried whereas £2 10s worth of brass currency is an impossible medium of exchange.

In the nineteenth century, manufacturing in the major industrial states was dominated by heavy engineering based on working pig iron and steel. The construction of ships and locomotives was particularly important. Textile production was also important. However, the industrial situation was one of flux. New products, such as cars, pharmaceuticals and telephones, provided opportunities and posed problems of adaptability. Many of these consumer products required new investment and were more dependent on skill and technology than some of the older 'metal bashing' industries. The balance of industrial power altered with the rise of Germany, which, by 1914, had forged ahead of Britain in iron and steel production, and was also particularly successful in chemicals, electrical engineering and optical goods.

By then, however, American output was equivalent to that of the whole of Europe. In large part, America's innovatory ethos derived from skilled labour shortages throughout the nineteenth century. Britain, by contrast, had invented and invested in heavy machinery in the early phases of the Industrial Revolution, making wholesale replace-ment expensive, while its plentiful supplies of cheap, skilled labour in any case militated against maximizing technological inputs. The American economy also ben-efited from substantial natural resources, including coal and iron, a large domestic market, extensive immigration, and an openness to foreign investment.

Alongside the economic 'winners' prior to 1914, there were also 'losers': economies or economic sectors that lost out to competition. Many resisted the globalization of the period by erecting tariffs, although tariffs were also used by states such as the USA concerned to support their own industries. Thus, prior to the outbreak of World War I in 1914, there were already threats to the liberal economic order. There were also problems with the financial system, not least a greater demand for gold (with which most currencies were convertible) than was available. This demand helped explain the importance of control over the South African gold mines. This had been won by Britain in the Boer War of 1899-1902 with the Afrikaner republics of Transvaal and the Orange Free State.

1914–1929

This very dynamic capitalist world was to be disrupted by war and inflation. World War I (1914–18) hit the European economies hard. Aside from the destruction of manufacturing plant, there was tremendous damage to trade and economic inter-dependence. On the global scale, European powers, especially Britain, sold much of their foreign investments in order to finance the war effort. The disruption of trade (and its total collapse outside Europe in the case of Germany) and the diversion, under state regulation, of manufacturing capacity to war production ensured that the European economies were less able to satisfy demand. This encouraged the growth of manufacturing elsewhere, not least in Latin America and in European colonies such as India. The USA, which did not enter the war until 1917, benefited most of all. The British war effort rapidly became heavily dependent on American financial and indus-trial resources.

After the war, the British sought to re-create the liberal economic order, but with only limited success. Instead, the terms of the world economy were set by America, which became not only the world's largest industrial power, but also the largest trader and banker. New York replaced London as the world's financial centre. American indus-trial growth satisfied domestic demand not only in well-established sectors, but also in the growing consumer markets for cars and 'white goods', such as refrigerators and radios. Consumerism was encouraged by the availability of credit. The spreading use of electricity helped economic growth, and the rise of plastic as a product affected several branches of manufacturing. New plant and scientific management techniques helped raise American productivity, which increased profitability and consumer income, and, therefore, the domestic market.

American economic expansion was not matched elsewhere, and the restriction on immigration by Asians and South and East Europeans with the Emergency Quota Act of 1921 and the Immigration Act of 1924 helped restrict the global benefit of American growth. The German and British economies revived slowly, with the Germans suffering serious inflation, and the Russian economy under communism played only a minor role in world trade. As a consequence, the USA became the major international lender in the 1920s. However, America's economic strength and protectionism lessened its ability to take imports and thus enable other countries to finance their borrowing.

THE GREAT DEPRESSION

The overheating American economy collapsed as a result of a bursting speculative boom in share prices in New York in October 1929, the Wall Street Crash. This bursting of an asset price bubble became far more serious as the inexperienced central bank cut the money supply. The tightening of the financial reins, including calling in of overseas loans, caused financial crisis elsewhere. The Kreditanstalt bank in Vienna collapsed in May 1931, leading to a major run, first on the German banks and then elsewhere. At the same time, the 1930 Hawley–Smoot Act put up American tariffs and depressed demand for imports. Other states followed suit, leading to a worldwide protectionism that dramatically cut world trade by 1932.

As export industries were hit, unemployment rose substantially across the industrial world. In the USA, the national unemployment rate rose to nearly 24 per cent in 1932, by when manufacturing was at only 40 per cent of capacity. The worldwide decline in consumer and business spending hit industrial production. At the same time, the industrial world's imports of raw materials declined, hitting commodity producers both in the industrial world (for example British coalfields) and elsewhere. The latter brought serious economic and political problems throughout the developing world, for example in Latin America and Australasia. In addition, these producers were now less able to finance imports.

The Slump and the subsequent Depression destroyed the liberal economic order, and led to a collapse of confidence in capitalist structures. As a result, states increasingly

THE SLUMP AND THE SUBSEQUENT DEPRESSION DESTROYED THE LIBERAL ECONOMIC ORDER, AND LED TO A COLLAPSE OF CONFIDENCE IN CAPITALIST STRUCTURES.

thought in national (rather than international) economic terms, and in many there was strong interest in government intervention in the domestic economy. Work creation schemes, such as the American Works Project Administration, were developed in order to fight unemployment. This led to an extensive development of infrastructure, especially roads.

Economic intervention was taken further in autocracies such as Nazi Germany. Intervention was already well developed in the communist Soviet Union, although its economy was characterized by public ownership, not the public regulation seen in Germany, as well as a range of other countries including Canada, Ireland and South Africa. In Britain, however, confidence in peacetime planning was limited until World War II. In part, it was discredited by its association with the Five-Year Plans of the Soviet Union and its command economy, but, more generally, such planning was unacceptable to the powerful financial community whose views were central to British economic strategy until 1940.

In some countries, there was a measure of recovery in the late 1930s from the depths of the Depression. Government borrowing and rearmament under Hitler helped lead the German economy to recovery, while its British counterpart was helped by the combination of loose monetary conditions (following departure from the Gold Standard in 1931) with orthodox fiscal policy, by low commodity prices, and by consumer demand from the prosperous section of the country. Public works played only a minor role in Britain: they were seen as likely to crowd out the private market. However, economic policy brought scant relief to the British heavy industrial sector, which did not grow appreciably until rearmament in the face of the German threat. In contrast, in the USA, unemployment was higher in 1935 than 1932, and, although it subsequently dropped, there were still over eight million unemployed in the late 1930s and unemployment only fell below 15 per cent in 1940.

The Depression gave rise to a critique of the traditional belief in 'sound finance', which had meant a balanced budget and low expenditure and taxation. This belief was criticized by an influential British economist, John Maynard Keynes (1883–1946), in his *General Theory of Employment, Interest and Money* (1936). He called for public spending to be raised in order to cut unemployment, and was ready to see very low interest rates and to tolerate inflation, a departure from conventional monetary policy.

It is far from clear, however, that such a policy was bound to work. Keynesian monetary policy really required a closed economy with very little liquidity. Even if public
investment is seen as a panacea for economic problems, it is too easy to be wise with
hindsight, and more appropriate to note the degree to which, for many academics and
politicians, economic performance was almost incomprehensible. Pump-priming
measures, such as those in the USA and Sweden, still left unemployment high.

Nevertheless, the welfare and economic reforms known as the New Deal, introduced
in America by Franklin Delano Roosevelt after he became president in 1933, satisfied
the political need to be seen to be doing something. In America, the Depression led to
a collapse of confidence in the old market economy and to greater federal economic
intervention. Roosevelt backed public works, but he also favoured balanced budgets
and put up taxes on the rich, neither of which conformed to Keynesian ideas (higher
taxes depress consumer demand), although the federal debt rose from $22.5 billion in
1933 to $40.5 billion in 1939. Roosevelt established social security, but it was a very
limited measure, not state socialism. A combination of the conservative nature of
American public opinion, hostility to interference with property rights, and growing
political opposition from 1937 prevented him from doing more. Furthermore,
American GNP per capita recovered and rose (from $615 in 1933 to $954 in 1940), and
those in work became considerably better off. Roosevelt was rewarded with easy re-
elections in 1936 (a particularly sweeping triumph) and 1940, although it was only in
World War II (1941–5 for the USA) that the major moves towards a stronger American
state were made.

State intervention in economic matters was increasingly common around the world
in the 1930s, and it led to a measure of corporatism as governments sought to direct
both labour and capital. Protectionism led to what was termed 'autarky': a quest for
self-sufficiency that was particularly strong in dictatorial regimes. They were also
motivated by a wish to prepare for war. Thus, Germany's Four-Year Plan, introduced in
1936, developed production of synthetic oil, rubber and textiles, while Japan stepped
up synthetic oil production in 1938. It was no accident that there was a focus on oil.
It had become more important with the spread of motorized transport, but was not
widely available, especially not in Western Europe or Japan, and therefore had to be
imported. Turkey introduced a Five-Year Plan for industrial development in 1934.

There was also important growth in the Soviet and Chinese economies in the interwar
period. In the Soviet Union, collectivization proved a disaster for much of the rural
community, particularly in the Ukraine, but there was a major expansion of the
industrial sector, and of electricity generation, albeit as a result of the state-driven

focus of resources on developing industry at a heavy cost in terms of the everyday life of the population. In China, the unification of the country by the Northern Expedition of 1926–8 was followed by important improvements in public finance, communications and industry. A unified currency and a central bank were introduced, and the tax on internal trade was ended, there was a major expansion in the road and, to a lesser extent, rail systems, and industrial output rose. Chinese growth continued during the Depression, but much of it was concentrated in Manchuria and the coastal provinces, and the impact on the rest of the country was restricted. Evidence about agrarian conditions is limited, and the extent of agricultural development is a matter of controversy. There appears to have been an important rise in output, but there was no transformation of agriculture. It is unclear that a movement of power and control over the land from landlords was politically acceptable to the Guomindang (Nationalist) government, but there were many other constraints on agricultural productivity.

WORLD WAR II, 1939–1945

World War II speeded up economic activity by forcing investment into industry. As in World War I, states taxed, borrowed, accepted inflation and directed resources, especially from the consumer, in order to boost industrial production. Unemployment fell very substantially, and there was also investment in new technologies, not least in electronics and aeronautics.

Oil played a major role in the conflict. It helped lead Japan to war in 1941 in order to gain oil fields in the Dutch East Indies and, to a lesser extent, Sarawak and Burma. Oil made the Germans determined to have the support of Romania, and led their forces in the Soviet Union towards the Caucasus in 1942. Control over most of the world's oil supplies was, however, retained by the Allies (from late 1941, most importantly Britain, the Soviet Union and the USA). Iraq and Iran were taken over by British and Anglo-Russian interventions in 1940 and 1941, and American entry into the war in 1941 was crucial in securing oil resources and refining capacity.

DURING THE WAR, AMERICAN INDUSTRY DEVELOPED RAPIDLY IN ONE OF THE MOST DRAMATIC ECONOMIC LEAPS OF THE CENTURY.

During the war, American industry developed rapidly in one of the most dramatic economic leaps of the century. The dynamic of American resource build-up relied on lightly regulated capitalism, not coercion. Having had cool relations with much of American business during the 1930s, Roosevelt turned to them to create a war machine, a task that was doubly difficult because there had not been a military build-up in the 1930s comparable to that of the Axis powers. The American army was in a particularly poor state, and smaller in 1939 than that of Portugal. That year, Congress agreed a major increase in military expenditure. Part of this was directed at creating a larger manufacturing base for war material. The War Resources Board was established in 1939, in order to ready industry for a war footing, and the Office of Production Management under William Knudsen, head of the leading car manufacturer General Motors, followed in 1941.

In the USA, the attitudes and techniques of the production line were focused on war. The Americans produced formidable quantities of munitions – $186 billion worth, including 297,000 aeroplanes and 86,000 tanks in 1941–5 – and an infrastructure to move them. Aside from massive resources, especially oil, and the fact that their industry was not being bombed as those of the other combatants were, the Americans benefited from a relative lack of need for imports, which contrasted greatly with the situation in Japan and Britain. In turn, American industry produced large quantities of goods for the Allies. These made a significant impact in particular operations: in North Africa in 1942 the British benefited from American tanks.

Production of weaponry was closely linked to the objective of movement. American forces were motorized to an extent greater than those of any other state, and this was not only a question of the armour. Infantry and artillery were also motorized. The capability of the American war economy was amply shown in shipbuilding. The global scope of Allied power depended on American shipbuilding. American production helped counteract the serious problems created by the boldness of Allied strategic planning, which had paid insufficient attention to logistical realities. Most of the 42 million tons of shipping built by the Allies during the war was constructed by the Americans. Many were Liberty ships, built often in as little as ten days, using prefabricated components on production lines. The organizational ability to manage large-scale projects and to introduce new production processes was important. All-welded ships replaced riveting, speeding up production. Despite losing oil tankers with a total tonnage of 1,421,000, mostly to German submarines, the tonnage of the American oil tanker fleet rose from 4,268,000 in 1942 to 12,875,000 in 1945. The war was very important to the growth of the American economy.

The flexibility of American society directly helped: by 1944, 11.5 per cent of the workers in the shipbuilding industry were women. Major changes in the geography of the American economy and population resulted as aircraft and ship productive capacity and production increased. The population of Washington, Oregon and, in particular, California, where many of the plants were located, rose greatly: by the end of the war, eight million people had moved permanently to different states. Some of the internal migrants were blacks: about 700,000 black civilians left the South, especially for California. The opportunities that war industrialization provided for black workers helped loosen racial, as well as gender and social, relations, although much segregation remained and racial tension led to serious outbreaks of violence, particularly in Detroit in 1943.

There was also an attempt to create new communication routes that would be outside the range of submarine attack. Pipelines were laid from Texas to the industrial centres of the North-East, including the 'Big Inch' from Houston to New York, in order to lessen coastal shipping. The coastal inland waterway system was improved. In 1942, the Alaska Highway was built in order to provide an overland route to the American bases there.

Turning to business led to a lack of co-ordination in economic management, but this was rectified by the establishment of the Office of War Mobilization in May 1943. Furthermore, the Americans benefited from their already sophisticated economic infrastructure, which helped in the shift to war production. Phenomenal quantities of weapons and weapons systems were produced, and the USA surmounted the domestic divisions of the 1930s in order to create a productivity-oriented political consensus that brought great international strength. The resources, commitments and role of the federal government grew greatly, and taxes and government expenditure both rose substantially. Government spending totalled $317 billion, and nearly 90 per cent of this was on the war.

Like America, Canada benefited in its wartime industrial mobilization from its distance from the combat zone. Thanks to production for the war, Canadian gross national product more than doubled in 1939–45, while federal government expenditure rose from $680 million in 1939 to $5,136 million in 1945. The War Measures Act was used to regulate industrial activity, and the Wartime Prices and Trade Board set wages and prices and allocated scarce commodities.

In Europe, there was a great degree of destruction. Owing to air attack and the extent of ground advances, much industrial plant was destroyed or damaged, far more so than in World War I. This was true of Germany, Japan, the Soviet Union and Britain, as well as of smaller economies. To fight on, these societies had to respond. Soviet industry displayed considerable adaptability, without which the USSR might well have collapsed. From the late 1920s, the Soviets had developed industrial production and mining in or east of the Urals, which were beyond the range of German air attack. This looked back to a long tradition of metallurgical production in the Urals, but was stepped up under Joseph Stalin (Soviet dictator from 1924 until 1953), such that about one-third of coal, iron and steel production was there. Major new industrial capacity was also developed near Novosibirsk in south-western Siberia, and new plants were built in Soviet Central Asia.

It was particularly in the Soviet Union that the mobilization of resources involved a marked degree of direction of the economy. Already an autocracy, where economic planning and the brutalization of society were mutually supporting, the Soviet system sustained the war effort despite the loss of many of its leading agricultural and industrial areas to German advances in 1941 and 1942. Indeed, although production statistics should only be used with care, the Soviet economy lost, in the first six months of the war, areas producing 68 per cent of its iron, 63 per cent of its coal and 58 per cent of its steel, as well as 40 per cent of its farmland, including, in the Ukraine, much of its most fertile area. These losses were but part of the profound wartime disruption caused by unexpected invasions.

The Germans knew that they were most likely to win through a rapid offensive war because they could not match the industrial, financial and demographic resources of their opponents; hence their emphasis on surprise, 'will power' and knocking a major opponent out of the conflict (the Japanese similarly put an emphasis on rapid success in the face of superior American resources). But none of this worked once the Allies had come to include the USA and had mobilized their superior capacity to produce and overwhelm their enemy.

The Germans tried to mobilize their industrial base from 1939, a major conversion of industrial capacity to war production beginning with the outbreak of hostilities. However, they faced numerous difficulties, not least too many competing agencies being involved, especially in 1939–41. The highest level of German armaments production did not come until towards the close of the war in September 1944, when, despite devastating Allied bombing, the rationalization plans of Albert Speer (1905–81), who had been appointed Minister for Armaments in 1942, came to fruition. For a variety of reasons, including Hitler's views on the role of woman as mother, unlike their opponents, the Germans failed to mobilize female labour thoroughly. Instead, they preferred to use slave labour, an inefficient as well as cruel policy: millions of foreign workers, especially Soviet, Polish and French, were brought to Germany, while, elsewhere in occupied Europe, workers were forced to work in often brutal conditions in order to produce resources for the German war effort. Aside from prisoners of war, 5.7 million foreign workers were registered in the Greater German Reich in August 1944; combined with the prisoners-of-war, they provided half the workforce in agriculture and in the manufacture of munitions.

Furthermore, the Germans failed to exploit mass-production techniques as successfully as had their opponents because they put a premium on responding to military requests for custom-made weapons, rather than on the mass-production of a more limited range of weapons. This reflected a military culture that emphasized duty and tactics, not logistics (nor indeed intelligence), a political culture in which there was a reluctance to understand the exigencies and potential of the economy, and a simple expectation that it would produce resources as required without consultation and to order. The Germans were also fascinated with potent weapons – moving towards bigger and bigger tanks and guns – rather than with weapons that were less effective individually, but easier to mass-produce. Hitler's interventions in the allocation of resources for weapon production and, subsequently, in the use of weapons were frequently deleterious, as also was his choice of the extermination of Jews over the harnessing of their labour and talents. He was convinced that late in the war Germany would suddenly produce a wonder weapon that would enable it to win; such a weapon existed in the atom bomb, but Germany missed the chance of developing it. Nevertheless, however inefficient, the German regime was able to direct and enforce a major expansion in the war economy, and a devotion of activity and production to the war, with personal consumption levels pushed down below those in Britain and the USA. Its major European ally, Italy, was far less effective.

HITLER WAS CONVINCED THAT LATE IN THE WAR GERMANY WOULD SUDDENLY PRODUCE A WONDER WEAPON THAT WOULD ENABLE IT TO WIN.

POSTWAR BOOM, 1945–1973

The war ended in 1945 with America even more the dominant economy in the world than at its start. Germany and Japan had been greatly affected by bombing and were occupied by the victorious powers, Britain had large debts and the Soviet economy had been devastated. The new economic order was established by the Americans. The international free trade and international capital markets that had characterized the global economy of the 1900s were slowly re-established. The availability of American credit and investment was crucial. Among the major powers, only the USA enjoyed real liquidity in 1945. Under the Bretton Woods Agreement of 1944, American-supported monetary agencies, the World Bank and the International Monetary Fund (both of which had American headquarters), were established in order to play an active role in strengthening the global financial system. The International Monetary Fund was designed to ensure currency stability by enabling countries with short-term liquidity problems to handle balance of payment problems within the fixed currency system. The Americans did not want a return to the beggar-my-neighbour devaluation policies of the 1930s.

Free trade was also actively supported as part of a liberal economic order, and this was furthered as America backed decolonization and the creation of independent capitalist states. The General Agreement on Tariffs and Trade (GATT), signed in 1947, began a major cut in tariffs that slowly re-established free trade and helped trade to boom. From 1945 to 1973, there was what was subsequently to be termed the 'Long Boom', a period of rapid economic development. This had a number of interrelated causes, and played out differently in various parts of the world, but the net effect was a synergy in which free trade and readily-available investment encouraged profitable interaction. Germany, Japan and South Korea, states that saw some of the highest economic growth of the period, were major exporters benefiting considerably from free trade.

The application of new technology in manufacturing and agriculture led to important productivity gains. In agriculture, mechanization led to a movement of workers from the land, especially in France and Germany. In manufacturing, the employment of mass-production in new purpose-built plants permitted a more effective introduction of new technology and organizational methods. This was a continuing process. Despite major earlier gains, productivity, in terms of production per worker, in the steel industry in the USA, Japan and Europe rose by 50 per cent in the 1990s alone. Manufacturing growth was seen not only in the developed world, but also in the developing world, where manufacturing output rose markedly and became more diverse and sophisticated in, for example, Brazil.

PRODUCTIVITY IN THE STEEL INDUSTRY IN THE USA, JAPAN AND EUROPE ROSE BY 50 PER CENT IN THE 1990S ALONE.

Economic growth was pushed by governments. Freeing international trade was a return to liberal economics, but government intervention in the domestic economy was not. Regulation was pushed furthest in communist states, where the government owned the means of production and directed the economy, and major concerns such as Gazprom, the Soviet Union's gas company, were branches of government. Elsewhere, there was also much state ownership or control. This was true not only of Europe, but also of much of the developing world. State control or public ownership, the choice of term is instructive, was pushed hard in many formerly colonized states.

Thus, private industries were nationalized in Egypt and Syria in 1961, helping ensure an over-reliance on a state direction that was to have damaging effects for both economies. Government regulation of the economy was least the case with the USA. There, however, as in Europe, state expenditure – in the case of America for defence – helped sustain economic growth and employment. The number of American government (federal and non-federal) employees rose from 4.5 million in 1940 to 15 million by the mid-1970s.

The wartime expansion of the American economy was followed in the late 1940s by a period of slackened growth, but expansion resumed markedly in the 1950s, and rose even faster in the 1960s. A buoyant domestic demand was accentuated by rapid population growth and by the American ability to export, not least to areas whose industries were still recovering from the war, particularly Western Europe. The recovery of the global economy provided further markets for the Americans, while their high level of personal consumption in turn made America an attractive market, both for American producers and for those elsewhere attracted by the mighty dollar. America became Canada's biggest export market after World War II. In the 1920s, it had already replaced Britain as the biggest source of foreign investment in Canada, and by 1960 its share of this investment in Canada was 75 per cent. In addition, the American war economy became entrenched as the military-industrial complex assumed an all-encompassing social and political relevance and prominence.

Growth rates in Western Europe and Japan were higher than in the USA, although that, in part, reflected their recovery from wartime damage, and also the possibility of making rapid advances by introducing American techniques. The economies of the non-communist world benefited from the growing availability of capital and from a major growth in trade, which encouraged specialization and economies of scale. The efficiency of the system was increased by structural reforms and also by improved communications. For example, agricultural productivity rose as large numbers of workers left the land with mechanization in the 1950s, while the containerization of freight, introduced on shipping in the USA in 1956, and then spreading to rail and road, increased the speed, and decreased the cost, of freight movements. Containerization was linked to the needs for labour productivity and product predictability that played a major role in Western manufacturing and helped it to sustain a powerful competitive edge.

In the late 1960s, however, there were increasing economic problems in the USA and more generally. In part, these reflected inflationary pressures that owed much to the American decision to pay for the Vietnam War and the Great Society programme of social improvement by borrowing rather than taxation. The resulting inflation spread through the global economy. In addition, it was difficult to control financial flows. Whereas liquidity had been restricted to the USA in 1945, and the American government had then extended it to other governments in small packets, especially under Marshall Aid, by the late 1960s liquidity was widely distributed and therefore difficult to control. Now employing Keynesian demand management, the USA was more prepared to tolerate inflation and price pressures than Germany and Japan. The different levels of inflation in particular economies made it very difficult to manage the international economy and exchange rates, and eventually shattered the Bretton Woods system: in 1971, Richard M. Nixon (US President 1969–74) suspended the convertibility of the dollar into gold. In addition, across the West, it proved difficult to sustain earlier rates of innovation and productivity growth. For example, the boost given by farm mechanization and the movement of rural workers to provide a cheap urban workforce could not be repeated in countries that had experienced it (although it was subsequently to spread to parts of the developing world). Labour costs rose in much of the developed world, as did the burden of supporting the large state sectors that had developed since the war.

THE WORLD ECONOMY 1973–2001

Difficulties were turned into crisis in 1973 when the price of oil was dramatically pushed up by the major producers in the Middle East. They were angry with Western support for Israel in its war that year with Egypt and Syria, but also keen to exploit growing world dependence on oil, which was the key energy source of the period. The price of oil per barrel rose from $3 to $18. This was devastating for oil importers, in both the developed and the developing world. The rise in oil prices led to a global upsurge in inflation (although that was already causing problems) and to a loss of confidence. As economic growth ceased or declined, unemployment rose, although, on the global scale, the crisis did not match that of the 1930s and indeed the world gross domestic product (GDP) continued to rise: capitalism delivered the goods in terms of rising living standards, not only in the boom period of 1950-73, but also in the more troubled period that followed. The price of oil was raised again in 1979 as OPEC (the Organization of Petroleum Exporting Countries, founded in 1960) restricted supply.

The crisis was not lasting in its effects. Growth resumed, especially in countries that were able to contain labour inflation, raise productivity and move into new areas of demand. This was particularly true of Japan, although it was a major oil importer. The Japanese economy made a major impact through concentrating on advanced electronics and engineering. Having passed Britain, West Germany and France in GNP in the 1960s, Japan became the second wealthiest country in the world (after the USA). The buoyancy of the Japanese economy led to significant Japanese overseas investment.

In the mid-1980s, real energy prices fell, partly because the oil hike in 1973 had encouraged the development of new fields, for example in the North Sea and in Alaska, and because OPEC members ignored the organization's limitations on exports. The American economy returned to significant growth in the 1980s and, even more, the 1990s and American consumerism helped drive production elsewhere. This was especially true of the Pacific region. By 1987 the American trade deficit with Japan had reached $60 billion, and in the 1990s this was followed by a marked rise in American imports from other developing Asian economies, particularly South Korea, Taiwan and China. In 2000, close to 40 per cent of Japanese car exports went to the USA. In 2000, the USA and Japan were responsible for 46 per cent of world output.

CHINA 1978–

The change in the Chinese economy was one of the major developments of the 1990s. The communist regime had long been concerned to further industrialization, but this process had been slowed by the rigidities of central planning and by the failure to raise agricultural productivity sufficiently, which was in part a consequence of the doctrinaire land policies of Mao Zedong. Mao died in 1976, having ruled since 1949, and in 1978 he was eventually succeeded by Deng Xiaoping, who pushed hard in the 1980s to move China towards economic liberalization. Deng believed it possible to keep political control of the communist state while abandoning the Maoist policies of economic direction. Recent Chinese politics have not been short of slogans and the 1978 constitution called for 'Four Modernizations' – agriculture, industry, defence, science and technology – which led to 'economics in command' and 'planning through guidance'. Reform-driven growth became the government's goal.

Slogans were not enough. Freeing prices, permitting private businesses, giving farmers the right to retain surpluses and attracting foreign investment helped ensure a boom that also owed much to the availability of foreign markets, particularly in Japan and the USA. Economic opportunities and liberalism further encouraged investment in industrial plant, and, in the 1990s, market reforms were pushed further. In place of sectionalized liberalization, not least in the Special Economic Zones created in 1984, came a more determined effort to make a 'socialist market economy' work and trade competitively. Growth rates in the 1990s shot up, and in the 1980s and 1990s Chinese

GNP rose more than seven-fold, increasing incomes and taking large numbers of Chinese out of poverty, although the reliability of Chinese government statistics is a matter for debate.

There was, as always in Chinese history, a powerful regional dimension, with expansion particularly apparent in coastal areas of the south, while government remained in the north. Resulting economic differences led to significant internal migration and to problems in meeting the resource demands of the booming regions, especially for food and water, without causing shortages and price rises elsewhere. Furthermore, economic reform meant an end to the Maoist social politics that had included full employment and universal housing and health care. Instead, came serious unemployment as uncompetitive factories, many the heavy industrial plants built in the Maoist years, closed, and consequent widespread poverty. The state-owned enterprises that were responsible for about 75 per cent of Chinese output in the late 1970s produced only about 28 per cent in 2000, although they were responsible for about 44 per cent of urban employment. The decline of the role of such enterprises was a major shift not only in China's economy but also in its society and politics. The failure of central planning that the decline of such enterprises represented reflected a failure to match production and demand that had an obvious counterpart in Chinese political history. Capital products and financial management were also poor; a classic feature of economies that were heavily politicized. Although official figures were unreliable, they suggested that in the 1990s inequality grew.

China's post-1978 growth represented a response to the opportunities for development offered by the demise of communist central planning and the introduction of Western technology and management skills, although the latter process was difficult. The range of resources, not least of population, was also important, as was a combination of entrepreneurship and social control that the Soviet Union could not match. Social control helped ensure a low standard of living that kept labour costs down. The plentiful labour supply helped China gain an important advantage in labour-intensive areas of manufacture such as textiles, shoes and toys. China came to enjoy an important comparative advantage over other exporters, both regional and further afield. This combination attracted inward investment, which, by 2000, was the second largest in the world after the USA. The economy also increasingly focused on more sophisticated manufacturing. Economic growth, however, posed serious environmental problems. For example, the expansion of the road system in the 1990s, which was praised as assisting economic integration, also led to an

INWARD INVESTMENT IN CHINA BY 2000 WAS THE SECOND LARGEST IN THE WORLD AFTER THE USA.

increase in pollution. In addition, corruption became a more serious problem in government.

EAST AND SOUTH-EAST ASIA 1960s–

A major source of goods, China also became a major market, for example for steel producers in Japan and South Korea. China's economic links with the USA came to match those of Japan in importance, complexity and political sensitivity. Elsewhere in what was termed the Pacific Rim, there was also significant growth, although being there was not alone a sufficient condition of growth, as shown by Ecuador and the Soviet Far East, Pacific regions whose economies remained weak. Instead, growth was highest in East and South-East Asia, especially in Taiwan, South Korea, Singapore, Thailand and Malaysia. As with Australia (67 per cent of exports went to Asia in 1991) and New Zealand, these countries benefited from the markets and opportunities created by expansion in Japan and the USA (where Pacific Rim California was the state with the largest economy). The USA and Japan also provided much of the investment which the states of East and South-East Asia were not able to generate domestically, despite very high savings ratios.

The economies and per capita income of the so-called 'Four Dragons' – South Korea, Hong Kong (not reunified with China until 1997), Singapore and Taiwan – rose markedly from the 1960s. Cheap and flexible labour and heavy investment with borrowed capital enabled them to benefit from the growing world economy through export-led growth. This pattern was also followed by Malaysia, Indonesia, Thailand and the Philippines as they, in turn, benefited from export opportunities and investment sources in the Pacific Rim, not least from Japanese foreign investment. Much growth derived from catching up with Western economies, in large part by borrowing technology and capital. Nevertheless, the quality of economic activity increased in East and South-East Asia. The Pacific Rim countries became each other's consumers and suppliers in a synergy of economic activity. At the political level, this was due to supportive home governments and to global liberalization in trade and investment. There was no organized regional drive, or controls, as the Association of South-East Asian Nations (ASEAN), created in 1967, lacked the necessary authority and power.

However, some parts of the region did not witness sustained growth. Laos earned only $1.3 billion in 1998. Moreover, regional growth was not without its weaknesses, and these were seen in 1997–8 in an emerging markets crisis that began in Thailand and spread rapidly, particularly to Indonesia. Related, though separate, there was also a serious problem with declining growth in Japan in the 1990s and early 2000s. In both

cases, there were serious problems with financial systems, reflecting a lack of control over lending during the period of rapid growth, combined with speculative pressures, for example over real estate in Japan, and a degree of corruption involving overly close links between politics and finance. This crony capitalism ensured that governmental investment in the economy was not properly costed; there was no adequate debate about economic policy.

Japan faced a serious banking crisis in 1997. Japanese deflation was linked to the failure to introduce structural reforms in the economy, and to serious fiscal mismanagement. Public investment failed to bring economic recovery. As a very different problem, a lack of openness to the free market ensured that attempts in the 1990s by Vietnam to follow China's economic growth proved unsuccessful. Helped by exports to a booming America, some regional economies, such as Malaysia and South Korea, rebounded rapidly from the crisis of the late 1990s, but it revealed important problems with economic fundamentals, and other economies, such as Indonesia, did not enjoy a comparable revival.

> **THUS DOUBT WAS SHED ON THE BOLD CLAIMS MADE IN THE EARLY AND MID-1990S THAT THE AGE OF AMERICAN ASCENDANCY WAS DRAWING TO A CLOSE.**

Thus doubt was shed on the bold claims made in the early and mid-1990s that the age of American ascendancy, economic and otherwise, was drawing to a close and that it would be replaced by that of East Asia. The ratio of economic indicators between America and Japan moved back in the favour of the former. Instead, talk of Asian dominance, and of the challenge to the USA, came to focus on China, although its growth did not match that of Hong Kong (prior to unification with China in 1997), where property rights were protected and liberal capitalism fostered.

THE USA IN THE 1990s

The American economy enjoyed considerable growth in the 1990s. Capital invested per American worker remained high, and the openness of the internal economy and market encouraged the speedy diffusion of most efficient economic practices. The American economy benefited from earlier important structural reforms in the late 1970s and 1980s. There were continuing difficulties, not least a high rate of indebtedness and the persistence of poverty, but the rate of poverty fell, to reach a twenty-year low in 1999, while the real median income of households rose that year to a record high: $40,816. Furthermore, the American poverty line – $17,029 for a family of four –

would have counted as riches across the world. The prestige of the dollar remained very high, and indeed led in 2000 to an attempt to dollarize Ecuador's economy. The role of the dollar reflected the extent to which the international monetary system was detached from any form of commodity. Gold, earlier in the century the basis of the freely convertible international currency system, had been demonetized, and, instead, the world money system was dependent on transactions of paper units, the value of which rested on governmental policy and investor confidence.

America also benefited most from the major development of multinational companies, which operated in many countries. A large number of these were American. Some companies had net worths and annual turnovers greater than that of many states. In 2000, the world's largest drug company, Glaxo SmithKline, itself the result of numerous mergers, had a market capitalization of $172 billion. On the national scale, capitalization and profits could also be huge. Citigroup, America's most profitable bank, declared profits of $9.87 billion for 1999. Successful in one country, companies repeatedly expanded into foreign markets.

America's position in the global economy was indicated by the rise in its share of global exports, from 15.7 per cent in 1993 to 17.7 per cent in 1999, and that in a period of a major growth in world trade. At the same time, more than simply the strength of the American economy was involved. America also benefited from trade policies, such as export subsidies for crops, which, alongside comparable European subsidies, hit producers elsewhere in the world. Nevertheless, the Uruguay round of GATT talks (1986–94) brought agriculture and textiles more fully into GATT and a measure of liberalization to trade in those sectors.

WESTERN EUROPE 1945–

No other region of the world achieved comparable economic growth to East Asia. Postwar Western Europe grew as a result of trade liberalization, American investment, agricultural productivity and the catch-up factor of applying advanced, mostly American, technology and production methods. Britain, France and Italy developed mixed economies with much state planning and nationalization. West Germany grew faster. This owed much to the economic liberalization pushed by Ludwig Erhard, Federal Chancellor 1963–6 (and earlier an influential Economics Minister), and other leaders, which was a major break from the cartels characteristic of earlier German history. Influenced by liberal-minded economists, the West German government adopted pro-competition policies and fostered currency stability. Furthermore, the West German economic and financial system contrasted with the nationalizations and state control seen in France and Britain, let alone communist East Germany. West Germany also benefited from the skill of its engineering industry and from more harmonious labour relations than those in Britain. Formed in 1957, the European Economic Community brought together what had been much of the industrial world (outside the USA) at the beginning of the century.

However, European growth rates were particularly badly hit in the 1970s and early 1980s. Although the subsequent expansion in the world economy also helped Europe, growth did not match that in East Asia. Western Europe was affected by higher labour costs and by expensive social welfare systems. The fiscal consequences of the reunification of West and East Germany in 1990 hit the West German economy. As a clear sign of a fall in competitiveness, the percentage of trade between the member states of the European Union as a percentage of their total trade rose markedly in the 1990s, and this encouraged the currency union of most of the European Union, with the adoption of the Euro in 1999–2002. Furthermore, investment in Western Europe in the 1990s rose far less than in the USA, in part because of lower productivity. Unemployment levels were far higher than in the USA. Nevertheless, the Western European economy was in a better shape than that of Eastern Europe or Latin America. In some fields, especially the financial services industry in London, Western Europe did particularly well.

THE SOVIET UNION AND EASTERN EUROPE 1945–

The Soviet Union and Eastern Europe apparently enjoyed appreciable growth during the Long Boom, in part as a consequence of recovery from the war, as well as agricultural mechanization and industrial modernization, although there is room for considerable scepticism about the available figures. The state put a heavy emphasis on heavy industry. In Hungary, for example, there was an attempt to create 'a country of iron and steel', while agriculture was collectivized. In the late 1950s and early 1960s, the Soviet Union boasted that it was overtaking the USA and Western Europe, not simply in rockets and military hardware, but also in technological capability and better standards of living. This was totally wrong, in part because statistics were manipulated but also because of a systemic failure to ensure that accurate figures were obtained and that proper balance sheets were produced.

Furthermore, the communist economies were hit by the economic downturn of the 1970s. They also suffered from the degree of investment directed to armaments, an investment that was pushed up in successive bouts of the arms race with the USA. This investment badly distorted the Soviet economy, but, more generally, it suffered from the role of state planning, particularly by Gosplan, the State Planning Commission, and from the failure to develop the consumer spending that was so important in the USA and Western Europe. Attempts from 1985 to achieve economic and political reform faced the structural economic and fiscal weakness of the Soviet system, not least the preference for Gossnab, the State Supply Commission, over any price system that reflected cost and availability. These attempts led to an unpredicted public response that caused the end of communist rule in 1989–91.

Subsequently, the former communist states faced serious economic difficulties as the dismantling of the old command economy exposed the uncompetitive nature of much of Soviet-era industry. It proved difficult to establish effective monetary and fiscal mechanisms. Western loans were necessary in order to prevent a total collapse of Russia in the 1990s. Its debt payments caused a severe crisis in 1998, leading to default and devaluation. Both there and in Eastern Europe there was no smooth transition to capitalism and democracy. Instead, the bankruptcy of large areas of the former command economy and the dismantling of social welfare led to a major rise in unemployment, poverty and social polarization, while public culture was affected by disillusionment and government corruption, and privatized economies displayed a new vulnerability to international trends. By 2000, Poland, Slovenia and Hungary had recovered to surpass their GDP of 1990, while the Czech Republic only managed to equalize this, and in Estonia, Romania, Bulgaria and Russia there had been a decline.

WESTERN LOANS WERE NECESSARY IN ORDER TO PREVENT A TOTAL COLLAPSE OF RUSSIA IN THE 1990S.

SOUTH ASIA 1945–

In South Asia, one of the most populous parts of the world, economic growth did not match that in South-East and East Asia. In part, this was due to the lack of economic liberalism seen in India and, even more, Burma. The Indians did not open their economy to global pressures, but, instead, followed a policy of import substitution and looked to a socialist model of state direction and Five-Year Plans. The influence of Western European socialism and of communist planning both had a deleterious impact on Indian economic management. Government policies built up Indian industry, but failed to match growth rates in East and South-East Asia, or in Pakistan. There, although democratic government was interrupted by periods of military rule, a less illiberal economic regime helped growth rates to average 6 per cent per annum in the 1980s, although they subsequently fell. Furthermore, the Indian economy was hit by the rapid rise in population, which ensured that per capita demand remained low and focused on essentials, rather than consumer goods. In 1991, the Indian government responded to the global move towards liberalization, abandoning economic planning, including industrial licences, and opening up to global markets, including dropping trade barriers. However, this process encountered serious political obstacles, and the opening up was only partial. More generally, South Asia suffered from serious resource problems, particularly a shortage of oil and natural gas, and from political instability.

LATIN AMERICA

Latin America also failed to realize its potential, in part because of its ambivalent relationship with global economic pressures. The economic nationalism of the 1930s, especially protectionism and state direction and subsidy, long prevailed over liberalization. Governments pushed hard for industrialization, in large part as a substitute for imports. Some progress was made in the 1950s, especially in Brazil and Colombia, although, elsewhere, industrialization was less successful. Argentina, Chile and Mexico, each of which had had important manufacturing sectors (as a percentage of total economic activity) in 1945, saw scant growth in this percentage by 1960. In the 1960s, Latin America failed to match the growth rates seen in East Asia, while industrial expansion was hit by the limited demand of the largely poor population and by the difficulty of breaking into high-skill, high-value manufacturing. Inflation, social tension and political instability accentuated the problems in the 1960s and early 1970s. Governments responded by borrowing, especially from the USA, but this money was not used to finance economic restructuring.

In the early 1980s, a major rise in American interest rates made it impossible for the Latin American countries to service the debt. In 1982, the situation collapsed when Mexico defaulted on its international debt (over $85 billion), to be followed by other Latin American debtor states. This was particularly serious as both the USA and Western Europe were then in recession, and the combination helped produce the most serious global economic and financial crisis since the 1930s. The resulting rescheduling of the debt greatly increased the power of international financial bodies, especially the International Monetary Fund and the World Bank, and led to policies that hit government spending and cut living standards, as lenders insisted that exports be pushed in order to permit interest payments. Large amounts of capital were lost to the region. Communist Cuba, which faced growing economic problems and defaulted on debt payments in 1986, was unwilling to accept the social costs of rescheduling. Its economy partly depended on Soviet support.

With the old system of state direction discredited across most of Latin America, new political groupings pledged to economic liberalism, as well as democracy, came to power. This led to a removal of state controls and economic ownership, and an encouragement of foreign investment. In Bolivia, Victor Paz Estenssoro, who, as President in 1952–64, had nationalized the tin mines, backed free-market policies when he returned to power in 1985–9. Across South America, inflation fell and economic growth picked up, although only to an average of 3 per cent per annum in the 1990s, compared to 2 per cent per annum in the 1980s. The growth of Chile in 1989–97 and Mexico in 1996–2000 was not matched across most of the continent. Having grown rapidly in the mid-1990s, Peru's economy failed to do so subsequently. Combined with the 1980s recession and population growth, this ensured that in real terms GDP per person in Peru in 2000 was no higher than in 1970; and that figure – $2,350 – was low. Heavily indebted, Brazil and, even more, Argentina faced serious monetary crises in 2001. At over half of GDP, Brazil's public debt ensured that debt interest was the major call on state spending. Ecuador suffered recession and bankruptcy in 1999 and in 2000 withdrew its currency in order to switch to the dollar; followed by El Salvador in 2001. In contrast, thanks to the North American Free-Trade Agreement (NAFTA), which came into effect in 1994, Mexico benefited from a major expansion in exports to the USA, especially in regions close to the border.

In many Latin American countries, serious economic problems and the widespread nature of poverty were potential challenges to support for democracy and to political stability. It was not clear that the long-term fundamentals of stable political structures and societies had been addressed.

AFRICA

Sub-Saharan Africa was also harshly hit by developments in the last quarter-century. Under colonial rule, the production of cash crops, such as cocoa in Ghana and coffee and vanilla in Madagascar, and of raw materials, such as copper in Northern Rhodesia (from 1964 Zambia) and the Belgian Congo, had been encouraged. These remained the staples of their international economy after independence. Some progress was made in industrialization, but it was limited. The infrastructure, for example good communications, was often lacking, domestic demand was hit by poverty and local capital sources were scant. Technology had to be imported, while industry could not provide the employment necessary for a rising population. Instead, it seemed central to modernization strategies that they developed with insufficient attention to agriculture. Nevertheless, the long economic boom brought profit to African commodity producers, and there was sustained economic growth in the 1960s and early 1970s, albeit from a low base.

However, sub-Saharan Africa was badly hit by the oil shock and the consequent economic downturn. The dependence of most of Africa on oil imports was a serious problem, but so also was the fall in demand for commodities that resulted from economic difficulties elsewhere. Economic hardship accentuated the consequences of mistaken public policy after independence, specifically nationalizations, poor investment and state planning. Thus in Tanzania under Julius Nyerere (Prime Minister and then President 1961–85) there was widespread nationalization, including of banks and all the land, while peasants were forced into collectives. Nyerere's socialist theory of development, outlined in the Arusha Declaration (1967), attracted praise from sympathetic outsiders, but its economic consequences were less happy. Both industry and agriculture were hit.

In the late 1970s and 1980s, economic growth declined, and many African countries, for example Zambia, Niger and the Ivory Coast, experienced a fall in GNP. By the end of the century, African economies were heavily indebted, and also affected by high rates of population growth, which accentuated poverty. Some African commodity producers were hit by the nature of the new industries of the 1980s and 1990s, such as advanced electronics, which relied on semi-conductors, not large bits of metal, for their manufacture. The industrial sector remained small, and commodity exports, for example oil from Nigeria and Gabon, were crucial. Attempts to develop heavy industry, for example steel in Nigeria, were mismanaged and suffered from inadequate infrastructure. In contrast, consumer production was helped by urbanization. By the end of the century, Coca-Cola was the continent's biggest employer. Africa's economic problems discredited the policies followed since independence, including nationalization and the establishment of heavy industries. Benjamin Mkapa, President of Tanzania from 1995, liberalized and privatized the country Nyerere had nationalized. In 2000, the Zambian state sold its copper industry, much of it to Anglo-American, the company that originally developed the industry before nationalization in 1969.

BY THE END OF THE CENTURY, COCA-COLA WAS AFRICA'S BIGGEST EMPLOYER.

FROM MOROCCO TO IRAN

The Islamic states of North Africa, the Middle East and Iran had very varied economic histories as a consequence of very different government policies, and of sharply contrasting ratios between oil production and population (high in Saudi Arabia, Kuwait, Oman, the United Arab Emirates, Libya and Iraq; low in Egypt, Morocco and Syria). By 2001, the Middle Eastern members of OPEC produced 26 per cent of the world's supply of crude oil. Oil revenues served to bring much wealth in the region, and this led to a marked degree of economic modernization, seen, for example, in the provision of advanced communications infrastructure. Much of the wealth was spent on armaments and wars; and a large amount was poorly invested, not only in conspicuous consumption, but also on uneconomic industrial plant. Rapid population growth put the entire economic system of the Islamic world under pressure. A measure of economic integration had resulted from the large-scale movement of immigrant workers to Saudi Arabia and the Persian Gulf, where the population was far smaller. Thus, there were large-scale movements of Yemenis into Saudi Arabia and of Egyptians to Libya. Furthermore, economic services for the oil world were provided by entrepôt and financial centres such as Bahrain. There was also important economic co-operation through OPEC. However, pan-Arabist attempts to further economic co-operation have been no more successful than their political counterparts. Unlike coal in nineteenth-century Britain, oil has not produced an industrial revolution in producing areas, whether in the Middle East, Africa or Venezuela, and there has been no creation of jobs sufficient to cope with the rapidly rising population.

CONCLUSIONS

In the late twentieth century, economic development focused more on the skills and investment required by increasingly complex manufactured products than on the raw materials required for basic manufacturing processes. In the 1990s, the need for investment encouraged orthodox financial policies and economic liberalization, and states that had earlier avoided free-market policies, such as India and Madagascar, adopted them. However, the political response to the consequences was often uncomfortable, if not antagonistic. The very nature of the global economy was that it was both dynamic and prone to bring the far-distant and different into contact. This was destabilizing, although, on the world scale, the productivity gains more than offset the pressures of rising numbers of people. In the 1990s, the great decade of globalization, the GDP of the world increased by possibly close to 40 per cent, although many did not share in this benefit. Furthermore, the economic problems that gathered pace in 2001 led to a serious fall in economic confidence and anticipated growth.

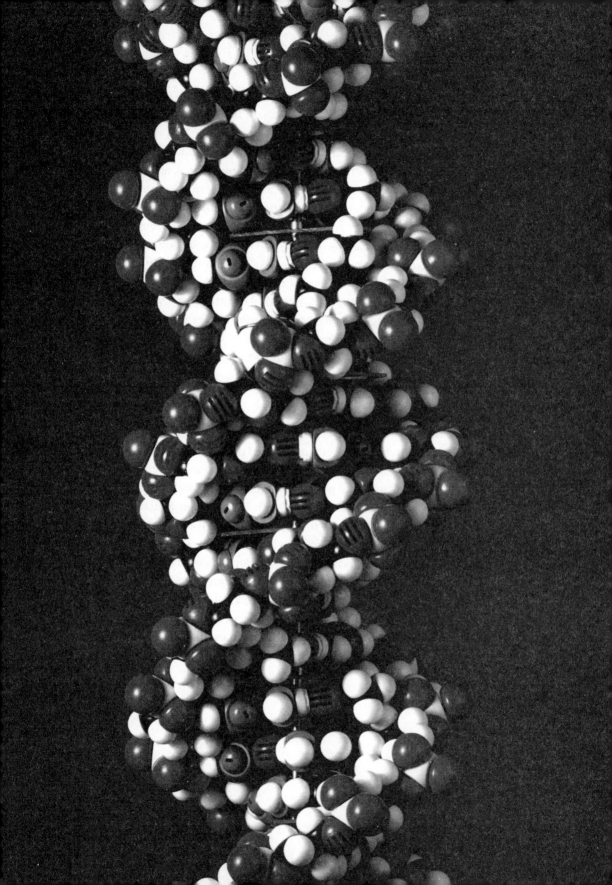

six

PROMETHEUS
UNBOUND
MACHINES AND
GOODS

INTRODUCTION

Machines shaped the twentieth century, and technology and science had a sweeping impact. Technology had become a freed genie in the nineteenth century, and the cumulative character of change became more striking in the twentieth century. Railway and telegraphy were succeeded by motor car and telephone, electricity and wireless. The growth of the genre of 'scientific romance' testified to the seemingly inexorable advance of human potential through technology and its impact on the collective imagination. The nineteenth-century fascination with the machine remained strong and influenced both popular and high culture. The *Manifesto* issued by Emilio Filippo Marinetti in 1909 and the *Manifesto of Futurist Painters* that followed in 1910 launched the artistic movement Futurism as a creed of science expressed in part through glorification of the machine. *391*, the magazine of the avant-garde Dada artistic movement, launched in Barcelona

TECHNOLOGY HAD BECOME A FREED GENIE IN THE NINETEENTH CENTURY, AND THE CUMULATIVE CHARACTER OF CHANGE BECAME MORE STRIKING IN THE TWENTIETH CENTURY.

by Francis Picabia in 1917, presented images of machines as symbols of life. This was also seen in Picabia's painting *Parade Amoureuse* (1917), in which the machine had the threatening capacity to be amorous.

SCIENCE

The twentieth century saw great intellectual achievements in science, particularly in physics, which was transformed by Albert Einstein (1879–1955), who developed the theory of relativity. The century also saw revolutionary transformations in theoretical and applied science and technology in most fields, whether transport, the generation and distribution of power, medicine, contraception, agricultural yields, cloning or the accumulation, storing, transmission and manipulation of information. Wealth was created and the means were provided that would make it feasible to suggest that humanity's lot on earth could be substantially improved, and that science should therefore be employed to ensure that such an improvement took place.

Furthermore, the relationship between humanity and the world was altered with the realization, through the combination of telescopic investigation of the universe and advanced mathematics, that there were other galaxies apart from our Milky Way (1923) and that, as the galaxies were moving apart, the universe was expanding (1929). This led to the reconceptualization of time, which was presented as originating from an original Big Bang when the universe began. This process of investigation and speculation extended to the more precise analysis of the building blocks of life. This analysis included the discovery and utilization of subatomic particles, an understanding of how light travels, the explanation in 1953 of the correct atomic structure of the genetic material DNA, and research on neurobiology and the workings of the brain. All this underlined the nature of knowledge as a process of change. A comparable sense of human capability arose from the human ability to synthesize new experiences, which culminated in the early 1990s with the development of virtual reality imaging. In addition, for example in the development of recycling technologies, science was able to display an ability to respond to environmental problems. At the start of the new millennium, the pace of change, and its insistent impact on the tempos of life, appeared greater than ever.

At the same time, disquiet about the pace of technological change, and the process and consequences of scientific advance, increased markedly. The use of the atom bomb in 1945 led to concern, and this was seen more generally from the 1960s as the environmental movement became more vocal and popular. Anxiety about technology was linked to a wider questioning of the rationale of economic growth, although such growth was required in order to fund environmental rehabilitation.

THE EXTENT OF CHANGE

For the elderly at the close of the century, and the aged were a growing percentage of the population, it was not only the individual major technological innovations of their lifetimes, whether atomic energy or contraceptive pill, television or microchip, jet engine or computer, bio-technology or artificial hip, that were of importance in affecting, directly or indirectly, insistently or episodically, their lives. Added to this was also the cumulative impact of change. The past ceased to be a recoverable world, a source of reference, value and values for lives that changed very little, and became, instead, a world that was truly lost, a theme-park for nostalgia, regret or curiosity.

Sensory experiences were altered as a consequence of these changes. For example, at the start of the century, power, heat and light across the world were dependent on coal and wood, and the associated sights, smells, sounds and tasks made up much of the fabric of life, and were also crucial to economies. By the end of the century, natural gas, oil and nuclear power had all become important sources of power. Furthermore, power was increasingly used as electricity, with associated changes for both the fabric of life and economic activity.

SCIENCE AND TECHNOLOGY

In the twentieth century, science affected ordinary people through technological advance. The ability to secure the latter helped ensure substantial public and private investment in science. Thus, there were far more scientists and scientific institutions than ever before, and this became more marked during the century. At the same time, the distribution of scientific research remained very unequal, with a heavy concentration in the USA and, to a lesser extent, Europe and Japan. As a result, their economies were better able to apply knowledge, and to make a productive use of new technologies. However, the existence of large scientific establishments in the Soviet Union and India, which did not enjoy comparable growth, underlines the need for caution before drawing simple links.

Science and technology most affected people through medical advances (as discussed in chapter 2), developments in energy provision, a transformation of communications and the creation of synthetic products. Science also threatened to destroy the world, but the potential change that a nuclear holocaust would have brought was averted, through restraint, a balance of terror and the limited diffusion of nuclear weapons.

RADIO, TELEPHONE, AND TELEVISION

The transformation of communications was seen throughout the century, and played a major role in the spread of knowledge and opinion. In 1896, Guglielmo Marconi arrived in London to try to interest the Admiralty in his primitive radio. Radio technology was rapidly improved, not least as crystal sets were replaced by valve sets in the 1930s, improving reception. The telephone also spread rapidly. This was particularly so in the USA, where it was invented in 1876, and where the dispersed nature of much settlement encouraged use. By 1910, there were nine million telephones in the USA, and the number there rapidly rose in the following decades. Telephone systems also developed in Europe, where, in 1925, it was decided to link them in order to create a long-distance communication system. In the developing world, however, the use of telephones remained small-scale, and during the 1930s there was only a modest rise in their global use.

Meanwhile, television had developed, with television services from the British Broadcasting Corporation (BBC) beginning in 1936. That year, Germany provided television coverage of the Berlin Olympics, and also a system of video-telephoning between Berlin and Leipzig. The lessening of consumer demand during World War II (1939–45) in order to focus on war production ensured that the expansion in telecommunications then was restricted. Indeed, in Britain, television was suspended, although during the war the radio, with its greater capacity for immediacy and its access to government, and not the press, became the main source of news. However, the war also brought research on telecommunications that increased their capability.

After the war, developments were carried forward on a prolonged wave of consumer demand in the developed world. The rise of television was seen in more sets, more channels and longer periods of broadcasting. Television came to mould lifestyles. By 1994, 99 per cent of British households had a television. From the 1950s, television succeeded radio as a central determinant of the leisure time of many, a moulder of opinions and fashions, a source of conversation and controversy, a cause of noise, an occasion of family cohesion or dispute and a major feature of the household. A force for change, a great contributor to the making of the consumer society and a 'window on the world' that demanded the right to enter everywhere and report everything, television became, increasingly, both moulder and reflector of popular taste. It took over from radio the function of providing common experience. Television became central to the trend-setting and advertising that were crucial to the consumer society, and to politics. It also increasingly set the idioms and vocabulary of public and private life. The ownership of telephones across the world also shot up after the war: from about 51 million in 1950 to 520 million in 1990; and that was before the mobile phone made its impact.

New technology made an impact. Colour was introduced to television, while the American development of the transistor in 1948 made smaller radios (and other equipment) possible. Like the laser, the transistor reflected an understanding of the wave-like character of the electron that arose from research in the 1920s. In the field of computing, Alan Turing's theoretical work in the 1930s and 1940s helped pave the way for the Manchester Mk1, the first all-electronic computer to function: it went into action in 1948.

Over the following half-century, as the use of telecommunications became more insistent in the developed world, they increasingly spread to the developing world, while there were also important technological developments. The spread of televisions was such that by 1986 there were 26 million in Brazil, 10.5 million in India and 6.6 million in Indonesia. However, such figures were put in perspective by the 195 million in the USA. Per head, television and telephone use was far higher in the developed world, and both were particularly patchy in sub-Saharan Africa and South-East Asia. However, the numbers of people involved were such that a rise in the per capita rate, especially in China and India, was very important. Furthermore, the growth of telecommunications in the developed world intensified their global impact.

COMMUNICATIONS FROM THE 1950s

In 1956, Europe was linked to the USA by underwater telephone cable, emulating the telegraph cables of the previous century, but satellite communication was soon to offer a very different system. In 1957, the first space satellite, Sputnik I, was launched, while silicon was found to be a good way to store electronic information. These changes led to communications satellites, able to provide a global system for transmitting words and images; and the silicon microchip, which enabled the creation of more effective communication systems. Satellite television brought cross-border influences that hit monopolies on control of information. The miniaturization of electronic components made it possible to create complete electronic circuits on a small slice of silicon. The Intel 4004, the first microprocessor chip, was created in the USA in 1971. Gordon Moore, the co-founder of the company responsible, predicted a dramatic revolution in capability as the result of the doubling of the number of transistors on chips every eighteen months. From the 1950s, cybernetics, the study of information systems, developed. As an instance of the extent to which analogies between humans and machines were pressed, this was applied to both brains and computers.

An advance of the 1970s, fibre-optic cables, increased the capacity of cable systems, and the volume of telephone and computer messages they could carry. A single optical fibre could carry ten billion bits per second. Fax machines and mobile phones became important from the 1980s. The rapid development of the latter increased the convenience of personal communications. In the developing world, they also served to 'leapfrog' technology beyond the stage of requiring landlines. By 1999, there were about one billion phones and nearly 500 million mobile phones in the world.

Initially, in the absence of miniaturization, computers were an industrial product, of great scale and cost, but, from the late 1970s, they became widely available as office and then household tools. Improvements in capability ensured that computing power became cheaper and thus more accessible. Size, specifically miniaturization, was a key element in the popularity of new consumer goods, such as mobile phones, laptop computers, mini-disc sound systems and, earlier, transistor radios.

THE INTERNET

In addition, the capacity of the electro-magnetic spectrum to transmit messages was utilized. Thanks to computers and electronic mail, more messages were sent and more information was stored in the 1990s than ever before. The growing number of company and personal computers facilitated the use of electronic mail and access to the Internet. The number of people with Internet access in the world rose to about 130 million in 1998, with nearly half in the USA. Although in China the government sought to limit access to the Internet, there were thirty million users there by 2000.

THANKS TO COMPUTERS AND ELECTRONIC MAIL, MORE MESSAGES WERE SENT AND MORE INFORMATION WAS STORED IN THE 1990S THAN EVER BEFORE.

As earlier with telephones and other innovations, the Internet only really became efficient when there were sufficient users to create a widespread system. Nevertheless, the lapse factor between innovation and widespread use greatly diminished during the century. Thus, in contrast to telecommunications and the Internet, electricity, the impact of which across the world was only fully felt in the 1950s, represented the most important use of steam power, initially a development of the eighteenth century. Electricity was seen as a major step forward and a sign and means of progress. Thus displays of electrical industries played a major role in international exhibitions, such as that in Barcelona in 1929, while electric power stations were designed as stylistic factories of power.

Successive improvements in technology enhanced not only communications, but also other aspects of organizational activity, such as information storage and analysis, and accounting systems. This contributed to governmental and economic activities, making it easier to exercise control and to engage in planning. Technology was an enabler of new notions of efficiency, effectiveness and control, and these, in particular, came to characterize American corporate culture, helping American business to grow. It is also important to appreciate the degree to which the uses and benefits of technological advances frequently proved unexpected.

The NGOs (non-government organizations), which became more prominent in political and social activism in the 1980s and 1990s, benefited from the extent to which new technology, and its capacity for enhanced organizational capability, was not limited to government. New social, economic and political networks and groupings were created, and this established new patterns and hierarchies of communication. However, the overload, management and accessibility of information became major problems for both institutions and individuals.

The spread of the Internet as a worldwide interactive medium, and the dominance of computing by American operating systems, ensured that English became more prominent as a language than ever before. The growth of English as the global language of business and international political and cultural links was of major importance in global integration. It also increased the need for, and profitability of, communications systems. If, at the same time, as a reminder of diversity, English was only known by a minority of the world's population (and this was particularly apparent in East Asia and Latin America), it was, nevertheless, a larger minority. Furthermore, the impact of the language spread in countries where Britain had never been the colonial power. Yet, there was also a class and age dimension. The poorer and older had less knowledge of English (and other foreign languages) than had the more affluent and younger. Alongside the rise of English, Spanish and Mandarin Chinese, the latter two due to demographic expansion, came the extinction of a host of languages that each had few speakers, for example the Northern Pomo language in California in 1995.

THE NEW MACHINE ECONOMY

At the end of the century, Internet links were followed by digital technology. This was part of a continuous process of change that affected communications and, in a characteristic of twentieth-century economic and technological development, sought out the market of the individual consumer. Users were the key figure in the computer revolution, with systems designed for the benefit of individuals.

The rise in telecommunications made the manufacture of the necessary equipment and related electronics an important field of industrial activity. It also greatly affected the world of goods. There was a marked fall in the centrality of paper products and records, and in the need for cash transactions. Credit cards facilitated telephone purchases and therefore helped to limit the importance of face-to-face commercial transactions in the 1990s. By 2000, 21 per cent of consumer spending in the USA was by credit cards. In the developed world, purchasing was increasingly divorced from shops and other retail premises. The same shift affected other economic sectors. Telephone banking was introduced in the 1980s and Internet banking in the 1990s. Pornography became a more accessible industry as a result of the Internet, and computer fraud spread.

The developed world increasingly manifested a knowledge economy, with information a key product and 'messaging' a major form of work. In parts of the developing world, there was an openness to the opportunities of new technology and an attempt to use it in order to 'leapfrog' earlier stages of industrial change in the developed world. Indeed, thanks to telecommunications, the role of distance shrank in the 1990s, and it became possible to integrate production and service activities with consumers around the world. This was a major contributor to longer working hours in the USA and Britain.

As a reminder, however, of the continued, and indeed growing, importance of older technologies, the world of print also spread in the twentieth century. Thanks to a marked increase in education, particularly for women and the poor (both of whom earlier had largely been marginalized in educational terms), literacy rose greatly. This was particularly impressive given the rapid rate of population growth. By the end of the century, literacy levels in the developed world were close to the level of all those possessing the necessary intellectual level. In addition, the literacy rate in China had risen to about 80 per cent, and rates had risen rapidly in the rest of Asia, as well as in the Middle East, Africa and Latin America. However, they were still lower in these areas than in the developing world, and in 1995 about 900 million people in the world were illiterate. The majority were in India, a country where social welfare had not been secured under independence. In general, not least in India, illiteracy rates were higher for women than for men. The rapid growth in literacy in the developing world, which was particularly marked in the 1980s and early 1990s, provided new markets for the culture of print, not least newspapers, books and letters. All have been underrated because of the focus on cutting-edge technology.

FLIGHT

More rapid telecommunications contributed greatly to the impression of an 'accelerated' world, which also owed much to advances in transport. Apart from cars (see chapter 3), planes also had a major impact. Manned heavier-than-air flight, first officially achieved by the Americans Orville and Wilbur Wright in 1903 (there were several significant predecessors), was rapidly followed by the development of the military and commercial possibilities of air power, and by its technological range: in 1965 the first (unmanned) spaceship flew past Mars, and in 1969 the first men were to land on the Moon.

Change in air capability was greatly accelerated thanks to World War I. The use of aeroplanes for combat led to considerable investment in their development, and to a marked rise in specifications. Air power exemplified the growing role of scientific research in military capability: wind tunnels were constructed for the purpose of research. Strutless wings and all-metal aeroplanes were developed. Engine power increased and size fell. The speed and rate of climb of aeroplanes rose.

In 1919, a converted British bomber was the first aeroplane to cross the Atlantic non-stop. By the end of the 1920s, about twenty aeroplanes were daily leaving London's airport, Croydon aerodrome, which had been opened in 1921. Imperial Airways developed long-distance air travel from London. From 1930, the journey to Australia took two weeks. Planes held sixteen passengers and stopped each evening for refuelling and for passengers to stay in luxury hotels. The model was clearly leisurely sea travel, rather than swift air travel. At the same time, air services developed rapidly in the USA and the Soviet Union. Air routes in both greatly expanded, as did the number of airports and planes. The 1930s also saw the establishment of what became the conventions of passenger travel, with air hostesses (1930) and reclining seats (1931). Journey times were progressively cut, but the range of most planes was such that frequent refuelling was necessary. It was not until 1939 that a passenger aircraft was introduced that was able to fly the Atlantic non-stop.

Again, wartime advances in applied technology, in the case of World War II gas turbine jet engines, were important for postwar trends. The possibilities of long-distance travel were enhanced with the building of the first jet-propelled airliner: the British Comet, which had its maiden flight in 1949, and went into commercial service in 1952. However, it was to be the American Boeing 707 that dominated jet transport, becoming the fleet aircraft not only in America but also for many carriers throughout the non-communist world. Jet transport pushed forward both domestic and international flights, although the passenger mileage flown was to be much greater from 1960 and, even more, 1975. Air travel took over from long-distance liner services, for example across the Atlantic. Again, aircraft specifications improved, with the 1960s bringing both more powerful engines and the wide-body design seen most successfully with the Boeing 747, the original Jumbo Jet. Demand rose in the long economic boom of 1945–73, and travelling by air became normative. This had a range of effects, including an encouragement of long-distance tourism, which transformed the holiday parameters and experience of people in the developed world. Thus, large numbers of Americans flew to the West Indies and the Yucatan peninsula in Mexico, Australians to Bali and Japanese to Australasia, while northern Europeans travelled extensively first to the Mediterranean and then further afield, for example to the USA, South Africa, Australasia and South Asia, especially Thailand.

Aircraft were not only important for long-distance passenger travel. They also became increasingly important for the movement of freight and helped ensure the growing importance in the international economy of high-value low-bulk goods. Aircraft were also used for a range of other activities, including the application of pesticides and fertilizers to crops.

TRAVEL

At the same time, older technologies remained important in transport. This was especially true of rail. Although it declined in the USA, with the growth of long-distance road and air travel in the second half of the century, and became proportionately less important in Europe, rail still remained particularly significant for freight: in the late 1990s, in the USA, rail provided 1.2 trillion tonne-miles compared to 900 billion tonne-miles for road. Both were formidable figures reflecting the synergy between economic demand and transport provision. Furthermore, where car ownership was lower and air travel less important, rail retained a major role in passenger travel. At the end of the century, Indian Railways sold 4.5 billion tickets annually. Rail services continued to expand in both the developed and the developing world. In China, the railway was extended to Urumqi, capital of Xinjiang, in 1960, to

Kashgar in 1999, and was projected to Lhasa, capital of Tibet, in the early 2000s. These extensions provided economic links and facilitated Chinese control of frontier provinces, not least by transporting Chinese immigrants.

Long-distance travel was of great economic importance, literally transferring wealth, but also had a major social impact. Although many tourists took with them impressions that were not challenged by travel, and frequently went to purpose-built resorts that reproduced much of what they were used to at home, with the addition of sun and sea, others were affected by the experience of visiting new countries. The impact of tourism on areas that were visited was considerable, not least the challenging of established patterns of activity.

As with many changes during the century, what had been an elite activity, largely open only to the wealthy, was democratized within the developed world. This reflected increased leisure time, and greater affluence, the two combining in the paid holiday, which became increasingly important in the interwar period. While most popular tourism was domestic in that period, from the 1950s it increasingly became international, thanks not only to jet aircraft and affluence but also to the active selling of package holidays, which covered travel, hotels and food. By the end of the century, over 1.5 billion air tickets were sold annually.

Conversely, for much of the developing world, tourism could not be afforded. This was true of much of the population of Africa, Latin America, South Asia and China. Their experience of tourism, insofar as it occurred, was that of servicing it, or of having environments affected to provide for tourists, for example by the creation of game reserves in Southern and East Africa or by the pressure on water supplies of the needs of hotels.

FOR MUCH OF THE DEVELOPING WORLD, THEIR EXPERIENCE OF TOURISM, INSOFAR AS IT OCCURRED, WAS THAT OF SERVICING IT.

This was an aspect of a global economy in which Third World workers and resources were in many eyes exploited. Thus, in the 1990s, children in the Third World worked for little pay to satisfy the market for 'trainers' (or 'sneakers') for the affluent young of the West.

CONSUMERISM

There were also problems with consumerism in the developed world. The ownership of material possessions rose, especially as teenage and child markets expanded, but problems were created by the massive rise in personal indebtedness made possible by purchase on credit, as well as by the peer pressure for consumer conformity (and related exclusion of those unable to participate), the extension of adult 'tastes' onto teens and pre-teens, and by what can be seen as the reverse infantilizing of adults in their twenties and even thirties.

More than the quantity of goods was at stake. Much of the consumer revolution related to labour-saving devices, such as washing machines, that reduced domestic drudgery, and encouraged higher female participation in the labour force. This can be seen in the 1930s, but became more common after 1945 when real wages rose, while redistributive taxation and benefit policies helped to spread income.

FOOD

The role of increased wealth and rising consumerism was also reflected in the greater commodification of food and the fashionability of particular foods. In the late nineteenth century, transoceanic products, brought in refrigerated ship-holds, had had a major impact on Western Europe, but in the early twentieth century there were relatively few changes in the diet of the developed world, or in other aspects of eating, such as outlets and meal-times, certainly compared to the following half-century. Meals heavy in carbohydrate predominated in most homes and restaurants, and there was little fresh fruit. There was a high consumption of sugar in hot drinks, desserts and confectionery. Dairy products were important, and butter and lard were widely used for cooking. The poor ate much cold food – bread, cheese and cold meat – and potatoes were also very important in their diet. Traditional dishes retained great popularity, and there was only limited interest in alternatives.

The disruptions of the two World Wars and the protectionism of the 1930s increased the emphasis on local foodstuffs, and in the 1950s the return to prosperity generally meant more of the same: increased consumption of the proteins and carbohydrates that was the staple of much of the Western diet. Given the precarious nature of the diet of the poor prior to World War II, this was no mean achievement. It also ensured that the nutritional standard of life in the developed world rose. Daily calorie supply per capita was particularly high in North America, Western Europe and Australasia.

From the 1960s, the national diet in these areas was increasingly affected by new ingredients and by dishes introduced from foreign countries, the latter an aspect of globalization. Italian, Chinese and Indian restaurants expanded outside their home areas, while American fast-food chains, such as McDonald's, became ubiquitous, enjoying a particular impact in Europe and Latin America. Traditional national dishes became less dominant. Supermarkets also increasingly stocked foreign dishes, although this varied by country, with France and Italy more resistant to foreign food than was Britain.

The shift towards new foodstuffs reflected aspects of the late twentieth-century world other than greater purchasing power and increased trade. Information, fashionability and technology all had an impact. There was a willingness to try new dishes and also far more information about how to prepare them. Households were no longer pre-pared to accept inherited recipes or one biblical cookbook. Instead, they purchased several, while cookery became very important in the media. The increased consump-tion of convenience foods, generally stored in deep freezers and reheated rapidly by microwave cookers, provided a major market for new dishes. Refrigeration trans-formed eating habits by making it possible to preserve foodstuffs. Seasons were ban-ished for consumers who wanted year-long supplies of products.

Changing diet interacted in the Western world with concern about what was seen as healthy eating to lead to a shift in the consumption of various types of food. Red meat, such as beef, mutton and lamb, became less popular, in favour of chicken, and the consumption of fats, such as butter and cheese, dropped, in favour of low-fat alterna-tives. Nevertheless, fast foods remained popular, and these tended to contain too much salt, fat and sugar. In general, the traditional diet, which had been formed largely in accordance with the needs of men, became less widespread for both men and women. The consumption of calories fell, in part as the role of physical labour in employment declined, while vegetarianism became more common, particularly among women. There were related changes in other consumer products, with a rise in the 1990s of toiletries and products linked to aromatherapy, a fashionable alternative medicine, designed, in particular, to combat stress, while decaffeinated hot drinks became more popular, and the range of teas, coffees, soft drinks, bottled water and alcoholic drinks all spread.

It need hardly be said that much of the world's population did not enjoy such a spread. Daily calorie supply per capita remained particularly low in sub-Saharan Africa, South Asia and parts of Latin America, and traditional foodstuffs and means of preparing food remained important. Cultural differences remained very significant in consumption patterns. Traditional taboos, such as the eating of pork by Muslims and Jews and beef by Hindus, proved resistant to change. Fundamentalist movements lent urgency to their enforcement, so that the consumption of alcohol by Muslims remained low and frequently illicit, although in more liberal Islamic societies, such as Turkey, it was more common.

SHOPPING AND SELLING

At the same time, the large number of urban workers in the developing world increasingly purchased processed and packaged food. As in developed societies, this was an aspect of the retail revolution of the second half of the century, which focused on economies of scale, such as mass purchasing. This enabled shopping chains to undermine independent retail activity through pricing structures. This was linked to the rise of the supermarket in the 1950s and the hypermarket, mainly out-of-town, in the 1980s. American models of car-borne shopping were particularly influential. 'Pink Dot', the USA's first telephone-order/delivery supermarket, operated in California from the 1950s. By 2000, there were 486 cars per 1,000 people in the USA, and 394 per 1,000 in Japan; although some countries, such as Italy and Germany, had an even higher rate. Mobility brought access to shopping opportunity, but the range of retail outlets diminished. The fate of local shops was linked to that of local economies, which were increasingly subordinated to national or regional suppliers.

The growth of advertising and the advertising industry transformed the world of shopping, and not only in the developed world. Traditional methods of advertising – on billboards, on the sides of buses, in shop windows and via 'sandwich men' – were supplemented by more novel methods: commercial television and, from the 1990s, the Internet. Advertising focused on entire countries and helped make products and activities national. This was true not only of foodstuffs but also of the fame of hitherto local or regional groups or products, such as football teams (Britain's Manchester United, for example, is hugely popular in China). National advertising both encouraged and helped to focus consumerism.

There was also an increasingly powerful international dimension to selling and advertising, which itself encouraged economic growth. This international dimension was due not only to the availability of investment and appeal of foreign models, but also to the enhancement of product range and possibilities through technological developments that had global impact far more rapidly than in the past. This was clearly seen with the development of synthetic fibres, such as nylon and polyester, and their impact on clothing. Fashion became more insistent due to the spread of colour photography, in magazines and newspaper supplements. It became common throughout wealthier societies to replace goods even when they were still functional. Thus, material culture was a focus of wider social currents as well as economic practices.

The world of goods was also an aspect and indicator of cultural trends. The images associated with desirable goods were the style of society. This relationship was accentuated by the growth of industrial design as a distinct practice and subject, especially from the 1960s, when the value of new design, as a device to improve sales and enhance the image of a good or service, was widely recognized. The impact of design consultants spread widely through society. The conflation of society and politics through the focus of consumerism led the devices of marketing and market research to encompass policies and votes. Politics had fully entered the world of goods.

POLITICS HAD FULLY ENTERED THE WORLD OF GOODS.

CONCERN ABOUT SCIENCE

At the same time, there was disquiet about consumerism and technology. The former was widely blamed from the 1960s for environmental pressures and contributed, in some circles, to a sense of cultural anxiety. Science was for long seen as crucial to modernization, but, whereas the scientist had been a heroic figure in the nineteenth century, in the twentieth his or her knowledge seemed incomprehensible. In an age when science made an ever greater impact, it was understood by only a minority. Furthermore, disquiet grew from the 1960s.

There had been initial optimism about the potential of nuclear power and a hope that it would bring cheap energy, symbolized by the Atomium, a gigantic model of an atom erected in Brussels in 1958. The expansion of the nuclear industry following the opening in 1956 of Calder Hall in Britain, the first nuclear plant to supply substantial quantities of electricity to a national system, was replaced by concerns, especially by worry about long-term problems of processing and storing nuclear waste. Such concerns proved stronger in some countries (Germany, Britain, USA) than others (France, Japan). Accidents at nuclear plants, especially at Chernobyl in the Soviet Union in 1986, led to an increase in public anxiety. After an accident at the Three Mile Island plant in 1979, no more plants were built in the USA, although, due to earlier construction, the USA remained the world's largest nuclear producer for the remainder of our period. In contrast, an accident at the Tokaimura plant in 1999 led to a scaling down of Japanese plans, but new reactors were still planned there, as well as in China, South Korea, Indonesia, Vietnam and Russia. However, European nuclear production fell as Germany began to close its nuclear plants in 2001. These very different policies illustrated the variety of responses to the complex issues of safety concerns and relative energy costs posed by nuclear power.

The development of nuclear power had owed much to the World War II race to produce the atomic bomb, a race won by the Americans, who dropped two bombs on Japan in 1945. Thereafter, the pace of technological development continued to owe much to military requirements, especially in those countries with a prominent military-industrial complex affecting multiple facets of society. Thus, from the Gulf War of 1991, the USA employed 'smart weaponry' making use of the precise prior mapping of target and traverse in order to follow predetermined courses to targets that were actualized for the weapons as grid references. Cruise missiles used digital terrain models of the intended flight path. In addition, precise positioning devices interacted with American satellites in a Global Positioning System. Advances in the capacity of satellites to provide effective surveillance aroused much concern among civil libertarians, but such concern did not halt subsequent advances, which continue today.

As another instance of the controversial nature of scientific advance, the oral contraceptive pill, a triumph of planned science, in that it was designed to mimic an enzyme in order to prevent ovulation, and thus stop the reproductive system, was rejected by the Catholic Church as an artificial infringement of a God-given natural process. Furthermore, the drug, which received its first trial in 1956, was to be found to have some harmful side-effects. Nevertheless, it was widely taken and greatly increased women's control over their own fertility.

Much of the religious critique of science was longstanding. Thus, fundamentalist Christians rejected the theory of evolution from the outset. Their stance enjoyed considerable popular support in the USA and a measure of institutional backing. In 1925, John Scopes was convicted for teaching evolution in the American state of Tennessee, where it was forbidden. Although the fundamentalists were castigated for intolerant ignorance, the law was not changed for several decades. In 1999, the Kansas Board of Education decided that creationism (the biblical account) should be taught alongside evolution, although the law was repealed in 2001 after considerable public protest.

Biotechnology, the manipulation of genes, which developed from the 1970s, especially in the pharmaceutical industry, led to particular disquiet. In Europe, this focused from the 1990s on opposition to genetically modified crops, such as soyabeans, maize and oil-seed rape. Biotechnology came to be regarded by many as a threat to human health and the physical environment, rather than an opportunity to continue earlier advances in enhancing crop productivity. The possibility of improving the stock of domestic animals or of gene therapy for humans led to widespread concern. In 1997, Dolly, the first cloned animal, appeared: the nucleus of an adult sheep cell was transferred to an egg cell from which the nucleus had been removed,

DOLLY, THE FIRST CLONED SHEEP, WOULD HAVE SEEMED A FANTASY A CENTURY EARLIER. and the egg developed to become a mature sheep. This would have seemed a fantasy a century earlier. Cloned cattle and pigs followed, although the problems of accelerated ageing still have to be resolved.

Nevertheless, there was a failure to reproduce the sense of achievement that had characterized much of the century up to and including the 1950s. Evil scientists and science-fiction stories about the dangers of abusing technology came to play an important role in popular culture. What had been seen as humanity's greatest adventure – space travel – lost its appeal and was increasingly criticized from the 1970s as expensive and irrelevant. Proposals for cloning human cells for scientific research, an essential preliminary for genetic research to help find cures for diseases, led to heated debate at the beginning of the twenty-first century, and in 2001 the American House of Representatives passed a bill banning all human cloning. Disastrous side-effects of scientific development, such as birth defects from the drug thalidomide in the 1960s, and unexpected consequences, as from exposure to asbestos, fuelled public alarm: the diminution in confidence in vaccination from the 1990s threatened public health as vaccination rates dropped. More generally, the 'ownership' of knowledge became an issue of scientific and public concern, not least with attempts from the 1990s both to patent genes and to stop 'pirated' AIDS drugs from being sold in Africa.

There was also disquiet about the development of robotics, another field in which science-fiction became reality. By the end of 1999, 750,000 robots were in use in manufacturing around the world. They were most commonly used in car manufacturing and were especially common (402,000) in Japan, a state that had invested heavily in state-of-the-art and futuristic technology. The distribution of robots also reflected the dominance of the developed world in technology. Thus, after Japan came the USA, Germany, Italy and France. Not a single country in Africa, Latin America or South Asia appeared in the list of the twenty countries with the most robots. As with computers, robots benefited after their introduction from subsequent capability improvements and from better production systems that reduced their cost, and helped them to raise the productivity of economic systems. However, the ability to create machines to tackle tasks, most of them highly repetitive, that formerly had been done by human workers led to considerable concern about issues of employment and control.

A very different qualification of reason, as well as an implicit criticism of the possibility of beneficial development defined by, and thanks to, improved technology, was offered by the popularity in the West of the School of Latin American fiction known as magic realism, for example the novels of the Colombian Gabriel García Márquez (1928–86), especially *One Hundred Years of Solitude* (1967). Such work made magical events both central and 'real', challenging the attempt to define the world by science and reason. The same was more generally true of the range of beliefs in the occult, as well as of providential religious creeds.

Yet, these doubts about technology have to be qualified by noting that the quest for living standards and national growth across the developing world led to anxiety about change playing only a small role in public policy there. In some countries, indeed, there was a determined attempt to reconcile the opportunities of technological change with traditional cultural norms, as with the strong emphasis on Islam and 'Asian values' in Malaysia in the 1990s. The extent and impact of anxiety about change varied greatly, but the net effect of a century of scientific and technological development was to enhance the range of options available in modern societies, and thus to increase the opportunity for debate about choices.

seven

HUMAN OR DIVINE?
IDEAS AND BELIEFS

INTRODUCTION

Over the century as a whole, the two major themes were consumerism and the persistence and, in many circumstances, resurgence, of religious beliefs and ways of interpreting the world. The first led to a commodification of Western culture and to a considerable degree of at least partial Westernization of popular culture around the world; while the second reflected the resilience of diverse cultures that might adopt modern technology, but not some other aspects of modernization. At the same time, it would be mistaken to assume that beliefs and ideologies have been roughly similar throughout the century, or to treat them essentially as a response to socio-economic conditions and pressures.

Political developments challenged cultural patterns and beliefs. Thus, although some colonial powers, particularly Britain, made important compromises with existing practices, others did not. Beliefs were challenged by the spread of Christianity under the aegis of Western power, while political practices that often played a major role in local culture, for example kingship in Burma and Vietnam, were overthrown. The same was to occur as a result of the two World Wars. The fall of the Russian imperial dynasty in 1917 was followed by a marked decline in the authority and presence of the Russian Orthodox Church, while, in reverse, Japan's defeat in World War II in 1945 led to the abolition of the imperial cult there, but not of the position of the Emperor.

It is also possible to point to a host of developments already mentioned in the book that challenged local cultures. The international consumerist culture was linked, however imperfectly, to a set of beliefs that 'empowered' women and the young (see chapter 4). Both the latter became more prominent in public culture from the 1960s, and the independent role of youth was accentuated by demographic trends and by the decline of deference. Technology facilitated this process. Satellite television ensured that images could more easily become global. Another aspect of demographics was unprecedented migration both within and, even more, between countries. The diverse cultural richness that immigrant societies produced challenged notions of ethnic homogeneity and created a source of disruption in particular national cultural traditions.

It is therefore easy to see cultural change and the remoulding of ideas and beliefs as imposed from 'outside'. At the same time, it is necessary to note the role of elites in encouraging change within their own countries, and the capacity of what is termed traditional or conservative to have a vitality and dynamism that encompassed the possibility of change. There is too often a tendency to imagine that traditional and conservative equate with unchanging and rigid, but this was frequently not the case.

> **THERE IS TOO OFTEN A TENDENCY TO IMAGINE THAT TRADITIONAL AND CONSERVATIVE EQUATE WITH UNCHANGING AND RIGID, BUT THIS WAS FREQUENTLY NOT THE CASE.**

CHINA, JAPAN AND TURKEY

The role of modernizing elites can be seen in states that avoided colonial control. It was true of China, Japan and Turkey in the early decades of the century. Thus, in China, the teaching of Western subjects was encouraged from 1901, while the long-established Confucian educational and examination system was abolished in 1905, furthering a process in which new ideas played a greater role in education (although only of a small minority). This helped lead to a spread of radicalism, but, at the same time, the government was pressing ahead with modernization, including the creation of provincial assemblies with elected representatives. In many respects, the situation was similar to France in the 1780s and 1790s. As there, it led to a

145

revolution (1911), a republic (1912), prolonged instability, and then the imposition in 1926-8 of a strong man, Chiang Kai-shek, who acted as a successful warlord with national pretensions.

In Turkey, there was a similar trajectory, although the particular steps were different. The Young Turks led, via World War I, to a new modernizing, republican state of Turkey under Kemal Atatürk, President from his foundation of the republic in 1923 until his death in 1938. Adult men gained the vote in 1924, women achieving equal electoral rights in 1934. Determined to Westernize Turkey, Atatürk introduced the Christian calendar (moving the day of rest from Friday to Sunday) and the Latin alphabet (1928), changed the language, introduced surnames (1934) and outlawed the fez, the traditional male headgear, although his attack on the veil was less successful. The capital was moved from Istanbul to Ankara. Atatürk regarded culture as integral to change and pushed through what has been presented as a Turkish cultural revolution. Its Western character was shown by the state opera and symphony orchestra he created.

In Japan, modernization had been long established, and took a fresh turn in the 1920s with a powerful boost from American culture. This affected industry, leisure and finances. Adult men gained the vote in 1925, although women did not follow until 1946. In Persia, men had gained the vote in 1906. Thailand introduced compulsory primary education in 1921 and became a constitutional monarchy in 1932.

RELIGION

If change was not therefore the monopoly of the West, it was also the case that important aspects of twentieth-century culture, both Western and non-Western, were discussed in simplistic terms of change versus conservatism. This was certainly true of religion, one of the most underrated forces of the century. The public role of religion, as a source of ideology and morality, was widely condemned by self-styled progressives for much of the century, while, as a private source of meaning, hope and faith, religion was treated in some circles as a delusion best clarified, like sexuality, by an understanding of anthropology, psychology and sociology. As such, it was subject to the scrutiny of relativism. More generally, the stress on the subconscious and, in particular, on repressed sexuality, in the psychoanalytical methods developed by the Austrian Sigmund Freud (1856-1939) and the psychological theories of the Swiss psychiatrist Carl Gustav Jung (1875-1961), challenged conventional ideas of human behaviour, and affected the arts as writers, composers and others sought to explore psychological states.

Secularization was pushed hardest in authoritarian states that saw religion as a threat to popular loyalty. Thus, the Soviet Union and communist China both made atheism their official creed and took major steps to extirpate religious customs. In Tibet, independence was brought to an end by Chinese conquest in 1950, and the unsuccessful Tibetan revolt of 1959 was followed by a major assault on institutional aspects of Buddhism, especially monasteries, as they were seen as reactionary and as expressions of Tibetan identity. In China, Christianity lost the important position it had acquired in the interwar period. Missionaries were expelled. The officially registered Catholic Church was not allowed to recognize papal authority, and the Catholics who did had to operate in a clandestine fashion. Gong Pinmei, the Catholic Archbishop of Shanghai, was sentenced to life imprisonment in 1960. The Chinese also found themselves in conflict with Islam among the minority peoples of north-west China, and, in the 1990s, with the Falun Gong, a quasi-religious sect that practiced a form of meditative exercise. In Vietnam, the communist regime took steps against the major religions: Buddhism and Christianity. More generally, authoritarian regimes challenged the independence of religious bodies.

In Turkey, the rivalry between government ideology and Islam that stemmed from Atatürk's policies remained strong. Regarding Islam as an obstacle to reason and progress, he abolished religious courts and put religious schools under secular authority (1924). From the ruins of the Ottoman empire, the strongest Islamic power, Atatürk created a secular Muslim country, not an atheistical state. Individuals were able to follow their own religion and Islam remained dominant, but under the watchful eye of Atatürk and those who subsequently acted as protectors of his powerful Kemalist legacy, particularly the army. As an example of the compromise that this represented, the senior Patriarch of the Greek Orthodox Church remained that of Istanbul (formerly Constantinople), but only Turkish citizens were elected, and the current holder, like other Turks, has performed his military service.

Hostile governments were not the sole challenges to established faiths. There was also a widespread current of secularism and scepticism, as well as a marginalization of the role of religion among many who considered themselves religious. The expansion of state agencies in education, health and social welfare hit the role of religious bodies, while the pace of social change, particularly of migration, put great pressure on the religious ministry and its ability to reach out successfully to the population. Across much of the West, but also in Japan, established religions were hit from the 1960s by general social currents, especially the decline of deference, patriarchal authority, social paternalism, the nuclear family and respect for age. These had also been challenged in communist states.

CHRISTIANITY

In Europe, permissive 'social legislation' flew in the face of Church teachings and left the churches confused and apparently lacking in 'relevance'. This was particularly serious for an age that placed more of an emphasis on present-mindedness than on continuity with historical roots and teachings. Belief lessened in orthodox Christian theology, especially on the nature of Jesus, and in the after-life, the last judgement and the existence of hell. The public perception of religion, as captured on television or in plays, was frequently critical. Furthermore, the churches found the laity willing to condemn as well as to cease religious observance.

BELIEF LESSENED IN ORTHODOX CHRISTIAN THEOLOGY, ESPECIALLY ON THE NATURE OF JESUS, AND IN THE AFTER-LIFE, THE LAST JUDGEMENT AND THE EXISTENCE OF HELL.

Responding to social and intellectual currents, the Catholic Church showed a willingness to follow new paths, such as a modernized liturgy, in 1962 when John XXIII (Pope 1958–63) summoned the Second Vatican Council, a general council of bishops. However, the Church's hold over many of its communicants was lessened by widespread hostility towards the ban on artificial methods of contraception in the 1968 papal encyclical *Humanae Vitae*, which was written by Paul VI (Pope 1963–78) himself.

There were important cross-currents within Catholicism in the closing decades of the century. In Latin America, there was the growing importance of 'liberation theology', a term first coined by Gustavo Gutierrez, a Peruvian priest, as an expression of the social message of Christianity to relieve the poor and oppressed. Liberationist priests were encouraged by Latin American Catholic bishops to promote liberation theology among the poor, but John Paul II (Pope 1978–) criticized liberationists for supporting Marxism in the 1980s, and, indeed, some did so, for example joining Nicaragua's Sandinista guerrillas. Behind this Catholic phalanx, other denominations, such as Presbyterians, have followed. Liberation theology spread to embrace feminist theology and black theology.

A very different movement was *Opus Dei*, which was founded in Madrid in 1928 as a body answering directly to the Pope. By 2000, it had about 80,000–100,000 members worldwide. *Opus Dei*'s ostensible goal was evangelism, but its opponents accused it of cult-like tendencies in aggressive recruitment through 'front' organizations, and control of individual members through opening post, compulsory salary donation and separating them from their families. *Opus Dei* was strongly conservative, anti-Marxist and intolerant of other religions. It rejected a major role for women in Christianity.

Conservative influences were challenged and resisted by liberal theologians, most prominently Hans Kung (1928–), a Swiss Catholic priest, professor of theology at Tübingen and adviser to the Second Vatican Council. He denied papal infallibility in *Infallible? An Inquiry* (1971) and was eventually stripped of his right to teach as a Catholic theologian (1979). Thereafter, Kung became a leader of liberal Catholicism, accusing John Paul II of turning the Church against the Second Vatican Council and toward extreme conservative doctrines. Kung eventually embraced the idea of married clergy.

More generally, there were numerous signs of Christian vitality through the century, not least in the world's leading state, the USA. Here, in the last quarter of the century, the role of religion in public life became more important, and the overwhelming majority of Americans described themselves as religious. American religiosity also had an impact elsewhere. Missionary activity in China in the first half of the century, which was by no means limited to Americans, helped encourage a degree of Westernization. The first six Chinese bishops were consecrated by Pope Pius XI in 1926.

In contrast, in Europe, the Americas and Australasia, traditional non-Christian faiths had only a limited appeal to Christians. Instead, these faiths essentially catered there for immigrant groups and their descendants: their logic was ethnic and exclusive. This was true of Jews, Muslims and Sikhs, particularly the first and the last. Judaism was seen as a religion for those who were ethnically Jewish. The claims of these faiths that they should be part of multi-cultural societies challenged Christian churches and became increasingly important as immigrant communities grew.

There was also a long-established challenge to Christianity from cults. Spiritualism enjoyed a marked revival in popularity and prestige during World War I. In addition, both 'new age' religions (sometimes based on pre-Christian animist beliefs) and Buddhism appealed from the 1960s to many who would otherwise have been active Christians. They proved better able than the churches to capture the enthusiasm of many who wished to believe amidst a material world where faith had become just another commodity. The popularity of cults was also a reflection of the atomization of societies that now placed a premium on individualism and on personal responses. Such societies were peculiarly unsuited to the coherence and historical basis of doctrine, liturgy, practice and organization that was characteristic of long-established churches, although this did not prove a problem in the more individualistic Christian culture of America. Several cults had a strong millenarian and apocalyptic element, and this was dramatized in periodic violent episodes, as in the confrontation between federal agents and the Branch Davidian sect in Waco, Texas, in 1993.

Cults were also prominent in some other parts of the world. They flourished in particular in Japan in the second half of the century in the more liberal conditions that followed the demise of authoritarianism at the close of World War II. Japanese cults were very varied in character, and many were fraudulent. By 1999, the government claimed that there were 200,000 cults and sects in Japan. Their diversity, with an enormous range of gurus and deities, encompassed the Aum Shinrikyo doomsday cult founded by Shoko Asahara. The cult manufactured large quantities of sarin nerve-gas and planned to disperse what might have killed 36 million people. An exploratory attack in the Tokyo metro in 1995 led to a government attempt to suppress the cult. Some Asian cults proved particularly effective in Europe and the USA. This was especially true of the Indian-based Krishna Consciousness movement and the Divine Light Mission of Guru Maharaj-ji, and also of the South Korean cult of the Reverend Moon.

As far as Western Europe was concerned, it can be asked whether an earlier decline of religious practice and belief had not itself permitted the development of a more individualistic society in the 1960s, or whether the society had caused the decline. It is necessary to stress the diversity of the 1960s and subsequent decades, and to note our limited knowledge and understanding of popular religion and what is termed folk belief. It is unclear, for example, how best to understand the popularity of astrology, and, in particular, how far this was an aspect of a magical or non-Christian religious worldview. Christianity did not collapse in Western Europe; it declined, but there were still many committed Christians, as well as a large number of conforming non-believers. However, both for most believers and for the less or non-religious, faith became less important not only to the fabric of life, but also to many of the turning points of individual lives, such as death. Events such as marriage ceremonies and baptisms declined in significance as occasions for displays of family and social cohesion. This was due to the simple fact that more couples were choosing to live together and more parents were choosing not to have their children baptized. This shift was true of Christian societies formerly noted for their devotion and for the authority of the Church. Contraception became more common in Italy, while in Ireland there were legal and political battles over divorce, homosexuality, abortion and contraception as the authority of the Catholic Church was contested.

There was also a major shift in the character of Christian worship, not least with a greater role for feminine ministry and an associated feminization of aspects of theology. This reflected the degree to which religious practice and belief variously recorded, refracted and resisted social and intellectual changes. As a reflection of political aspirations, there was also, particularly within Christianity, a development of ecumenicalism that lessened earlier divisions. Ecumenicalism had more of an impact intellectually and socially than institutionally, but it was still important.

The secularist position that can be seen in Western Europe was not matched in Eastern Europe and Russia. There, communism failed to engage the affection of most of the population, although party membership was often considered a wise career move and the figures for membership reflected this. Instead, religion provided a powerful sense of identity as well as spiritual meaning. This was true both of countries trying to respond to Soviet hegemony, most particularly Poland and Lithuania, in each of which Catholicism was strong, but also of Russia, where the Orthodox Church retained the support of much of the population, and revived rapidly as a public force from 1991. Similarly, in Yugoslavia, religion combined with (and helped to define) ethnicity from 1991 in order to wreck the unity of the country and then to cause a bloody and protracted series of conflicts. Catholic Croats, Orthodox Serbs and Muslim Bosnians and Albanians proved the major protagonists. These developments caused more of a surprise for commentators, who had assumed that religion was in some fashion a redundant force, than for those aware of its central role in popular culture and social structures.

> **IN YUGOSLAVIA, RELIGION COMBINED WITH ETHNICITY FROM 1991 IN ORDER TO WRECK THE UNITY OF THE COUNTRY AND THEN TO CAUSE A BLOODY AND PROTRACTED SERIES OF CONFLICTS.**

Outside Europe, Christianity also displayed an important ability to retain support and to expand, continuing the long period of expansion that was co-terminous with, but not confined to, Western imperialism. Missionary activity was particularly important in the early decades of the century, not least for colonies where traditional religious beliefs and structures had been disrupted and had lost prestige as a result of Western conquest. This helped lead to mass conversion movements that ended with the creation of local churches. The translation of the Bible into a host of languages was a testimony to the energy of the missionary effort, and also reflected the technical ability of a culture able to produce large numbers of inexpensive books and tracts.

The experience of converted areas varied. Latin America, which had been converted after Spanish and Portuguese conquest from the sixteenth century, remained very much a Catholic society, helping to ensure that Catholics made up the majority of Christians in the world (59% in 1985, just over a billion people in 1998), although there were attacks on Church power, for example in Mexico in the 1930s, and an atheist government in Cuba under Fidel Castro, who held power from 1959.

Protestant evangelicalism was important over much of Latin America, particularly in the last three decades, for example in Brazil. Owing partly to this and partly to growing secularism, the percentage of Brazilians calling themselves Catholics fell from 93 per cent in 1950 to 83 per cent in 1991. In Amazonia and Patagonia, Christianity remained a missionary religion contesting tribal beliefs, and this was linked to a more widespread assault on the Amerindian position and culture that included active discrimination. In Haiti, voodoo rites proved resilient.

There was also a clash between Christianity and tribal beliefs among the indigenous (non-European) population of Canada and Australia, and also in sub-Saharan Africa. Joseph Kiwanuka of Uganda, the first African Catholic bishop of the Latin rite, was consecrated by Pope Pius XII in 1939. The Christian advance was less violent in these areas than in Latin America, but it involved an attempt to extirpate what were seen as pagan and backward practices. Thus in Canada, until 1996, large numbers of native children were sent to Church-run residential schools, supposedly intended to raise them up the hierarchy of civilization. The same policy was also followed in Australia, and in both countries the children were forbidden to use their native languages. In interwar Papua, the Australian colonial government banned what was defined as sorcery. Christianity also continued to be the main religion in the Philippines, while it made important advances in South Korea.

In sub-Saharan Africa and the Philippines, however, Christianity faced an important challenge from Islam. This contributed to violence in some areas, such as Sudan, Nigeria and the southern Philippines. Religious belief was linked to ethnic differences, for example between Muslim Hausa and Christian Yoruba in Nigeria, while in the Ivory Coast in the 1990s, Muslim northerners competed with Christian southerners. Elsewhere, this tension contributed to the massacre of Armenian Christians by the Turks in the 1910s, to tensions between Copts and Muslims in Egypt throughout the century, and to violence in the Moluccan Islands in Indonesia in the late 1990s.

ISLAM

As with Christianity, Islam was not a united force. Aside from important ethnic, cultural, political and economic differences in the Islamic world, there were major theological rifts. The most important divided the Shia, who predominated in Iran (with important communities elsewhere, for example in Kuwait, Lebanon and Yemen), from the Sunni, who predominated across most of the Islamic world and treated the Shias as schismatics, with consequent restrictions of public patronage, and, often, harsh discrimination. However, there were also important religious differences among the Sunni.

Religious divisions interacted with political strains. This was especially the case during the war of 1980–8 between Shia Iran and Sunni-ruled Iraq under Saddam Hussein (President from 1979). Religious divisions also encouraged hostility to the rule of Syria by Hafez Assad (1970–2000), leading to a rebellion in Hama in 1982 that was brutally suppressed. The political character and context of Islam varied greatly by country. In some states, ruling dynasties enjoyed a crucial degree of religious authority and prestige, for example the Saud dynasty in Saudi Arabia and the Sharifian dynasty in Morocco. The Pahlevi rulers of Iran (1925–79) enjoyed no such prestige, and Muhammed Reza Shah Pahlevi (1941–79) was easily overthrown as a consequence. In Indonesia, the world's most populous Islamic country, there was tension between Muslim assertiveness, especially, but not only in Sumatra, and governmental attempts to make a multi-religious society work effectively.

RELIGIOUS ASSERTIVENESS

Aside from tensions with Christianity, Islam advanced against tribal beliefs, particularly in Indonesia. The clash between Islam and Hinduism proved a major aspect of the political tension in South Asia that led to the partition between India and Pakistan in 1947 and to subsequent clashes, particularly over Kashmir. Islam was frequently presented as a 'fundamentalist' creed, but that greatly simplifies a religion whose manifestations are very diverse. This was also true of Christianity. In both cases, it is worth noting this diversity, which could entail a syncretic adaptation to other faiths, alongside discussion of the century in terms of globalization. This diversity is too readily overlooked, but it reflected in part the determination of individuals and communities to develop their own versions of faith, hope and salvation. Some of these also reflected the pressures of events on patterns of belief and on the human capacity to bear misery and understand change. This helped to encourage millenarian creeds. Some religious movements posed political challenges. Thus, the Holy Spirit Movement, which began in northern Uganda in 1986, interwove Christianity with the traditions of the Acholi people, and caused serious problems for the government.

THE DIVERSITY OF CHRISTIANITY AND ISLAM IS TOO READILY OVERLOOKED.

A belief that smearing with shea butter provided protection against bullets could not offer lasting success, but the balance of commitment put government forces at a disadvantage; nor did the discrediting of the Movement put an end to their difficulties, for it was replaced by the equally tenacious Lord's Resistance Army.

In parts of Asia, religion served as a prime focus for identity. This was true for example of Buddhism in Tibet, of Sikhism in the Punjab and of Judaism in Israel. In India, there was a determined attempt by the nationalist independence movement under Mahatma Gandhi (1869–1948) and by the dominant political grouping after independence, the Congress Party, to create a secular state that could incorporate all religious groups. This helped ensure that Congress received an important measure of political support from the untouchables and from religious minorities, especially Muslims, but Congress's domination of the political process eventually fell victim not only to its own weakness but also, in the 'saffron wave', to the rise of a Hindu nationalist party, the Bharatiya Janata Party (BJP), which, for the first time, did very well in the election of 1991.

The BJP, which evolved from a nationalist Hindu body, Rashtriya Swayamsevak Sangh, drew on longstanding Hindu notions of India as a Hindu nation and civilization, and on longstanding Hindu revivalism. The party was a response to the strong sense of communal identities in India and to Hindu concern about the assertiveness of minority groups. Thus, the volatility of Indian politics and society led to a strong expression of concern that produced calls for national renewal as defined by, and in the interests of, those expressing the concern, a situation analogous to that in other societies under strain, such as Germany in the early 1930s. After a long campaign, in 1992, the BJP were responsible for the very controversial destruction of a mosque at Ayodhya, where they wanted to build a Hindu temple. In Pakistan, by contrast, religious (Muslim) identity had been central to the state ever since independence. Candidates in the local government elections in 2000 had to prove they were 'good Muslims'.

India, whose constitution was drafted under Pandit Nehru (1889–1964, Prime Minister 1947–64) on deliberately secular lines, serves as an instance of the wider resilience of religious identities and of the drive by religious groups for a major public role. Other examples can be found in opposition to secularist governments or governments perceived as insufficiently religious, especially by Muslims, for example in Iran and, less successfully, Algeria, Morocco and Turkey. The Muslim Brotherhood, the major opposition group in Egypt, was banned in 1954. In contrast, after decolonization and the decline of Western control, strict Islamic law was enforced in a number of countries, such as Sudan. Islamic fervour played a major role in inspiring much of the opposition to the Soviet-backed regimes in Afghanistan in 1979–89, and, after the Soviet forces were withdrawn, in the continued conflict that led to the overthrow of the communist President Mohammad Najibullah in 1992. Four years later, the Pakistani-backed Taleban overthrew the government, captured Kabul and imposed a fundamentalist religious, cultural, social and political order in which their interpretation of the Koran played a central role. The Taleban was overthrown in late 2001 when Afghan opponents received powerful support from American air power. Jewish fundamentalists played a major role in Israeli politics, in large part because of their role in coalition governments.

RELIGION IN THE USA

The USA presents a very different picture in that the leading activist religion there is Christianity, albeit, in accordance with the constitutional ban on an established church, a Christianity fractured among a variety of creeds as a reflection of the individualistic nature of American society, and with a major role for faith communities, such as Jewish communities, as a whole. The individualistic context of American religion ensured that new denominations were founded there and flourished more readily than in other countries. This was taken a long way in Pentecostalism, with its notion that individuals could receive the gift of speaking in tongues, and furthest in the creation of messianic cults. The modern form of Pentecostalism began in Los Angeles in 1906 with the Azusa Street Revival.

A willingness to compromise with others was not encouraged in the evangelical Protestantism and millennialism that flourished in much of American society. Protestant fundamentalism was a strong presence throughout the century, encouraging, for example, prohibition (the banning of alcohol), which was passed with the 18th amendment to the constitution in 1919, as well as creationist attacks on the theory of evolution, support for school prayers and opposition to homosexuality. The polygamy that was distinctive to the Mormons proved unacceptable and was officially forbidden in 1890 in order to promote Utah's claims to statehood, although some 30,000 polygamous relationships still continue there today.

The religious situation was far from constant in the USA. In the late nineteenth century, Protestantism had in part defined itself in opposition to the Catholicism of recent immigrants, especially Irish, Poles and Italians. This remained important in the first half of the twentieth century, and local and national differences between the Democrats and Republicans frequently related to religious divides. The Democrats were more open to minorities, both Catholics and Jews, and the first Catholic presidential candidate (Al Smith in 1928) and later, in 1960, the first Catholic elected President (John F. Kennedy) were both Democrats.

Although anti-Catholicism continued to play a role with some religious groups, the full integration of Catholics into American public life was followed by a religious reconfiguration in which many of them, alongside many evangelical Protestants, sought to resist and roll back what they presented as the irreligious and destructive social revolution of the 1960s. This trend was given added force by a shift in Protestantism that saw the long-established and more liberal denominations – the Episcopalians, Methodists and Presbyterians – lose support and energy in the 1960s–1980s. Instead, the 'born-again' conservative churches, particularly the Southern Baptists and the Assemblies of God, became far more prominent. Americans inspired a 'fundamentalist' Christianity that focused on a direct relationship between God and worshipper, without any necessary intervention by clerics and without much, if any, role for the sacraments. Certain aspects of this Christianity, especially its charismatic quality, epitomized by the American evangelist Billy Graham (1918– , a Southern Baptist minister), had considerable appeal to other Christians. Non-Trinitarian religions (which did not regard Jesus as the Son of God), such as the Christadelphians and Jehovah's Witnesses, grew in popularity, while the long-established Mormons expanded outside Utah. Modern technology was utilized by television evangelists, such as Pat Robertson, and they became prominent figures. Accepting no barrier between religious conviction and public politics, the evangelical groups pushed hard to back particular candidates (Jimmy Carter in 1976, Ronald Reagan in 1980 and 1984) and causes. Christian conservatism led first to the 'Moral Majority' movement and then to the Christian Coalition. Opposition to abortion and other social policies linked them to the Catholic Church, whose leadership became more conservative under John Paul II.

The election as President of Bill Clinton in 1992 and, even more, his re-election in 1996 was a blow to the political cause of American evangelicalism, and the movement failed to achieve many of its goals, but it also contributed to, and reflected, a sense that religion was normative in public life, as well as a strong private faith, which separated the USA from Western Europe and, indeed, most of the Western world. In the 2000 presidential election, candidates vied to assert their born-again piety in a fashion that did not characterize, for example, Canadian, French or German politics. Naming the political philosopher who had most influenced him, the winning candidate, George W. Bush, replied 'Christ. Because he changed my heart.'

CONCLUSIONS

If America was exceptional in this context, consideration of the role of religion there and over much of the world suggests the need to put it foremost in any discussion of ideas and beliefs. Not only foremost, but of growing importance. The Muslim political revival that led to and followed the Iranian revolution of 1979 was succeeded by the impressive revival in religious activism in Russia and Eastern Europe in the 1990s. At a basic level, religious affiliation, especially Christianity and Islam, grew with the world's population, although Buddhism failed to show much of an increase. More significantly, religion, which had been regarded as an anachronism, made redundant by scientific progress and marginal by secularism, instead displayed far greater vitality than the political cults that seemed on the cusp of the future and generally receive more attention in works of this sort.

RELIGION, WHICH HAD BEEN REGARDED AS AN ANACHRONISM, DISPLAYED FAR GREATER VITALITY THAN THE POLITICAL CULTS THAT SEEMED ON THE CUSP OF THE FUTURE.

SECULAR IDEOLOGIES

The debate over the extent and impact of religious commitment interacts with the question of how far secular ideologies provided a sense of identity, value and purpose to individuals and the community. Like all important questions about modern society, this is one that can be answered differently by commentators, and, as valuably, by readers. Secular ideologies in the twentieth century tended to depend on the notion of progress and human improvability, and thus rejected the Christian lapsarian view of human existence with its emphasis on sin and on humankind's fallible nature. Although they varied in their political, economic, social and cultural analyses and prescriptions, such ideologies shared a belief that it is possible and necessary to improve the human condition, and that such a goal gives meaning to politics and society. In short, reform was seen as a goal in itself, and progress as attainable. There was only limited support for continuity and stability, as opposed to reform, as public goals; and for an institution or government to pledge itself to inaction was unthinkable. Instead, as with Islamic and Christian fundamentalism, conservative policies were primarily propounded in terms of a return to an earlier situation (true or mythical), and thus as reform through reaction against a perception of the present, rather than as a static maintenance of the present position.

The sway of reform reflected the major role of the state in the economy and social welfare, and its power. All of these factors increased in most countries during the century, even where the authority of the dynasties that had ruled at the beginning of the century was replaced by governments that could be removed by the electorate. Commitment to change rested on prudential considerations, especially the need to modernize in order to compete successfully on the international scale, but also on powerful ideological currents. Reform, as a means and goal, was the foremost secular ideology of the century, and one that was shared by governments of very different political outlook, and there is no sign that this will change.

However, across the world, reform meant very different attitudes and policies, and focused both on improving and on abandoning the past. This was true not only of domestic policies but also of those abroad, both foreign policies and imperialism. Thus reform could entail the development of empires, but also their dissolution. Like 'freedom', 'liberty' and 'justice', 'reform' was a value-laden term. Reform could mean both more and less government intervention, and this helped to contribute to controversy. The general thrust during the century was for more intervention. From the 1920s and, even more, 1930s until the advance of neo-liberalism in the late 1970s and 1980s, state intervention in the economy was conventionally seen in terms of reform. Planning reflected a strong current of collectivism.

Prior to World War I, the liberal (i.e. progressive) reform movements that had been so important in the late nineteenth century had enjoyed a fresh activist burst, with the 'New Liberalism' in power in Britain from 1905 and the consequent enactment of social welfare reforms, and with the Progressive Era in the USA. However, there was an ambiguous relationship between liberalism and the socialism that was becoming increasingly influential among the working classes of the developed world.

World War I put a brake on progressivism, although, for the combatants, it led to a major extension of state power and enabled governments to circumvent many of the constraints and exigencies of prewar politics. The war was followed by a conservative reaction, not least in the USA, that reflected hostility to socialism and concern about the example of the Russian Revolution. As a consequence, the 1920s, especially in the USA, saw an emphasis on a non-interventionist role by the state, although such a bland remark does not do justice to the depths of social tension in 1919–22, which included a very heavy level of labour conflict that had wider political and ethnic resonances. These included high levels of race violence between blacks and whites in 1917–21, and widespread concern about anarchism and radicalism that focused on immigrants and led to repressive government action. Republicans (Warren Harding, Calvin Coolidge and Herbert Hoover) occupied the White House in 1921–33). They benefited from a reaction against change, immigration and urban life that led to a

stress on supposed white and Protestant values. This contributed directly to Prohibition (1920–33) and to a powerful revival of the racist Ku Klux Klan in 1921–6.

Across most of the world, the combination of the 1930s Depression and World War II put paid to the *laissez-faire* state and to self-help in social welfare. Elected President of the USA in 1932, Franklin Delano Roosevelt pushed through what he called his New Deal to help revive the economy, which already had twelve million unemployed, and a political system where despair had led from 1930 to higher levels of protest and violence. Political will provided the means. In 1933–4, the federal government spent $7.1 billion, despite revenues of only $3.1 billion. Work schemes helped create a sense that a corner had been turned (see chapter 5). In Japan, ties between government and the major industrial conglomerates came closer in the 1930s in an effort to manage the response to economic problems.

EGALITARIANISM

More generally, both in the 1930s and throughout the century, 'welfare' in part represented the triumph of human agencies in society over spiritual responses to life. Expressed through a variety of political systems, egalitarianism – the belief that all people should have equal shares in society's rights, benefits and duties – encouraged planning in order to offset what was seen as the less equal character of liberal (i.e. capitalist) economies, as well as to counteract the problems that they encountered.

The belief that people are equal and should be treated equally was classically associated with the left. In societies that had 'mixed economies', with much of industry outside state control, this created the problem of how best to manage the relationship between socialism and capitalism. It proved difficult to turn the rhetoric of egalitarianism on the left into reality. Indeed, it can be argued that a belief in equality of opportunity was employed, on both left and right, to justify inequality in the name of meritocracy, with the assumption that meritocracy would lessen the social costs of inequality. In India, under the Congress Party, the attempt to use socialism and nationalism to offer an Indian identity that could replace or contain loyalties based on caste and community had only limited success. The rhetoric of socialism extended in India to removing the powers of princely rulers, but not to land reform.

Egalitarianism as a goal or rhetorical strategy was not restricted to the left. Right-wing populists, with their talk of the people or nation, advocated a notion of community. Paternalist conservatives were inspired by a number of views, including a sense that a nation has an organic character (is like a body), and, therefore, that the health of one was the health of all. Other conservatives stressed the need for opportunity for all. This led to a 'Social Darwinism', seen strongly in American attitudes, in which the possibility of social mobility was seen as providing judgement on, and the excuse for, very different levels of material success, and employed to deny the need for redistributive state action. Other right-wing groups advocated policies of simple class interest or a reactionary opposition to change, particularly in the first half of the century.

In the second half of the century, it became more common for all regimes, whatever their character, to proclaim a support for human rights for all. This was even true of dictatorships and limited democracies across the world. Thus, although an Islamic dictatorship, the Sudanese government issued a new constitution in 1999 that promised freedom of religion, expression and association. The Green Book that contained the thoughts of Colonel Qaddafi, leader of Libya from 1969, declared that 'Wealth, weapons and power lie with the people', but there was neither democracy nor free debate in the country. Hafez Assad, leader of Syria from 1970 (officially President from 1971) until his death in 2000, gained power as a result of a coup and relied heavily on the secret police, but claimed to rule in accordance with the constitution and preserved a parliament. The governing Baath party in Syria was socialist and republican, but the reality of power was a dictatorship. The same was true of post-Soviet Uzbekistan under Islam Karimov (President 1990–), who cancelled the election due in 1996, and of post-Soviet Belarus under Alexander Lukashenka (President 1994–). One-party states claimed that their non-existent democracy represented 'real democracy'.

ONE-PARTY STATES CLAIMED THAT THEIR NON-EXISTENT DEMOCRACY REPRESENTED 'REAL DEMOCRACY'.

Elections were set aside in the name of progress. The military rulers of Myanmar (Burma) refused to heed the election of 1990 and, as first the State Law and Order Council and, from 1997, the State Peace and Development Council, claimed to secure stability and development. Communist China is a 'people's republic' and holds elections, but there is no alternative to the governing group.

Across the world, countries proclaimed equal justice for all as central to the state-supported rule of law. However, many people lacked access to law. This was true not only of the administration of justice by the agencies of the state, but also of the absence of legally protected rights to property and other assets. Thus, for much of the world's population across the entire century, the world of law was not that of the state and its agents, who frequently appeared either distant and unwilling, or too close and corruptly self-serving, to help, but really a searching after expedients, especially the help of local kinship networks. This does not conform to the usual formulations of political thought, but the notion of loyalty to kin and connection was a powerful adhesive, not least in the face of hostile public institutions, but not only in response to them.

INDIVIDUALISM

Interacting with these varied positions came the political spectrum from corporatism – the amalgamation of people into blocs, which were then seen as representing them – to libertarianism. In the shape of individualism, the latter was a powerful social current that became more potent from the 1960s, although it was also important earlier. Thus, the notion, among those championing female emancipation, that women did not need to behave in accordance with the dominant behaviour pattern ascribed to them was designed to be liberating. Migration can be seen as another important aspect of individualism. It represented a rejection of homeland, generally in order to provide opportunity and improve material circumstances, as well, frequently, as to obtain liberty. This was important throughout the century and for all parts of the world, bringing an interdependence that challenged notions of community and politics based on ethnicity.

The most successful countries were able to define a different basis for community and politics to that of ethnicity. Thus, the USA, which took in nearly a million immigrants annually in 1901–14, and approaching double that figure in some years of the 1990s, created an American culture that was more successful than most in overcoming sectoral differences, although this, like immigration, was not without serious difficulties. The position of African Americans/Blacks/Negroes (terms varied during the century, as did their acceptability) was a particular scar on American notions of opportunity and inclusion. Although no longer slaves, they were actively segregated not just in the southern states (where they were most numerous and had been slaves), but also at the national level, in, for example, the armed forces and sport. This segregation led to the Civil Rights movement, which achieved considerable success in the 1950s and, even more, 1960s, especially with the Voting Rights Act of 1965. However, these reforms did not fully address the issue of social inequality, and a sense of anger at discrimination helped to fuel widespread disturbances, particularly in the 1960s. Nevertheless, black separatism and radicalism failed to develop as mass movements, and most black leaders pursued community interests through mainstream politics, particularly the Democratic Party. The fluid character of America was shown in the 2000 census, when, thanks to Latino and other immigration, the number of Californians describing themselves as 'white' became a minority. In addition, by 2000, there were at least seven million illegal immigrants in the USA. The demographic shift in the second half of the century led to a multi-culturalism that was important to the nature of American political culture.

Libertarianism became more powerful in the West in the 1960s, first as an aspect of lifestyles that were uneasily contained within existing social structures, and eventually as an anti-authoritarian individualism that helped, in much of the world, in the overthrow of collectivist notions in the 1980s and 1990s. Libertarianism was the cult of self, and was linked with a whole transformation in the language of politics and society away from duties and responsibilities and towards rights. This was related to the triumph of capitalism in the shape of consumerism, and also reached back to the period before large-scale government intervention in social and economic life.

PARTICIPATION IN POLITICS

Other variations in the world of ideas included the extent of popular participation in politics and the nature of wealth. Many political systems deliberately sought to restrict popular participation. In others, repeatedly, throughout the century, it was notable how active participation in the political process was limited. Many people chose not to vote and even more never belonged to a political party. This offers an interesting dimension on the world of ideology: much of it did not have an impact insofar as eliciting popular participation and strong enthusiasm is concerned. Religions were more effective under this head, as were political movements, especially Nazism, that were pseudo- or quasi-religions, characterized by messianic fervour, millenarian vision, apocalyptic imagery and charismatic leadership. It is depressing to note that liberal values generally lacked strong populist appeal.

The nature of wealth in the community was also important to political ideologies. Where capital ownership was widely distributed, through the direct ownership of wealth, indirect ownership in pension funds or as a consequence of property ownership, this generally created a political culture that was more liberal and less sympathetic to state controls than in other societies. In all countries, the desire to own property had a greater capacity to focus aspirations than had wider political movements. This is not a tendency that plays a major role in political thought, but home ownership was the prime ideological commitment in many societies, not least the most powerful, America. These policies were encouraged by public policy in the shape of relief on mortgages.

HOME OWNERSHIP WAS THE PRIME IDEOLOGICAL COMMITMENT IN MANY SOCIETIES.

DEMOCRATIZATION AND ITS OPPONENTS

Alongside these factors, it is necessary to emphasize the importance, in social and political thought and change, of democratization: the process of becoming responsive to the popular will, or to aspects and impressions thereof. The popular will is a concept that is difficult to judge, but is no less important for that. The struggle for democracy is generally thought of in terms of gaining representative government and the vote, but that was incomplete without democratization. Indeed, democracy created a new means for validating a power structure and social system that was frequently essentially impervious to democratic pressures. This impervious characteristic was contested by democratization, which entailed both a reconceptualization of the state, so that it represented, at least in theory, the organized will of the people, and, building on this, the use of the state to try to change society.

That democracy would entail such changes led, in opposition, to a powerful assertion of elitist practices, and sometimes views in many countries. What was known in East Asia as 'money politics' – the frequently corrupt shared direction of government and the economy by political and economic cliques – was widespread across the world. Indeed corruption subverted both the popular will in democracies and the reforming, or at least controlling, aspirations of authoritarian regimes, and lessened support for both forms of government. Corruption received a powerful impetus from the major expansion of the illegal narcotic drug industry from the 1960s. Crime took to globalization as readily as other forms of free enterprise. In some countries, such as Burma, Colombia and Peru, insurrectionary movements derived much of their revenue from criminal activities, especially the drug trade, and this challenged governmental authority, law and order, and social peace, in autocracies and democracies alike. In Colombia, where guerrilla groups competed with right-wing paramilitaries, and both attacked the public, civil society broke down in the late 1990s, with 23,172 killings alone reported in 1999, and the flight abroad of large numbers in response to the chaos.

Hostility to accountability was also, frequently effectively, demonstrated in many democracies, albeit in an implicit, not overt, manner, by the unwillingness of, often self-defining, elites, such as judiciaries or town planners, to accept popular beliefs and pastimes as worthy of value and attention, and their conviction that they were best placed to manage and define social values. The extension of the scope of government during the century exacerbated this paternalistic tendency, because much of it entailed social policing. Both in authoritarian societies and in democracies, behaviour deemed anti-social in the spheres of education, health, housing, personal conduct and law and order all became a matter for scrutiny, admonition and, in many cases, control by the agencies of the state. This was pushed far in Singapore, a democracy that had one-party rule under the People's Action Party from 1959.

THE EXPANSION OF THE STATE

Alongside social policing, there was a major expansion in the surveillance apparatus of the state, and it was directed against both domestic and foreign targets. Thus, state intelligence bodies, such as the American Central Intelligence Agency (CIA), created under the National Security Act of 1947, and the British MI6, became larger and more sophisticated. By the end of the century, the USA, Britain, Australia, Canada and New Zealand were joined in Echelon, an electronic eavesdropping service, while France and Germany also co-operated in such covert monitoring. In addition, citizens judged unreliable were the target of surveillance and intelligence operations. The potential of this approach for misuse was shown in the USA under Richard M. Nixon (President 1969–74) when the government used illicit means to spy on and discredit opponents. Eventual revelation, in the Watergate scandal, led to Nixon's forced resignation and fed American paranoia over the nature and ambitions of the state.

State spending as a percentage of GDP in the wealthy OECD (Organization for Economic Co-operation and Development) countries rose from 25 in 1965 to 37 in 2000, by when GDP was far greater. However, the expansion of the public sector created a serious burden on the remainder of the economy. In addition, across the world, the expansion of government agencies and extension of state control brought income and status to those who ran, or benefited from, government. In many countries, state employees were able to negotiate their way into a relatively safe and comfortable position, and in some, such as Portugal in the 1990s, they were also better paid on average. This expansion of government often had a powerful class component, and was linked to the prestige of 'white-collar' over 'blue-collar' occupations. In addition, the continuation and spread of Western-style bureaucracies in states that gained their independence from colonial rule were important in the definition of new patterns of social ranking and behaviour. These bureaucracies frequently absorbed a large share of state revenues, and helped ensure that a prime function of government appeared to be the employment of public officials. Thus, from the 1950s until 1985, Egypt provided such jobs for all university graduates, and, in 2001, there were still about six million people employed by the Egyptian government.

Much of the domestic history of states across the world can be presented in terms of the demands and tensions created by democratization. These were not simply material, but could be seen in social politics, namely the workings of society understood as reflecting the distribution and nature of power within society. The impact of democratization could be seen clearly in education policy and in welfare. In most countries, at least in theory, inclusive governmental practices, stemming from universal provision in crucial fields such as education, health and military service, were important. So also was populism. This was encouraged by the explicitly democratic political language of left-wing political movements, many of whose activists came from the trade unions. Right-wing populism was also important. From the 1960s, there was also a widespread reaction against deference and hierarchy that affected most organizations and careers, and also relations between people and organizations such as the police. More widely, pressure groups challenged existing arrangements and sought to stir up and/or direct public demand for change.

Far from suggesting that democratization implied one social agenda or political programme, its importance lay in the degree to which it gave vitality to democracy, translating it, in particular, from politics to society. At the same time, democratization tended, in its focus on customers/voters/members, and its emphasis on rights, not responsibilities, to make it harder for institutions to operate. This helped undermine communism in Eastern Europe.

A powerful contrary pressure arose from globalization, specifically the rise of multinational companies in national economies and their extension into the service sector. With foreign bases and ownerships, such companies were, in part, removed from the scrutiny and control of national agencies and opinion. Globalization also posed a potential challenge to national identity. The tension between globalization and democratization was readily apparent in the second half of the century, not least in countries that dismantled command economies and embraced pluralistic democratic systems. This tension, in states such as South Africa in the 1990s, was exacerbated by high levels of poverty and by expectations of improvement of living conditions through public policy. It proved difficult to win popular support for neo-liberal policies of privatization and the free market (see chapter 5), and this posed a question mark about the stability of states that embraced them in the 1990s. This was particularly true in Latin America. However, the failing economies of states that did not do so, such as Cuba, Syria and Zimbabwe, were scarcely an advertisement for opposition to liberalization; and nor were many (although far from all) state-run companies and services. Furthermore, with most economies increasingly dependent on outside trade, investment and energy supplies, there was a need to satisfy external demands for economic openness and political reliability, if not accountability.

NATIONAL AND LOCAL GOVERNMENT

At a different level, it is important to note the widespread failure to address localism when considering ideas and beliefs. This is part of a more general neglect of local

IT IS IMPORTANT TO NOTE THE WIDESPREAD FAILURE TO ADDRESS LOCALISM WHEN CONSIDERING IDEAS AND BELIEFS.

identities and government. It is easy to understand because, on the whole, the expanded role for government throughout the world led to a development in the power and pretensions of the central state, rather than of local government. In part, this was due to the traditionalism of local authorities, but the dynamic of central planning and financial control was more important. Across the world, the greater role of local government, where it occurred, generally arose from initiatives by central government and was usually not matched by an ability to formulate policy.

The relationship between central and local government was a prime instance of the competition for power and scarce resources that affected and shaped government and politics throughout the century. In some countries, for example Lebanon in the 1980s and Sierra Leone in the 1990s, the state collapsed and power atomized, but in countries where the state maintained coherence it was rare for the central government not to gain power. In the USA, the federal principle remained active and state governments continued to have a central role in domestic government, but the focus, from the early 1940s, on international threats and global responsibilities – the rise of the 'national security state' – ensured that the central government played a greater role than hitherto, fuelled by the military-industrial complex.

In India, the greater authority of the central government from the 1960s reflected not the response to external challenges but rather a shift, also seen in many other countries, from politics and government understood as an accommodation of a number of interests and centres of power, to a more centralized and less pluralist notion of authority. This owed much to a conviction of the value of government intervention and planning as a means to modernization and growth, and also reflected the difficulty of fulfilling goals for the latter.

POLITICS AND ETHNICITY

An account of ideas and beliefs that says so little about fascism and communism may seem perverse, but they will be mentioned in chapters 8 and 9 and each, anyway, was a failure. Fascism was destroyed as a significant force with Adolf Hitler, dictator of Germany in 1933–45. His National Socialism rested on a personality cult and a confused mixture of racialism, nationalism and a belief in modernization through force. Force certainly characterized Hitler's regime, with a brutal attitude towards those judged unacceptable that culminated as a genocidal attack on what were seen as lesser species, particularly Jews.

In a horrific form, the Nazi concentration and extermination camps, such as Dachau, Belsen and Auschwitz, testified to a far more widespread use of concepts of race in order to rank peoples and develop and express national and international cohesion. This was more common in the political thought of the century than is generally appreciated, and was particularly important in the state-building that followed decolonization and the ebbing of traditional political allegiances. Thus, in Egypt in the 1950s, the republican revolution of 1952 was followed by pan-Arab nationalism. This, however, proved weaker than state power, and most attempts to link Arab countries, such as the union of Egypt and Syria in the United Arab Republic (1958–61), were shortlived. The 1990 merger between North and South Yemen was more durable, although the achievement rested on many years of conflict.

However, whatever its weakness as a basis for international movements, ethnicity proved more successful as an ideology for countries and ruling groups. This was true in the Third World, for example the Malay nationalism of the United Malays National Organization, which has governed the country since independence in 1957. The Mongolian state based its identity on an ethnic consciousness that included concern about how best to sustain racial purity. This also led to the expulsion of large numbers of ethnic Chinese in the 1960s. At the same time the Halh-majority language and culture in Mongolia was supported at the expense of other Mongolian groupings, some of which were referred to as half-breeds.

The religious logic of Pakistan as the Islamic state created out of British India in 1947 was subverted by ethnic politics, specifically the mistreatment of the Bengali majority of East Pakistan by governments based in West Pakistan, leading in 1971 to an unsuccessful revolt, and, after an Indian invasion, the Indian-supported creation of the new state of Bangladesh. In turn, Bangladesh's governments mistreated minority non-Bengalis, particularly the Chakmas near Chittagong. Like many other peoples across the world, these and other Bangladeshi tribal peoples were subjected to assimilationist pressures, and also found that both autocratic and civilian governments followed hostile policies. The power of the state was generally directed against those judged outside the fold of patronage structures and the government's image of its people. Aside from land seizures, the Chakmas suffered from the flooding of land by a dam, the Kaptai dam; a fate similar to that of others across the world with a weak hold in the political system.

Ethnicity also increasingly became a national ideology in Europe after the fall of the Romanov (1917) and Habsburg (1918) empires and, again, in the 1990s, after the fall of communism. Yet, the new states faced decolonization struggles of their own, as the principle and practice of national self-determination confronted the inchoate and controverted nature of nationhood across much of the world. Countries were rarely homogeneous ethnic groups separated by clear-cut boundaries. As a result, although it was welcomed as a progressive idea, self-determination as the basis for nation-creation, like nationalism and decolonization, was also a cause of international instability. The principle of self-determination failed to address the issue of who was allowed to seek it. In 1960, the United Nations stated that all 'peoples' had the right to self-determination, but it was not clear how 'peoples' were to be defined. They could be 'constructed' as much as nations. For example, the Ovimbundu of Angola were presented as a single 'polity' but, in practice, were a dozen warring tribes.

THE PRINCIPLE OF SELF-DETERMINATION FAILED TO ADDRESS THE ISSUE OF WHO WAS ALLOWED TO SEEK IT.

States sought to deny efforts by minorities to pursue self-determination. Across much of the world, force was used to suppress regional separatism. Successive Ethiopian regimes unsuccessfully sought to control Eritrea, where a war of secession was waged between 1961 and 1991, eventually leading to the creation of a new state. Katanganese separatism was suppressed by Congo with United Nations support in 1963, while in 1966 the Ugandan army suppressed a secession attempt by the Kingdom of Buganda: the new state taking precedence over other loyalties.

In 1967–70, Biafra, the political expression of Ibo nationalism, unsuccessfully sought independence from Nigeria in a conflict fuelled by ethnic fear and hatred. The slaughter of possibly 30,000 Ibos after a coup in 1966 led to a collapse of Ibo support for the notion of Nigeria. The Nigerian government was unsympathetic to the Ibo demand for a looser confederation, while the Ibo leadership challenged the legality of the federal government and increasingly took steps towards autonomy. The resulting 'police operation' led to a full-scale civil war. The 'warfulness' of the domestic political situation was readily translated into civil war, thanks to the prominent role of the military in government and because there was already a high level of violence in Nigerian society. The atrocities committed against civilians by both sides in the Biafran conflict were all too common in separatist wars, reflecting the crucial argument of ethnic numbers, the polarization of civil politics and the commitment of military regimes to holding states together.

Such attitudes led to a politics of exclusion, seen at one level in hostility in many countries towards migrant workers. This exclusion culminated in periodic genocides, such as the Turkish slaughter of the Armenians in 1915, or the genocide in Hutu-ruled

Rwanda in 1994 in which about 800,000 Tutsis were killed, as well as the harsh treat-ment of Hutus by Tutsi-ruled Burundi, or the brutal assertion and expansionism attempted by Croatia and Serbia in the 1990s. The Croatian Democratic Union was typical in the authoritarianism of its leader, Franjo Tudjman, who was President of Croatia between 1991 and 1999, and in its use of nationalism to provide both identity and rationale.

Such ethnic nationalism was not always on behalf of the largest community within a country. Indeed, in South Africa, Afrikaner supremacism was specifically designed to keep power from the majority black community. This led to the concept of apartheid, or separate development, which culminated in the idea of creating Bantustans: appar-ently independent states in which most black South Africans were to be confined. Developed by Hendrik Verwoerd and Johannes Vorster, Prime Ministers in 1958–66 and 1966–79, respectively, this concept is a reminder of the need to avoid glib remarks about 1960s values as if they enjoyed a global following. Apartheid legislation had been propagated from 1948, when the National Party gained power under Daniel Malan (Prime Minister until 1954). Crucial legislation included the Prohibition of Mixed Marriages Act (1949), the Population Registration and Group

APARTHEID IS A REMINDER OF THE NEED TO AVOID GLIB REMARKS ABOUT 1960S VALUES AS IF THEY ENJOYED A GLOBAL FOLLOWING.

Areas Acts (1950) and the Bantu Homelands Citizenship Act (1970). Apartheid existed at a number of levels. There was detailed segregation at the level of parts of buildings and transport facilities; a re-spatialization of cities, as blacks were moved, for residen-tial, although not employment, purposes, out of town centres; and the redefinition and resettlement of large parts of the rural hinterland as homelands were created by dictat. Four of these Bantustans were declared independent: Transkei (1976), Bophuthatswana (1977), Venda (1979) and Ciskei (1981). None was to last. At the same time, the hostile international response to South Africa, which led to an arms boycott and to economic sanctions which denied the country foreign investment, indicated that some regimes were, at least publicly, unacceptable.

Ethnic consciousness challenged states that sought to offer a pan-ethnic national consciousness, such as Indonesia or post-apartheid South Africa, where, in the 1990s, the Zulu Inkatha movement opposed the inclusiveness of the African National Congress. Czechoslovakia, a state created in 1918 from the ruins of the Habsburg empire, faced longstanding tensions between Czechs and Slovaks that led to separate states in 1939–45 and then again from 1992, while difficulties with German and Hungarian minorities led to the expulsion of the Germans in 1945. In Cyprus, tension between Greek and Turkish Cypriots, and the intervention of Greece and Turkey, culminating with a Turkish invasion in 1974, led to a partition of the island on ethnic grounds, with large-scale movements of people.

In Indonesia, the 1990s brought a strengthening of ethnic tension and regional consciousness, with widespread violence. Thus, in Kalimantan (Indonesian Borneo), from 1997, native Dayaks fought Madurans who had immigrated from the 1950s, in part with government encouragement: thinking of Indonesia as a unit, the government sought to move people from areas of overcrowding, although without any consultation with the population in the receiving areas. Adding to the horror of this conflict, beheading played a major role in the violence: it was important in traditional Dayak culture, was seen as the way to win favourable magic and is a reminder of the persistence of such ideas. In Indonesia, ethnic rivalry was linked to tension over resources, particularly land and jobs. This could also be seen in less violent confrontations, for example in the central highlands of Vietnam in the 1990s, where long-established tribesmen resisted immigration by lowlanders who cleared the land they occupied for cash crops. Again, this was the reality of politics in a century where they have been too readily discussed in terms of clashing ideologies. Although the form of the slaughter in Kalimantan was very different to the gas chambers used in the Nazi concentration camps, the underlying reality was the same, and is a reminder of the grim durability of hatred during the century, and its role in politics. Under pressure, some societies, such as Somalia in the 1990s, moved from the state basis of a national government to the clan or ethnic basis of regional power.

Important differences between states in terms of their treatment of ethnic issues reflected and sustained distinct social and political circumstances: endogamy (marriage within the clan) was more common in some countries than others and the latter were more tolerant societies. Thus, in the USA, sexual and marital relations between members of different ethnic groups became more important during the century, particularly from the 1960s. Similarly, in Australia, a lessening of ethnicity as a source of identity led not only to a willingness to take large numbers of immigrants from Asia, but also, in 1962, to the granting of the vote to the Aborigines, the indigenous population. Five years later, the constitution of 1901 was changed so that Aborigines were included in the census. The Aborigines continued to have lower living standards and their cultural assumptions were not those of an increasingly urban society, but public discrimination diminished. In the 1960s, there was an abandonment of the policy of seizing the children of mixed parents from their Aborigine mothers and committing them to institutions where they were to be brought up as 'whites'. It had reflected the fusion of racism with the social policing and eugenics that were so strong in the first half of the century, when steps had also been taken to wipe out Aboriginal languages.

AUTHORITARIANISM

Alongside discussion of democratization, it is necessary to recall the number of occasions during the century in which democratic governments were replaced by the military, especially in Latin America and Africa, but also in Asia and Europe. This was particularly true of the creation of military regimes, for example Chile after the 1973 coup, but also of changes in civilian governments, such as those of Peru and Colombia in the 1980s and 1990s. In 1992, President Alberto Fujimori used the army to shut down Peru's Congress and courts. Although military leaders could act as reforming figures, with Atatürk in Turkey as the best example, most lacked any such intention and could only offer an authoritarianism they termed order. The creation of the Chinese republic as a result of the 1911 revolution saw power go to the strongest army commander, Yuan Shikai, and Sun Yatsen (1866–1925), the founder of China's Nationalist Party, felt obliged to resign the presidency to him in 1912. Unwilling to accept parliamentary opposition or provincial autonomy, Yuan acted as a dictator from 1913, and in 1916 became emperor. However, it proved difficult for a new ruler to recover the mystique of earlier monarchs and, in the face of growing opposition, Yuan rapidly ceased to call himself emperor and soon after died. An attempt in 1917 by another general to restore the last Manchu emperor also failed.

These events reflected the more general difficulty of creating new monarchical dynasties and the growing weakness of legitimist positions. Most monarchies were overthrown, and those that continued (for example Japan, Thailand, Britain, Sweden, Denmark, Norway, the Netherlands and Belgium) or were revived (Spain) did not wield political control. Most dictators sought to present themselves in populist terms, or at least as expressions of a supposed national will. In Indonesia, General Suharto, who became President in 1968, sought to establish a New Order designed to replace ethnic and religious divisions and to ensure economic growth, and created a party, Golkar, to rally support for his army-based regime. In Afghanistan, King Mohammed Zahir Shah was overthrown in 1973 in favour of his cousin, Mohammad Daud, who renounced his royal titles and made himself President and Prime Minister.

Dictators also appealed to a desire for order, stability and competence, rather than to a continuity based on legitimism, although in many states, for example Turkey in 1960 and 1980, the military staged coups in order to maintain what they saw as the constitution.

The frequency of violent seizures of power suggests that it is unwise to write about politics and government without taking note of them. In Latin America after 1945, there were coups in Venezuela in 1948 and 1958, Peru in 1948, 1961 and 1967, Bolivia in 1951, Colombia in 1953 and 1957, Guatemala in 1954, 1978, 1982 and 1983, Argentina in 1955, 1962, 1966, 1970 and 1976, the Dominican Republic in 1963, Brazil in 1964, Chile in 1973, Grenada in 1983 and Ecuador in 2000. In addition, there were military rebellions, for example in Brazil in 1954 and Argentina in 1988. Many of the military regimes were longlasting, in Brazil for example from 1964 until 1985. It was no accident that secret police forces, such as the Iranian Savak, became one of the most important props of such regimes. They also helped mould their ethos.

In the short term, such regimes, whether military or civilian dictatorships, were far less powerful or rigid in practice than they appeared, and could only operate by accepting the circumvention of their nostrums and structures by their own members, as well as by vested interests, and by the public itself, a situation that helped undermine confidence in autocracy and communism alike. In the long term, these regimes found it difficult to contain political problems and satisfy popular demands. This was true not only of Europe and Latin America but also of other cultures. Thus, in the Philippines, the civilian dictatorship of Ferdinand Marcos, who had become President in 1965, was overthrown by popular opposition in 1986, while, in Thailand, the military lost power in 1992 (and the government fell to popular disaffection again in 1997), and, in Indonesia, Suharto was forced to surrender power in 1998 after thirty-two years in office. This process revealed widespread popular hostility to the paternalistic views that state-backed economic growth enabled governments to dispense with democratic scrutiny. In Bahrain in the Persian Gulf, where Parliament was suspended in 1975 after a brief period of democracy, civil liberties and constitutional government were reintroduced from 1999. In 2000, the decade-long rule of Serbia by Slobodan Milošević came to an end when popular protest forced him to respect the results of an election; the rule of Peru by Alberto Fujimori also collapsed that year. In 2000, the Guomindang, which had ruled Taiwan from 1949, as the last relic of its earlier government of China, lost a presidential election, a convincing demonstration of the effectiveness of the multi-party politics that had not been tolerated there in the early decades of its rule.

The authoritarian regimes termed fascist after 1945, especially Paraguay under Alberto Stroessner (President 1954–89) and Spain under Francisco Franco (1939–75), were of no importance as a model for developments elsewhere, although they testified to the conservative social and cultural policies that many authoritarian states pursued. A different result from World War II would, however, have led to a situation in which fascist states, such as those allied to Hitler, for example Slovakia and Croatia, were more common. In Europe after 1945, the nationalist, traditional right was discredited by World War II, tainted by collaboration or, in Eastern Europe (bar Greece), brutally suppressed by the communists. Instead, Christian Democracy emerged as a powerful force, particularly in West Germany and Italy, but also in the Benelux countries. This movement reflected the corporatism that was so powerful in the Western world until the rise of neo-liberal free-market policies and anti-statist rhetoric in the last quarter of the century. Right-wing dictatorships came to an end in Greece (1974), Portugal (1974) and Spain (1975).

Some dictators, such as Idi Amin of Uganda (1971–9) and Mobutu Sese Soko of Congo (1965–97), only fell as a result of foreign invasions, while another invasion of Congo was launched in 1998 in an unsuccessful attempt to overthrow Mobutu's replacement, Laurent Kabila. Domestic coups and violence put paid to more dictators, including Kabila in 2001, although others, such as Colonel Qaddafi of Libya (President 1969–), proved more durable. The same was true of the military dictatorship in Myanmar (Burma), which crushed the 1988 democracy movement. In the closing years of the period, a number of dictators were succeeded by their sons, for example in North Korea (1996), Syria (2000) and Congo (2001). This reflected not so much the strength of a monarchical or dynastic attitude as the degree to which close-knit ruling groups were unwilling to destabilize their position.

THE DECLINE OF COMMUNISM

It is premature to write of communism's complete failure, given its continued role in the official ideology of the most populous country in the world, China, but, in Europe, communism was revealed as a failure in the 1980s and 1990s, unable to fulfil its policy objectives in government, and heavily rejected by the people. Furthermore, in China, the groups and attitudes condemned by the communists as they seized and consolidated power were, in many cases, prominent a half-century later, having revived following the death of Mao Zedong.

Born in civil war, the Chinese communist state was violent from the outset. Beijing was occupied and the People's Republic of China was proclaimed in 1949. Mao, who was both Chairman of the Chinese Communist Party and President of the Republic, was ready to use force. The Agrarian Reform Law of 1950 was enforced at the cost (estimates vary) of 200,000–2,000,000 landlords' lives, and, in other campaigns of the early 1950s against alleged counter-revolutionaries, capitalists and corrupt cadres, maybe 500,000–800,000 were killed. In the Great Proletarian Cultural Revolution

(1966–9), capitalism and bourgeois values were rejected and, under the 'Sixteen Points' adopted in 1966, a violent effort was made 'to transform education, literature and art and all other parts of the superstructure not in correspondence with the socialist economic base'. In both the short and the long term, this attempt to reverse the trend to 'revisionism' failed. The acute disruption, not to say anarchy, brought by the revolutionary Red Guards led to their disbandment and to a determined effort to restore stability. After the death of Mao in 1976, the radical 'Gang of Four', which included Mao's widow Jiang Qing, was kept from power. There was a marked reaction against Mao's policies. Communism lost its radical edge in China and became an official creed that adapted to capitalism, although dictatorial power was retained by a ruling group.

The brutality of communism's social politics was shown during the occupation of Hue by the Viet Cong in the Vietnam War in 1968. About 5,000 South Vietnamese civilians were slaughtered or 'disappeared'. Their crime was that they came from social categories judged unacceptable in the Maoist society that the communists were trying to create.

Although longer-lasting, so far, than its Chinese counterpart, Russian communism could not manage the transition to capitalism. Gaining power, as in China through violence – in Russia a civil war (1918–21) that followed a coup in 1917 – the communists forced through major changes, especially under Joseph Stalin, the dictator from 1924 until his death in 1953. Russia was taken into state ownership, the country was forced into industrialization, and the Orthodox Church was reduced. Terror and government-tolerated famine killed at least eleven million in Stalin's 'peacetime' years, warped the lives of the remainder of the population and made casualties of faith, hope and truth. The secret police were a crucial prop to the government, and were far more powerful than in democratic societies.

> **TERROR AND GOVERNMENT-TOLERATED FAMINE KILLED AT LEAST ELEVEN MILLION IN STALIN'S 'PEACETIME' YEARS, WARPED THE LIVES OF THE REMAINDER OF THE POPULATION AND MADE CASUALTIES OF FAITH, HOPE AND TRUTH.**

The Soviet regime became a military super-power, but was unable to build up a solid basis of support. A paranoid sense of vulnerability, which owed much to World War II and something to communist ideology, encouraged a major stress on military expenditure. Nearly a quarter of state expenditure went to military purposes in 1952, when the Soviet Union was not at war, and this figure increased as greater nuclear capability was added to the arsenal. Thus, the major economic gain of the 1950s and 1960s seen across most of the world brought only limited benefit in terms of Soviet living standards. Totalitarian regimes such as the Soviet Union and Nazi Germany were command systems that were inherently prone to impose inefficient direction, rather than to respond to advice and to interest groups. This had a serious long-term consequence for the stability of the Soviet system, for a lack of popularity made it difficult for the government to view change and reform with much confidence.

With time, the sham character of communist progress became more apparent, to the Russians, to other subjects of the Soviet state and of other communist states, and to foreign commentators. The reform policies of the Gorbachev government, the attempt from 1985 to create 'socialism with a human face', inadvertently destroyed both Soviet communism and the Soviet state. Communism could not be democratized, and it proved impossible to introduce market responsiveness to a planned economy. At the same time, there was no protracted attempt to use the military resources of the Soviet state to prevent this collapse.

WITH TIME, THE SHAM CHARACTER OF COMMUNIST PROGRESS BECAME MORE APPARENT, TO THE RUSSIANS, TO OTHER SUBJECTS OF THE SOVIET STATE AND OF OTHER COMMUNIST STATES, AND TO FOREIGN COMMENTATORS.

Radical governments outside the former Soviet bloc also lost power or changed policy. In Nicaragua, the radical Sandinista movement that had forced the dictatorial Somoza dynasty from power in 1979, and resisted American economic, political and military pressure thereafter, was defeated in a general election in 1990. In Ethiopia, Mengistu Haile Mariam, a Marxist who had seized power in 1974 from the feudal monarchy of the Emperor Haile Selassie, was driven out in 1991, and replaced by Meles Zenawi and his policies of economic liberalism. The transition from communist rule in the former Soviet bloc was sometimes to a state that combined formal democratic constitutionalism and economic liberalization with autocratic practice. This was particularly true of the former Soviet republics in Central Asia, such as Kazakhstan and Kirgizstan. Several of the ex-communist states, including Belarus and Turkmenistan, were dictatorships.

Elsewhere, the transition from communism also proved difficult and former communists were able to profit from resulting government unpopularity in order to return to power: in Bulgaria between 1994 and 1997. However, the combination of democratic accountability and the problems of economic management ensured that these communists operated in a very different context to that of their predecessors in the Soviet era.

Former communist states were an obvious instance of the more widespread problem of fragile democratic structures. Although it was easy to draw up democratic constitutions, it proved far harder to ensure governments that accepted the restraints of law, the creation of mature political institutions, parties and practices, and the development of public confidence in all three, as well as in the police, the judiciary and the government. This was also a particular problem in states where non-communist authoritarian regimes had yielded power, as well as where the social extent of democratic participation was limited, as in much of Latin America.

CONCLUSIONS

As the next two chapters will suggest, the most significant ideological development of the century was the drive for independence from colonial rule and the role this played in the most important shift in global power during the century. This process enjoyed greater popular support than the, later, move to economic liberalism seen across the world in the last quarter-century. Instead, it was nationalism and religion that were most successful in eliciting popular support during that period.

As a reminder of the general theme of this book, the major development within Christianity was the growing importance, vitality and relative independence of Christianity in Asia, Africa and Latin America. An account of religion written in terms of the First World appeared increasingly implausible. The failure of (some) intellectual argument and public policy to overcome religious belief can be, possibly fancifully, compared to the fragility of earlier confidence in human ability to control and manipulate the environment without cost. In each case, this served as a reminder of the complexity of the human condition.

With its discussion of the persistence, indeed revival, of religious belief, the pressures of democratisation, the extent of authoritarianism and the ambivalent character of the concept and language of reform, this chapter has underlined the variety of religious and political belief and practice during the century. Furthermore, it is clear that a narrative or analysis of either based on the First World is flawed. Instead, it is important to consider the character and impact of developments across the globe.

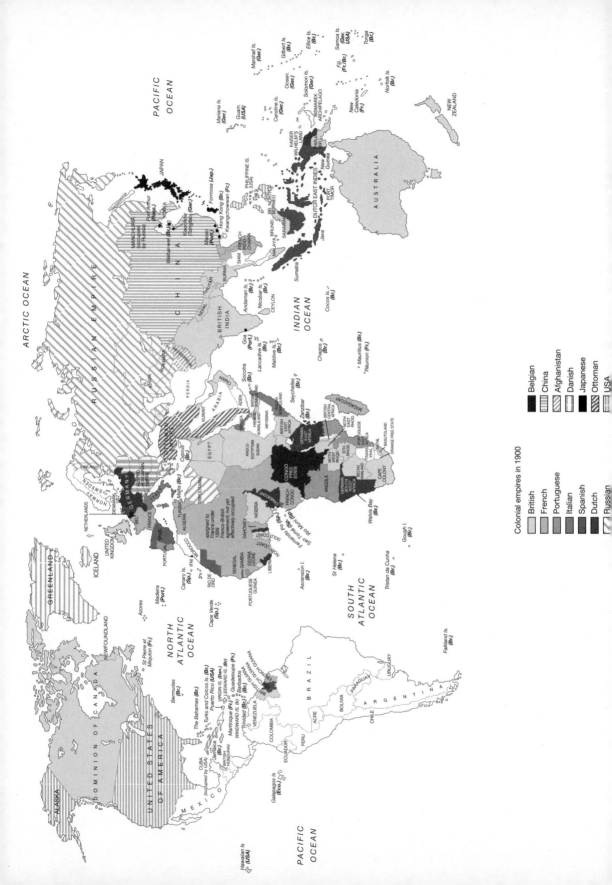

ARCTIC OCEAN

PACIFIC OCEAN

PACIFIC OCEAN

RUSSIAN EMPIRE

FINLAND

NORWAY

SWEDEN

DENMARK

NETHERLANDS

UNITED KINGDOM

ICELAND

GREENLAND

NEWFOUNDLAND

DOMINION OF CANADA

ALASKA

UNITED STATES OF AMERICA

MEXICO

NORTH ATLANTIC OCEAN

St Pierre et Miquelon (Fr.)

Bermudas (Br.)

Azores

Madeira (Port.)

The Bahamas (Br.)
Turks and Caicos Is. (Br.)
Puerto Rico (USA)
CUBA (occupied by USA)
Jamaica (Br.)
BRITISH HONDURAS
VIRGIN IS. (Dan.)
LEEWARD IS. (Br.)
Guadeloupe (Fr.)
Barbados (Br.)
Martinique (Fr.)
WINDWARD IS. (Fr.)
Trinidad (Br.)
VENEZUELA

COLOMBIA

ECUADOR

Galapagos Is (Ecu.)

PERU

BOLIVIA

ACRE

CHILE

BRAZIL

PARAGUAY

ARGENTINA

URUGUAY

BRITISH GUIANA
DUTCH GUIANA
French GUIANA (Fr.)

SOUTH ATLANTIC OCEAN

Falkland Is. (Br.)

Hawaiian Is (USA)

JAPAN

KOREA

CHINA

MANCHURIA OCCUPIED by RUSSIA

Port Arthur (Russia)
Weihaiwei (Br.)
Kiaochow (Tsingtau) (Ger.)
Kwangchowan (Fr.)
Hong Kong (Br.)
Macao (Port.)
Formosa (Jap.)

PHILIPPINE IS. (USA)

SIAM
BURMA
FRENCH INDO CHINA

NEPAL
BHUTAN
BRITISH INDIA
Andaman Is. (Br.)
Nicobar Is. (Br.)
CEYLON

Goa (Port.)
Laccadive Is. (Br.)
Maldive Is. (Br.)

INDIAN OCEAN

Chagos (Br.)

Mauritius (Br.)
Réunion (Fr.)

Cocos Is. (Br.)

PERSIA
AFGHANISTAN
KHIVA
Bokhara

ARABIA
OMAN
KUWAIT
ADEN (Br.)
Socotra (Br.)

EGYPT
ANGLO-EGYPTIAN SUDAN
ABYSSINIA
ERITREA
BRITISH SOMALILAND
FRENCH SOMALILAND
ITALIAN SOMALILAND
BRITISH EAST AFRICA
GERMAN EAST AFRICA
Zanzibar (Br.)
Seychelles (Br.)

NYASSA
MOZAMBIQUE PORT. EAST AFRICA
N'RTH RHO.
S'TH RHO.

MADAGASCAR

CONGO FREE STATE

ANGOLA

GERMAN SOUTH WEST AFRICA
Walvis Bay (Br.)

BECHUANALAND
TRANSVAAL
NATAL
BASUTOLAND
CAPE COLONY
ORANGE FREE STATE

PORTUGUESE GUINEA
Cape Verde (Sp.)

RIO DE ORO
IFNI
Canary Is. (Sp.)

MOROCCO

ALGERIA
TUNISIA (Fr.)
TRIPOLITANIA
Malta (Br.)
Cyprus (Br.)

GERMANY
AUSTRO-HUNGARIAN EMPIRE
FRANCE
BELG.
SPAIN
PORTUGAL

SENEGAL
GAMBIA
SIERRA LEONE
LIBERIA
IVORY COAST
GOLD COAST
TOGO
DAHOMEY
NIGERIA
CAMEROONS
Fernando Po (Sp.)
Rio Muni (Sp.)
São Tomé (Port.)
FRENCH CONGO

assigned to France under Franco-British agreement; not yet effectively occupied

St Helena (Br.)
Ascension I. (Br.)
Tristan da Cunha (Br.)
Gough I. (Br.)

DUTCH EAST INDIES
Sumatra
Java
Borneo
BRN.
BR. NORTH BORNEO
SARAWAK
BRUNEI
MALAYA
PORT. TIMOR

NEW GUINEA
KAISER WILHELM'S LAND
ADM.
BISMARCK ARCHIPELAGO
New Caledonia (Fr.)
Solomon Is. (Ger.)
Norfolk Is. (Br.)

AUSTRALIA

NEW ZEALAND

Mariana Is. (Ger.)
Guam (USA)
Caroline Is. (Ger.)
Marshall Is. (Ger.)
Ocean Is. (Ger.)
Gilbert Is. (Br.)
Ellice Is. (Br.)
Fiji (Fr.-Br./Br.)
Samoa Is. (Ger.-USA)
Tonga (Br.)

Colonial empires in 1900

British
French
Portuguese
Italian
Spanish
Dutch
Russian

Belgian
China
Afghanistan
Danish
Japanese
Ottoman
USA

eight

WORLD IN FLAMES
POLITICS AND WAR
1900–1950

PREAMBLE: NEW VIEWS OF THE WORLD

The world was literally redrawn several times in the century, most controversially in a map projection devised in 1967 by the German Marxist Arno Peters and publicly presented in 1973. This episode was of considerable importance as it demonstrated the politicized character of differing accounts of the globe. Peters' equal-area projection was contrasted with the traditional Mercator worldview, which, instead, had put the emphasis on accurate bearings. Arguing that the end of European colonialism and the advance of modern technology made a new cartography necessary and possible, Peters found a receptive international audience. His emphasis on the Tropics matched concern by and about the Third World, so that his projection was greatly praised by international aid agencies. The Peters' world map became a politically correct icon and was both praised in, and used for the cover of, *North–South: A Programme for Survival* (1980): the 'Brandt Report' of the Independent Commission on International Development Issues, a prominent work that conflated globalist perspectives, social concerns and redistributive strategies.

The Peters projection was in fact open to serious criticism. It was less novel than Peters suggested, while there was a serious shape distortion. Peters greatly elongated the Tropics, so that, for example, the length, but not the width, of Africa was much exaggerated. Coastal shapes were thus considerably distorted and the standard cartographic images of continents, the iconic language of map shapes, were changed. Ironically, the rectangular nature of the Peters map, its placing of north at the top and its use of a central meridian close to Greenwich all proclaimed its conventional character.

Nevertheless, Peters underlined the plasticity of our views of the world and dramatized the issue of how the world should best be presented. In the *Peters Atlas of the World* (1989), he produced all the maps at the same scale, ensuring that Africa, Asia and South America received more, and Europe and North America less, coverage than in traditional atlases.

Peters was not alone in offering new views. The Robinson projection of 1963, designed to offer the least possible area-scale distortion for major continents in an uninterrupted format map, was more accurate in terms of area than the hitherto influential Van der Grinten projection devised in 1898. The latter had continued the Mercator projection's practice of exaggerating the size of the temperate latitudes, and was particularly influential in the USA: in that projection, a large Soviet Union appeared menacing, a threat to the whole of Eurasia, and a dominant presence in the world that required containment. It was a cartographic image fitting for the Cold War. In contrast, the Robinson projection, adopted by the American National Geographic Society in 1988, made the Soviet Union appear smaller and therefore less threatening.

INTRODUCTION

Discussion of different projections serves as an instructive reminder that there is no single way to approach this chapter. The focus here and in the next chapter is on the fate of imperialism, not out of faddishness or political correctness, but because the areas of the world under direct or indirect imperial control in the first four decades of the century comprised much of the globe, while the issue can be continued beyond the collapse in 1974–5 of the Portuguese empire, the last of the European overseas empires, to include the fate of the Russian communist empire, the Soviet Union, in the early 1990s and, subsequently and, more generally, the question of ethnicity and rule at the present day. The fall of empire has a relevance not only to those who gained independence, but also to former imperial powers. It was also linked to other currents in global history. The combination of nationalism and the mass mobilization of people and resources that had characterized industrializing nations in the nineteenth century spread to the non-European world and helped to undermine the logic and practice of colonial control. The 'right to rule' colonial peoples could not be sustained in the political climate of the later twentieth century. There were examples of suc-

THE 'RIGHT TO RULE' COLONIAL PEOPLES COULD NOT BE SUSTAINED IN THE POLITICAL CLIMATE OF THE LATER TWENTIETH CENTURY.

cessful military counter-insurgency (and the Chinese empire continues to provide them in Tibet and Xinjiang), but the political contest was lost. Imperialism became ideologically and politically bankrupt, and this was to be more important in the collapse of European control over most of the world than changes in military capability.

THE HEIGHT OF EMPIRE

At the beginning of the century, decolonization did not appear a serious prospect. In the last two decades of the nineteenth century, a sizeable amount of the world's surface had been conquered by Western powers, particularly in Africa and South-East Asia. The West eventually prevailed in most places due to superior military force, improved disease control and enhanced communications. On the global scale, it was not a case of Western powers expanding into a passive void of decrepit states and undeveloped societies, but rather of the Westerners as an increasingly dominant element in the dynamic non-Western world. Precisely because these non-Western societies were not undeveloped, primitive, decrepit or weak, the Western success in conquering large areas was a formidable military achievement. By 1900, Britain had an empire covering a fifth of the world's land surface and including, mostly in South Asia, 400 million people; and France one, mostly in Africa, of six million square miles and 52 million people.

Territorial expansion owed much to an ability to deploy forces and to use imperial space, an ability in which railways and steamships played a major role. In 1896, the Russians obliged China to grant a concession for a railway to Vladivostok across Manchuria, and the Chinese Eastern Railway was accordingly constructed in 1897–1904. The German Berlin–Baghdad railway project was designed to create a new geopolitical axis in Eurasia. Enhanced communications also served lesser powers. The building of a railway across the rebel area in 1900 helped to end longstanding Mayan resistance to the Mexicans, although the impact of cholera, smallpox and whooping cough in weakening the defenders was also important. The role of rail as an enabler of Western power and modernization helped to ensure that track and trains became strategic targets for their opponents. In China, in 1900, the destruction by the Boxers, an anti-foreigner movement, of part of the track between Tianjin and Beijing forced the abandonment of the initial attempt to relieve the foreign legations in the capital. Significantly, no railways were built in Afghanistan, a country not brought under Western control.

In addition, Western expansion benefited from the ability to win local support, especially to recruit local levies. Politics within Western states were also important. There was a strong sense of imperial mission and a major emphasis on winning territorial control: sovereignty became more crucial than informal influence. The profit motive was subordinated to geopolitics: much imperial expansion arose from the response to the real or apparent plans of other Western powers, particularly in Africa, South-East Asia and Oceania, although the search for markets was also important.

The scramble for possessions continued without slackening in the early years of the twentieth century. Areas where the Westerners had not hitherto sent troops were made fully aware of the potential of their power. In 1900, the French seized the Touat oasis in the Sahara, the first loss of territory by Morocco for over a century. This campaign, which cost nearly twenty million francs and for which 35,000 camels were requisitioned in the neighbouring French colony of Algeria, indicated the ability and willingness of the colonial powers to spend in order to achieve results. The same year, the Pacific island of Tonga became a British protectorate. By 1912, the French had established a protectorate over most of Morocco, the remainder becoming a Spanish protectorate. With columns advancing from both north and south, the French also conquered the Sahara, where effective resistance ended in 1905.

The previous year, the British advanced to Lhasa, the capital of Tibet, a region that had never before experienced Western intervention, in order to dictate terms. In the East Indies, the Dutch expanded their power in the 1900s. On several occasions, their opponents ritually purified themselves for death and fought their final battle (*puputan*): armed only with daggers and lances, they were slaughtered by Dutch firepower. It was the end of the old order. In 1911, another area not hitherto conquered by Westerners in part succumbed when an Italian expeditionary force landed in Turkish-ruled Tripolitania and Cyrenaica and called their conquest Libya, restoring an ancient name for the region. This was the first war in which armoured cars and bombing aeroplanes were used. Another long-established empire lost power to a Western state when, in 1911–12, the Russians established a protectorate in Outer Mongolia, replacing Chinese influence. By the outbreak of World War I in 1914, the Western imperial powers had annexed most of the territories they sought in the world, and had defined spheres of influence in most of the countries still outside Western control, particularly China and Persia (Iran).

As the geographical range of conquest expanded, there was also an increase in rebellion against Western influence and rule. This was not new, but the extent of rebellion in the 1900s was noteworthy. In large part, rebellions occurred in response to the implementation of control in newly annexed territories, although the Boxer Rising in China in 1900 was an expression of hostility towards Westernization, especially Christian missionaries. In the Philippines, conquered from Spain by the USA in 1898, American annexation was resisted by Filippino nationalists who mounted a guerrilla war. This led the Americans to add counter-insurgency methods to their ideology of racialism and divine purpose. Prisoners were killed and prison camps were created in which 11,000 people died.

In 1905, the rebellion by the Nama and Hereros of South-West Africa against their German conquerors was finally crushed with great brutality. The Germans practised extermination, killing their opponents in large numbers, driving the Hereros into a waterless desert and treating the prisoners sent to labour camp with great cruelty, such that over half the population died there. In 1905, the Germans suppressed the Maji Maji rising in German East Africa (Tanganyika, now Tanzania) using a scorched-earth policy against guerrilla warfare: about 250,000 Africans died of famine. Revolts in Madagascar and Morocco against the French, and in Natal against the British, were suppressed in 1904, 1906 and 1907, respectively.

WORLD WAR I, 1914–1918

These Western imperial powers were themselves to wage a bitter war for, first, predominance and then survival. The origins of the war have inspired a vast historiography. For our purposes, it is important to note that war was seen by contemporaries as a way to achieve goals, but that anxiety as much as opportunity conditioned these goals. This was true of the Germans, who were concerned about growing Russian military preparedness on their eastern frontier, especially the construction of a strategic railroad network. The policy of a watchful prudence, resting on support for an international order based on a mutual acceptance of great power interests, that the German Chancellor, Otto von Bismarck, had managed in 1871–90 had been replaced under Emperor Wilhelm II (ruled 1888–1918), from the 1890s, by a more volatile search for German advantage. The Germans were also affected by a belief in the inevitability of war, which encouraged a desire to begin it at the most opportune moment for themselves. Furthermore, Germans could look back with pride and confidence to successful recent wars against Austria (1866) and France (1870–1).

Germany's main ally, Austro-Hungary (Austria for the sake of simplicity), was equally concerned about its apparently worsening strategic and political situation, specifically Russian-supported Serbian assertiveness and its challenge to the stability of Austria's Balkan possessions, particularly Bosnia, and even to the Dual Monarchy itself. There was a growing frustration amongst the Austrian leadership at not being able to shape their own destiny in external affairs, and Serbia had a great deal to do with that feeling. The same sense of being powerless was also strong in respect to politics within the Austrian empire, not least as a result of the demands of ethnic groups, and war with Serbia seemed the answer to this problem. The Russians, in contrast, were encouraged by Serb success and ready to see Serbia as a crucial protégé. As recently as the autumn of 1912, international tension over the position of Serbia had led Austria and Russia to deploy troops in mutually threatening positions, but the forces had withdrawn in the spring of 1913.

The Austrian heir, Archduke Franz Ferdinand, and his wife Sophia, were assassinated in Sarajevo on 28 June 1914 by Gavrilo Princip, a Bosnian Serb. The terrorist group to which he belonged was under the control of the Black Hand, a secret Serbian nationalist organization pledged to the overthrow of Habsburg control in South Slav territories. When the news reached Vienna, there was shock and the customary response to an unexpected and dramatic event: a sense that a display of action was needed. This interacted with an already powerful view that war with Serbia was necessary. The assassinations apparently provided the excuse to take care of Serbia. A promise of German support reflected the sense that a forceful response was necessary, appropriate and likely to profit Austrian and German interests. As a consequence, Germany found itself in a crisis in which it controlled neither the parameters nor the timetable.

GERMANY FOUND ITSELF IN A CRISIS IN WHICH IT CONTROLLED NEITHER THE PARAMETERS NOR THE TIMETABLE.

Austrian threats to Serbia in the aftermath of the assassinations posed a challenge to Russian interests and the Russian perception of international relations in Eastern Europe. Confident that German backing would deter Russia, the Austrians sought a limited war with Serbia, not agreement with the Serbs, who were, in fact, willing to make important concessions and prepared for binding arbitration on the points to which they objected. The Serb response to an Austrian ultimatum of 23 July was deemed inadequate, and on 28 July the Austrians began hostilities. The Russians had responded to the ultimatum by beginning military preparations on the 26th. They were confident of the support of their ally France and believed it necessary to act firmly in order to protect Serbia.

Efforts to contain the crisis, and localize the conflict, were pre-empted by its rapid escalation. On 30 July, rather than abandon Serbia, Russia ordered a general mobilization against both Austria and Germany. This put pressure on Germany, whose war plans called for action against France before Russia could act. The refusal of both Russia and France to halt their preparations led the German government – unwilling to back down and as if trapped by its strategic concepts – to attack. In addition, German leaders opportunistically sought to use the Balkan crisis to change the balance of power in their favour. They were willing to risk a war because no other crisis was as likely to produce a constellation of circumstances guaranteeing them the commitment of their main ally, Austria, and the support of the German public. General German mobilization was implemented on 1 August. Despite the international recognition of Belgium's perpetual neutrality in 1839, the Germans on 2 August issued an ultimatum to Brussels demanding acceptance of the passage of their troops in order to permit an advance on Paris from the north-east. When Belgium refused on the 3rd, Germany declared war. This led Britain, one of the guarantors of Belgian neutrality, to enter the war on 4 August, although a major reason for the government was to defend France as a vital element in the balance of power.

Military considerations, and the army leaderships themselves, played an important role in pushing governments to act; this was because mobilizations were seen as the crucial indicator of intentions and mobilizing faster than one's adversary bestowed a major advantage. The military were especially important in Austria, Germany and Russia. Military pressure in power politics rested on the argument of necessity. War was seen not as an easy challenge but as a danger in which it was vital to act first. It has been argued that the European war-plans of 1914, with their dynamic interaction of mobilization and deployment, made war 'by timetable' difficult to stop once a crisis occurred. This was clearly the case with the German war-plan, which required that hostilities rapidly follow mobilization.

WAR WAS SEEN NOT AS AN EASY CHALLENGE BUT AS A DANGER IN WHICH IT WAS VITAL TO ACT FIRST.

It has also been claimed that politicians were not trapped, and that their own roles and preferences were important. An awareness of precarious domestic and international situations did not inevitably have to lead to war. Furthermore, alliance did not dictate participation: despite being their ally, Italy did not join Germany and Austria. An awareness of likely risks had helped prevent former crises from leading to war. In 1914, the situation was different because Austria chose to fight, Germany to support it, and Russia to respond.

The political ambitions of the war helped to drive the offensive strategy of the participants. The Austrians sought to capture Belgrade, the capital of Serbia, and the

Germans Paris, while the French advanced to regain Alsace-Lorraine, lost to Germany in 1870–1, and the Russians to reduce pressure on their allies and both to overrun much of Austria and to march on Berlin. The goals of the powers altered during the war, but continued substantially to rest on gaining or regaining territory. This helped to sustain the central role of the offensive, both strategically and tactically, in the campaigning.

The manoeuvre stage of the war in the West, with its emphasis on a strategy of envelopment in order to secure total victory, and on a battle of annihilation, ended by October 1914. Generals were to try repeatedly to re-create this flexibility, and, in particular, to reopen a war of movement by breaking through their opponents' front line, but this goal was to prove elusive and risked losing large numbers without causing comparable casualties to the enemy. The alternative was a strategy of attrition, which focused primarily on killing large numbers of opponents.

The absence of a speedy military victory and France's membership in a powerful coalition ensured that the Germans could not repeat their rapid triumphs of 1866 and 1870–1. Instead, in contrast to these earlier wars, a front line, the Western Front, soon crystallized, with its stability expressed in trench systems. In the West, this was the basic strategic fact of the war: Germany had seized much of Belgium and part of France, and dug in to protect its gains. This put the Western allies, principally Britain and France, under the necessity to mount offensives; another need for attacks was provided by the wish to reduce German pressure on Russia and to prevent it from being knocked out of the war. Furthermore, there was a conviction that only through mounting an offensive would it be possible for the Allies to gain the initiative and, conversely, deny it to the Germans, and that both gaining the initiative and mounting an offensive were prerequisites for victory.

The horror of heavy casualties and what appeared to be military futility in World War I distracted attention from the effectiveness of the European military system. Despite the nature of the conflict on the Western Front in 1915–17, the war was not an impasse created by trench systems and by similarities in weapons systems. In Eastern Europe, the force-to-space ratio was lower, and it was easier to break through opposing lines and advance rapidly, as the Germans demonstrated at Russian expense in 1915.

German successes played a major role both in the collapse of the power of the Romanov dynasty within Russia in 1917, and in the subsequent weakness of the Kerensky regime, a moderate republican government; this provided the Bolsheviks (better known as communists) with an opportunity to seize power in November 1917.

Indeed, the fall of the Kerensky regime owed much to its failure on the battlefield in 1917 (or, alternatively, to its failure to pull out of the war altogether).

Vladimir Ilyich Lenin (1870–1924), the Bolshevik leader, had hoped that the spread of revolution to Germany would make negotiations unnecessary, but when the Bolsheviks refused to accept the terms offered, the Germans resumed the offensive. Their rapid success forced the Bolsheviks to accept even harsher terms in the Treaty of Brest-Litovsk, ratified, on 16 March 1918: they ceded sovereignty over Poland, Lithuania, Ukraine, Courland (modern western Latvia) and Finland.

In addition, the conquests of Serbia in 1915 and Romania in 1916 by Austria, Bulgaria and Germany demonstrated the ability of contemporary armies to achieve decisive victories in certain circumstances. Outside Europe, Britain, France and their allies also demonstrated the potential effectiveness of their military systems. They rapidly over-ran all the German colonies, bar German East Africa, but the Turks (an ally of Germany) were a more formidable foe, not least because their forces were neither small nor cut off by Allied seapower (as was the case with those of Germany outside Europe). The initial Allied advance into Mesopotamia (now Iraq) was unsuccessful, although Turkish resistance there was overcome in 1918. In 1917–18, the British drove the Turks from Palestine.

On the Western Front, the Germans were finally defeated in 1918. Their initially suc-cessful offensive that year was blocked and the Allies then outfought the Germans and drove them back. The Germans were also affected by the collapse of their allies, first Bulgaria and then Austria, and by the degree to which the exacerbation that year of Germany's military, economic and domestic problems destroyed the will to fight. There were serious food shortages. More specifically, manpower shortages hit not only the German army but also the economy. Thus, coal production declined in 1917, and both this and the shortage of manpower hit the rail system. The cumulative impact of such shortages was a rundown in the German economy and its growing atomization, which hindered attempts to co-ordinate and direct production. The Germans had no equivalent to the support provided to Britain and France by the Americans, who had entered the war in 1917, or to the prospect of future help that this offered. Pressing the domestic population harder to provide resources for the war only helped to under-mine German public support for the conflict.

The strain imposed upon German society by the attempt to mobilize the resources for total war was heightened by the failure of the 1918 spring offensive. Army morale col-lapsed. These factors helped to confound the Allied expectation that the war would continue until 1919. Instead, an armistice came into force on 11 November. The strains of war had gathered to a point of political crisis. Wilhelm II was forced to abdicate in the face of incipient revolution, and the new government was eager to end the conflict. In a sense, Russia in 1917–18 became Germany in 1918, although there was no comparable social collapse.

Important as American troops were on the Western Front in 1918, American financial resources and industrial capacity were even more crucial. The role of all three looked towards the decisive part played by the USA in World War II and subsequently. As World War I ended before American forces could play the role envisaged for the 1919 campaign, their potential was not yet clear to all contemporaries, although the German Supreme Army Command was well aware of the issue. Having failed to win a quick victory by unrestricted submarine warfare or by attacking in the West in spring 1918, Germany had lost. The example, and its implications, had not been adequately digested by Hitler and his circle when they declared war on the USA in December 1941. In World War I, America's industrial resources and technology were available to the Allies (for a price) from the outset, and the ability of the British to sustain trans-Atlantic shipping routes against German submarine attacks was crucial to the war economy. American resources were crucial because, in 1914, neither Britain nor France had an industrial system to match that of Germany. For machine tools, mass-production plant and much else, including the parts of shells, the Allies were dependent on the USA.

WORLD WAR I OUTSIDE EUROPE

World War I did not have a disruptive impact on the Western empires outside Europe akin to that of World War II. There was a major defeat for the British in Mesopotamia at the hands of the Turks at Kut in 1915 and the attempt that year in the Gallipoli campaign to force the Dardanelles and besiege Constantinople failed, but these did not have an impact on the prestige of the British empire comparable to the fall of Singapore to the Japanese in 1942. There were indeed rebellions against European empires – against the French in Tunisia in 1915–16 and against the Russians in Central Asia in 1916 – but none was successful or posed a more major threat to these empires. The widespread Muslim revolt in Central Asia against the Russian introduction of conscription was defeated, with great brutality and heavy casualties. In some respects, indeed, World War I, for a while, led to an intensification of European military control in the colonies. This was particularly so in, and near, areas of conflict, as imperial forces manoeuvred in the interior. Forces were also available to enforce imperial authority, as with the British expedition of 1918 against the Turkana of Kenya.

The successful articulation of imperial systems on a global scale was readily apparent. Both Britain and France benefited from the support of their empires. The French deployed about 140,000 West African troops on the Western Front, and more than 800,000 Indian soldiers fought for the British in the war, so that, far from the British having to garrison South Asia, it was a crucial source of manpower for them. The British used large numbers of Indians on the Western Front at first, as well as a substantial Canadian force. Indian troops captured Basra in 1914, protecting British oil interests in south-west Persia (Iran), and advanced into Mesopotamia the following year. The impact of raising troops in the Punjab in India was such that it became a virtual 'home front' for the British war effort. Without the empire, Britain would have been unable to mount offensive operations in the Middle East, would have been largely reduced to the use of the navy against German colonies, and would have been forced to introduce conscription earlier than 1916. The use of imperial forces was helped by the absence of an enemy in East Asia, with the exception of the German base at Tsingtao in China, which was captured by Britain's ally Japan in 1914. The situation was to be very different in the Second World War when Japan allied with Germany. To provide an indication of the far-ranging impact of the war, New Zealand, a dominion of the British crown, also introduced conscription in 1916. Forty per cent of New Zealand men of military age (between 19 and 45) served overseas; of this 120,000, over 50,000 were injured and 18,000 died.

INTERWAR IMPERIALISM

The war was followed not by a retreat of European empire, but by its advance. The imperial ethos remained strong, and the British in particular saw the events of the war outside Europe as reflecting the value and appeal of empire. The defeat of Germany and its allies ensured that Western control over the world's surface reached its maximum extent. Although the redistribution of Germany's colonies resulted in gains for Japan in the western Pacific, the partition of the Ottoman empire led, in 1920, to British rule over Palestine, Transjordan and Iraq, and French rule over Syria and Lebanon, all under League of Nations mandates. Whereas local consent, in the form of plebiscites, was used to determine some European frontiers after World War I, for example that between Denmark and Germany in 1920, such consent-frontiers were not granted outside Europe: the victors and the League of Nations introduced and maintained very different logics of territorial legitimacy outside and within Europe. Thus, in 1939, France, which held the mandate for Syria, accepted Turkish claims to the Alexandretta region without a plebiscite. This created the basis for a long postwar dispute between Syria and Turkey.

THE WAR WAS FOLLOWED NOT BY A RETREAT OF EUROPEAN EMPIRE, BUT BY ITS ADVANCE.

Throughout the colonial world, there was a deepening of imperial control as areas that, earlier, had been often only nominally annexed were brought under at least some colonial government. Thus, in southern Sudan posts were established by Arab troops under British officers and military patrols were launched. Road-building improved the British position on the North-West Frontier of India.

However, the European imperial powers, exhausted by World War I, began to sense that they had overreached themselves, particularly in the Islamic world. Revolts in Egypt (1919) and Iraq (1920–1) led to Britain granting their independence in 1922 and 1924, respectively, although Egypt remained under *de facto* British military control. British influence collapsed in Persia (1921), and the confrontation with Turkey in the Chanak Crisis (1922) caused a political crisis in London that led the British to back down. Prefiguring modern concerns, General Rawlinson, the Commander-in-Chief in India, argued in 1922 that war with Turkey would lead to trouble in India and the Middle East: 'To undertake offensive action against the Turk is merely to consolidate a Pan-Islamic Movement.'

Other European powers faced growing similar problems. The French and Spaniards encountered opposition in Morocco, while the Druze rebelled against the French in Syria in 1925–7, in reaction to attempts by the governor to introduce what he considered modernizing reforms in the Jebel Druze area. This alienated the notables, the crucial intermediaries in successful imperialism. In Spanish Morocco, the weak state of the colonial administration and military led to a severe defeat in 1921. The Dutch, meanwhile, came under attack in the Far East from the PKI (Indonesian Communist Party) in Java (1926) and Sumatra (1927).

The net effect of these risings might suggest a reduction in Western military superiority. This was further illustrated by the failure of Western powers to enforce their post-World War I settlement on Turkey. In particular, in 1922 the Turks totally defeated Greek attempts to subordinate them and force them to accept Greek control of much of western Turkey.

Nevertheless, an impression of Western failure would be misplaced. The colonial powers still had sufficient military superiority to reimpose control in most cases. France and Spain crushed the rebellion in Morocco in 1926. The French regained control in Syria and the Dutch, rapidly, in Indonesia in 1926–7. The French had used heavy artillery bombardments to thwart Druze progress in Damascus in 1926.

The Italians recognized Libyan self-government in 1919, but Benito Mussolini, the fascist leader who gained power in Italy in 1922, was not prepared to accept this.

Employing great brutality against civilians, of whom over 50,000 were probably killed, the Italians subdued the colony in 1928–32. Their tactics included the use of columns of armoured cars and motorized infantry, the dropping of gas bombs and the employment of Eritreans rather than Libyans as auxiliaries. These tactics were accompanied by a ruthless suppression of the population: wells were blocked and flocks slaughtered, both effective forms of economic warfare, and the Libyan population was disarmed and resettled in camps in which about 20,000 people died. A largely pastoral society, much of which was nomadic, was brought under control. The Bedouin population of Libya was halved.

UNDER MUSSOLINI, THE BEDOUIN POPULATION OF LIBYA WAS HALVED.

In the post-1918 world, although they were very different as states, it is also possible to see both the Soviet Union and the USA as empires. Having gained control in Russia in the Russian Civil War (1918–21), the communists ensured that Tsarist gains in the Caucasus and Central Asia were retained. Soviet forces occupied Armenia in 1920 and overran Georgia in 1921. A major rising in Georgia in 1924 was suppressed. The Basmachi rising, a Muslim attempt in the early 1920s to organize a government in Turkestan, was crushed by the local Russians, who had more modern weapons, as well as the benefit of control over the major towns and railways. Overwhelming force, the use of artillery against mountain villages and the ability to call on some local support, enabled the Soviets to crush an Islamic uprising in Daghestan and Chechnya in the northern Caucasus in 1920–1, and also subsequent uprisings in 1924, 1928, 1929, 1936 and 1940.

With their control over Alaska, Hawaii, Guam, American Samoa, Puerto Rico and the Philippines, the Americans were a major colonial power. In addition, they enjoyed a quasi-imperial position in the Caribbean and Mexico, supported by extensive and growing trade and investment. In both, they intervened with their armed forces to protect their interests, but they encountered nationalist resistance in Mexico and in parts of the Caribbean, especially Haiti. Popular guerrilla movements in Haiti and the Dominican Republic in the 1920s proved able to limit the degree of control enjoyed by occupying American marines, who found that rebel ambushes restricted their freedom of manoeuvre. American bombing was no substitute, particularly in face of guerrilla dominance of rural areas at night. Although the guerrillas in the Dominican Republic conditionally surrendered in 1922, American troops sent to Nicaragua in 1927 failed to defeat a rebel peasant army under Augusto Sandino (1895–1934); their occupation ended in 1932. Despite these checks, the Americans dominated the region in economic, military and political terms.

Opposition to, and risings against, imperial powers testified to the more general problems created for them by the steady growth of anti-imperial feeling and, sometimes, by the more positive emergence of national identity. In 1885, the Indian National Congress was founded, in 1897 the Egyptian National Party, and in 1906 the All-Indian Muslim League. In 1920, the Soviet Union hosted a Congress of Peoples of the East at Baku, although initial attempts by communists to exploit anti-imperialism, as in Indonesia, were of limited success. The National Congress of British West Africa was established in 1920, the Young Kikuyu Association in Kenya in 1921 and the African National Congress in South Africa in 1923. Within French Africa, there was the *Etoile Nord-Africaine* in Algeria and the *Destour* in Tunisia. The global diffusion of Western notions of community, identity and political action, and of practices of politicization, challenged imperial structures, although it is important, in addition, not to underrate indigenous notions of identity and practices of resistance, many of them central to a peasant culture of non-compliance with ruling groups. The protest in Samoa in 1929 that led to an armed police response and to the deployment of New Zealand troops arose from the suppression that year of the Fono of Faipule, Samoa's democratic assembly.

Military opposition to the imperial powers continued in the 1930s. The French crushed an uprising at Yen Bay in Vietnam in 1930 and had pacified the tribes of the Moroccan Atlas by 1933. An anti-Soviet rebellion in Mongolia was defeated in 1932, but the American withdrawal from Haiti in 1934 owed much to a sense of the intractability of the conflict; the Americans were unwilling to devote resources comparable to those of the French in Syria and lacked the same sense of mission. In 1936, the Americans established the self-governing Commonwealth of the Philippines, which was designed to lead to independence a decade later, as it indeed did.

The most farflung empire, that of Britain, faced the most widespread opposition. Aside from hostility from the Nationalist Party in Malta and Greek Cypriot nationalist riots in 1931, there was serious Arab violence in Palestine in 1936–9, which led to the deployment of 50,000 troops. In India, the growing strength of the non-violent Indian National Party created a serious political problem. Gandhi's non-violent criticism of British rule, in particular his flouting of tax on salt in 1930, led to a growing uneasiness in the British position there.

If some rebellions could be suppressed by small forces supported by air power, the overall burden of imperial security remained high. Nevertheless, real costs were lessened by the use of non-Western troops, both local forces and those from elsewhere in the empire. Regions that had been conquered in the late nineteenth century provided many soldiers for the colonial powers, and both they and troops from areas that had been ruled for longer were trained in Western methods of warfare and organized accordingly. Hitherto independent armies of local allies were similarly organized or were integrated into imperial forces. The result was a high level of military resource. For example, in response to the Arab rising against the British in Iraq in 1920, four divisions were sent from India.

Locally raised troops helped the French suppress the Druze rebellion. French military control of Syria and Lebanon substantially rested on the *Armée du Levant*, 70,000 strong in 1921, a force largely composed of colonial troops from Africa, as well as on local military and police forces: the *Troupes Spéciales du Levant*, 14,000 strong in 1935, and the Gendarmerie. Both had a strong element of local minority groups, such as Christians, that could be relied upon in the event of clashes with the rest of the population. Divide, recruit and rule was the crucial object and process of imperialist control.

DIVIDE, RECRUIT AND RULE WAS THE CRUCIAL OBJECT AND PROCESS OF IMPERIALIST CONTROL.

Two very different images of empire can be offered, reflecting the different and contradictory policies of repression and conciliation followed by the British after World War I. The Amritsar massacre in April 1919, when General Dyer ordered troops to fire on a demonstrating crowd, causing nearly 400 fatalities, dented British authority in India by suggesting that it had an inherently repressive nature (although it also revealed the nature of British strength: the troops were Indians). But, that same year, a Government of India Act established the principle of dyarchy: responsible self-government in certain areas. The Government of India Act of 1935 moved India further towards self-government, although it was also designed to ensure British retention of the substance of power. However, the provincial elections of 1937 were a success for the Indian National Congress, which sought independence.

A very different image of empire was offered by the successful Italian invasion of Ethiopia in 1935–6. This was a brutal conquest in which advanced weaponry was used alongside native auxiliaries: Eritreans bore much of the fighting. The new military technology was employed with harsh effectiveness. Motorized columns were supported by aeroplanes, and large quantities of mustard gas were also used. The new technology and the use of nearly 600,000 troops compensated for Ethiopian bravery, for the ineffectiveness of much Italian generalship, and for the logistical problems of campaigning in the difficult mountainous terrain; the last forced the Italians to devote much energy to road-building.

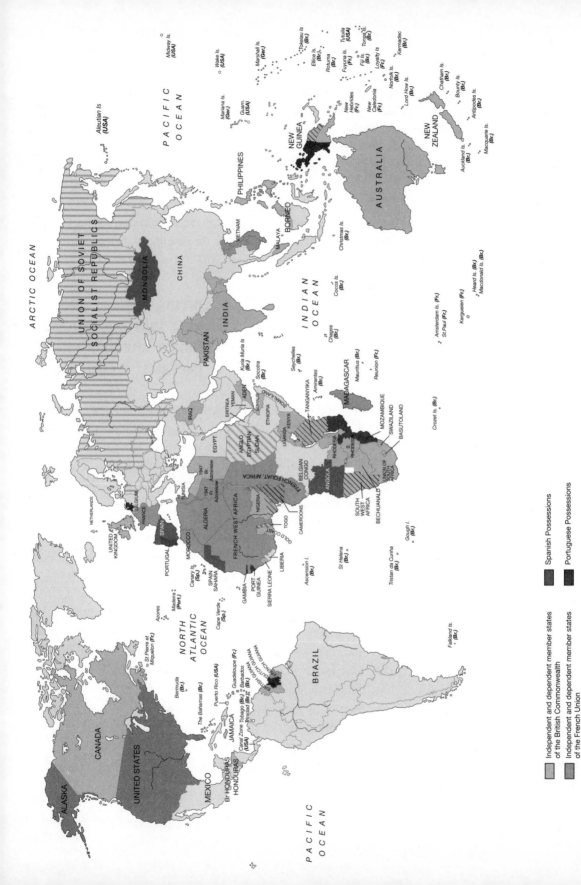

As with much else, it is unclear what would have happened to Western imperial control had World War II not broken out in 1939. The causes of the war have frequently been traced to the failures of the Peace of Versailles of 1919 that followed World War I. The peace terms, which included significant territorial losses to France and Poland, as well as heavy reparations, left Germany with a major sense of grievance.

As part of the peace settlement, the League of Nations was established in 1919 as the first pan-national organization with a global mission to prevent war and to deal with any unresolved peace settlement issues. However, it included neither the USA – despite President Woodrow Wilson's active championing of the League, the Senate refused to ratify the Peace of Versailles in 1919 – nor Russia, then in a bitter civil war and, from 1921, under the rule of communists whose call for world revolution was seen as a threat to international order. The Chinese delegation, meanwhile, refused to sign the peace agreement because it accepted the Japanese gain of German interests instead of returning them to China.

Some of the criticisms of the Versailles agreement were naïve. Having launched the war in the West in 1914 and then been defeated, it was understandable that Germany suffered, and the terms were designed to prevent it launching fresh aggression and thus to serve as a form of collective security. The principle of national self-determination actively pushed by Wilson (US President 1913–21) left a series of new countries in Eastern Europe (Poland, Czechoslovakia, Hungary, now separated from Austria; as well as an enlarged Romania and a Yugoslavia that was ruled by the Serbian dynasty) that were vulnerable to any revival of German or Russian power, but it would have been impossible to re-create the shattered humpty dumpty of the Habsburg (Austrian) empire.

On the whole, the international system worked reasonably well in the 1920s, at least from the perspective of Western interests. There was domestic instability and international tension in Europe, but this had also been the case prior to 1914, and World War I, the collapse of the European dynastic empires and the Versailles settlement had left many disputes. There was a widespread use of force in 1919 to settle territorial disputes in Eastern Europe and the politics of Germany; and, in Ireland in 1919–21, an insurgency that led to the abandonment of British control over most of the island was followed by a civil war (1922–3) in which the new Irish Free State suppressed domestic opposition.

Nevertheless, in Europe as a whole, economic recovery in the mid- and late 1920s facilitated a process of internal consolidation and a lessening of international tension. This, however, was overthrown in the 1930s by the consequences of the Depression (see chapter 5). Liberal democratic governments now appeared weak and unable to cope. The Depression encouraged social and political tensions and helped to lead to the rise of anti-democratic political movements. This was not only true of Europe. In the USA, tension rose, with clashes between the unemployed and the police, for example in New York in 1930. Demagogic populism became politically important, especially with Huey Long, the Governor of Louisiana, whose career was cut short by assassination in 1935, and also with, ultimately unsuccessful, fascist movements.

Authoritarian regimes came to power across most of Eastern and Southern Europe, where Mussolini had launched fascism as a governing system in 1922. Adolf Hitler benefited from the appeal of his nationalist and racist populism, and from right-wing concern about communism, in order to destabilize the democratic system in Germany. Once he had gained power in 1933, he transformed Germany into a dicta-torship, combining, in 1934, the office of President with that of Chancellor, which he already held.

Concern about the challenge from working-class political parties, and fear about the consequences of the economic crisis, encouraged support elsewhere for right-wing authoritarian solutions. In Spain, the right came to power after a brutal civil war in 1936-9. Other right-wing seizures of power included those by Antonio de Salazar in Portugal in 1932, Konstantin Päts in Estonia in 1934 and King Carol II in Romania in 1938. There were authoritarian regimes in Hungary and Poland. In Bulgaria, an army coup in 1934 was followed by the country becoming a military dictatorship under King Boris in 1935. Greece also became a military dictatorship in 1935.

The same process could be seen in Latin America, where there was serious political instability, not least as a consequence of acute economic pressures and social division, as well as of only limited support for democratic practices. In Brazil, the army removed the President in 1930, and prevented the inauguration of the President-elect, instead putting his defeated opponent, Getúlio Vargas (1883–1954), into office. Supported by the army, Vargas crushed the 'Constitutionalist' Revolt of 1932 and communist risings in 1935. In 1937, Vargas used troops to introduce a new constitutional policy, termed the *Estado Novo* (New State), in which he enjoyed near-dictatorial powers. There were coups in Argentina in 1930 and Uruguay in 1933, while the army overthrew the peasant-based government of El Salvador in 1931 and also smashed a peasant revolt the following year with much slaughter. The army seized power in Cuba in 1933, and suppressed peasant opposition in Honduras in 1932 and 1937. In Japan, the democratic practices of the 1920s were challenged by authoritarian nationalists who pursued a steadily more ambitious intervention in China, with the support of a growing militarism that threatened civil society.

Although democratic (and non-democratic) systems were overthrown by coups across much of the world, it would be mistaken to see a violent breach in governmental continuity as the only response to the social and economic problems of the 1930s. Democracy continued in many countries, especially (but not only) in Australasia, North America and parts of Western Europe. At the same time, one important response in democratic societies was a measure of greater cohesion, with an economic politics of corporatism and increased government intervention, and politics dominated by one party, as in the USA, Mexico and, from 1931 in the shape of the National Government, Britain.

WORLD WAR II, 1939–1945

ORIGINS

Japan shared with Nazi Germany, fascist Italy, the communist Soviet Union and Hungary (a right-wing dictatorship) a drive for a radical revision of the Versailles settlement. All of them built up their military. Breaking the provisions of the Versailles settlement, which had limited the German armed forces, Hitler rapidly increased German military spending, although this helped to unbalance the economy. The Four-Year Plan, initiated in 1936, was designed to ensure readiness to go to war in four years.

In the late 1930s, the revisionist powers increasingly relied on force to achieve their goals. In defiance of the Versailles settlement, Hitler unilaterally remilitarized the Rhineland on 7 March 1936: it provided military protection for the Ruhr, Germany's leading industrial region, and was also a springboard for action against France. Far from responding forcefully against this breach of the Versailles settlement, the British sought to discourage the French from acting. In hindsight, Western passivity marked a major step in Nazi expansionism, but, at the time, it was not seen in such a stark light. Furthermore, the very limited nature of Anglo-French military co-operation over the previous decade, and their lack of preparedness, were understood by contemporaries as a poor basis for joint action. But when Hitler occupied Austria on 12 March 1938, uniting it with Germany in the *Anschluss* (union) on the 13th, this was more than a revision of the Versailles settlement: it was a fundamental redrawing of the map of Europe.

WHEN HITLER OCCUPIED AUSTRIA, UNITING IT WITH GERMANY, THIS WAS MORE THAN A REVISION OF THE VERSAILLES SETTLEMENT: IT WAS A FUNDAMENTAL REDRAWING OF THE MAP OF EUROPE.

The Versailles settlement had left to Czechoslovakia those parts of Bohemia and Moravia where there was an ethnic majority of Germans (the Sudeten Germans). This was unacceptable to Hitler, who sought the union of all Germans in one state and was determined to destroy Czechoslovakia, a democratic state that looked to other great powers for support. His threat to attack Czechoslovakia in 1938 led to the satisfaction of his territorial demands in a settlement negotiated with Britain, France and Italy: the Munich agreement of 29 September. Eventually, in March 1939, Hitler destroyed his victim. He was able to do so without encountering armed resistance, because Czechoslovakia had been much weakened by internal dissent between Czechs and Slovaks. He was also aided by the terms of the Munich agreement, which resulted in its loss of the frontier fortifications in the areas annexed by Germany. Hungary and Poland used the crisis to make gains at Czechoslovakia's expense in 1938, and, in March 1939, Hungarian forces occupied Ruthenia, the easternmost part of Czechoslovakia. Also in March, the Germans bullied Lithuania into ceding the city of Memel, where there was a vocal German minority, plus the surrounding area. In intimidating the other powers in 1938, Hitler benefited from their understandable fear of war. In many respects, the Munich agreement was part of the legacy of World War I.

In April 1939, Mussolini invaded and annexed Albania. This followed on from his suppression of Libyan opposition and his conquest of Ethiopia. The fascist glorification of war and the revived notion of rebirth through conflict, so widely held before 1914, had a major impact on Italian policy, accentuating the consequences of an already extreme nationalism. Mussolini's rhetorical foreign policy placed an emphasis on force and power, often for their own sake.

In Japan in the 1930s, there were those in the army who believed devoutly in the idea of war as 'the father of creativity'. In 1931, the Japanese invaded Manchuria, China's industrial heartland, claiming that the Chinese had been sabotaging the Japanese-financed South Manchurian Railway. In 1937, Japan widened its aggression to a full-scale invasion of China that was based on a mistaken confidence that China would fall rapidly.

The dictators were increasingly acting as war-leaders in peacetime. The systems they had created lacked effective institutional and political restraints on their power and ideas, or the facility to offer any reasonable range of policy options. In Germany, control and direction of foreign and military policy was monopolized by Hitler, whose long-term views interacted with the short-term opportunities and anxieties presented by international developments. Opportunities and anxieties do not exist in the abstract, but are sensed and created, and Hitler's ideology largely conditioned the process. Far from being a nihilist without plans, Hitler sought a war for the extirpation of what he regarded as a Jewish-dominated Soviet Union, which he felt would secure his notions of racial superiority and *Lebensraum* (living-space) for Germany. To that end, Hitler aspired to control Eastern Europe, as well as to end the threat of a war on two fronts by defeating France, and to reach an agreement with Britain. The destruction of the Soviet Union was to be accompanied by the annihilation of the Jews, the two acts creating a Europe that could be dominated by the Germans, who were to be a master-race over the Slavs and others.

This agenda began long before the outbreak of World War II in 1939 with the violent suppression of political and economic freedoms, organizations and entities within Germany, including strikes, left-wing parties and Jews. Hitler might not have wanted a major conflict in 1939, but he anticipated such a war soon, and planned his economy accordingly. Import-substitution policies were pushed actively from 1936 in order to reduce Germany's vulnerability to blockade. Hitler did not invent racialism, anti-Semitism, the notion of *Lebensraum* or aggressive warfare, but they were combined to genocidal effect and given dynamic force by his evil determination to fulfil his vision. Hitler also believed that war was necessary and, even, a positive force.

Initially, the British and French governments had hoped that Hitler would be tamed by the responsibilities and exigencies of power, or that he would restrict his energies to ruling Germany. There was also a feeling in Britain that the Versailles terms had been overly harsh on Germany and that it was, therefore, understandable that Hitler should press for revision. It was anticipated that German revisionism could be accommodated, and that Hitler would prove to be just another episode in European power politics. Both Britain and France were unsure whether the Soviet Union was not a greater threat to the European system than was Nazi Germany. Furthermore, in both Britain and France, pacifism was strong, and fiscal restraint even stronger, although, outside Europe, both powers used troops to sustain their imperial interests.

The policy of the appeasement of dictators rested on the belief that it was possible to reach mutually acceptable settlements with them. The British government thought it both necessary and feasible to negotiate with Hitler, and it took time for the government to appreciate that this was not possible and, instead, was dangerous. Hitler wanted Germany to be a super-power, was happy to destroy both the balance of power and collective security in order to achieve this goal, and aimed at a new world order. By 1938, he appeared quite openly as a threat.

Once Hitler destroyed Czechoslovakia in March 1939, and renounced all the guarantees he had earlier made in the Munich agreement, showing that his ambitions were not restricted to bringing all Germans under one state, Neville Chamberlain, British Prime Minister 1937–40, lost confidence in negotiating directly with Germany. He sought, instead, to create an alliance system capable of intimidating Hitler. Despite the resulting guarantees of British support to Poland and Romania, Hitler persisted with his plan for an attack on Poland. He believed that Britain and France would not fight, especially after he secured a Non-Aggression Pact with the Soviet dictator, Joseph Stalin, signed on 23 August, which reflected the failure of the Western Allies to negotiate an alliance with the Soviet Union. Indeed, the British Chiefs of Staff had advised that it would not be possible to offer Poland any direct assistance. Despite this, the German attack on Poland on 1 September 1939 led Britain and France to declare war on 3 September.

THE CONFLICT

World War II is an umbrella term for a number of closely related struggles that, nevertheless, each had their own cause, course and consequences. Seen from the perspective of Italy or Iran, Japan or Jamaica, it can look very different. A war that began over Hitler's intimidation of Poland came to involve much of the world. This reflected the range of interests involved, the failure of the system of international adjudication and peacemaking (the League of Nations) and the vortex-like nature of war. In particular, the outbreak of hostilities led to a heightened pace of fear and opportunity. The unwillingness of the Germans to try to translate initial victories into a widely accepted peace ensured that the cessation of offensive operations with the conquest of Poland did not lead to an end to conflict. Britain and France were determined to fight on to prevent German hegemony, and this led Hitler to plan an attack on France, which was, eventually, successfully launched in May 1940.

A year later, Hitler's over-confidence and contempt for other political systems, his belief that Germany had to conquer the Soviet Union in order to fulfil its destiny and obtain *Lebensraum*, combined with his concern about Stalin's intentions, led him to mount Operation Barbarossa, his attack on the Soviet Union, even though Britain was unconquered, though largely neutered as a threat by being driven from the European mainland. Hitler was confident that the Soviet system would collapse rapidly and was happy to accept misleading intelligence assess-ments of the size and mobilization potential of the Red Army, although appreciable casualties were anticipated and the Germans deployed as many troops as they could. Hitler's refusal to accept what others might consider objective diplomatic and strategic considerations ensured that the local wars he had won were, from 1941, transformed into a world war he could not win. Such adventurism and conceit rested on Hitler's warped personality and were also the product of a political-ideological system in which conflict and hatred appeared natural, and genocide all too possible.

HITLER'S REFUSAL TO ACCEPT WHAT OTHERS MIGHT CONSIDER OBJECTIVE DIPLOMATIC AND STRATEGIC CONSIDERATIONS ENSURED THAT THE LOCAL WARS HE HAD WON WERE, FROM 1941, TRANSFORMED INTO A WORLD WAR HE COULD NOT WIN.

The process by which the war spread is important, because the course of the conflict is inseparable from its politics, and those helped to frame strategic goals and planning options. Franklin Delano Roosevelt (US President 1933–45), had responded to the escalation of Japanese attacks on China with a speech urging 'a quarantine of the patients in order to protect the health of the community against the spread of the dis-ease'. Such a policy eventually proved impossible for most of the world in the early 1940s. The vortex-like character of a major war can be seen at work in the extension of the German war, with, for example, the entry of Italy on the German side in June 1940, and the German attack on Yugoslavia and Greece in spring 1941; and also with the outbreak of the Pacific war in December 1941. German successes in 1939–41 led other states, willingly or otherwise, to become Axis allies and protégés, and to provide military resources to help the Germans, most obviously against the Soviet Union when Germany attacked on 22 June 1941. Romania, Hungary, Slovakia and Finland all made major contributions to the attack, and the composite force launched was simi-lar in this respect to that led by Napoleon in 1812. Earlier, the neutrality of states such as Denmark, Norway, Belgium and the Netherlands had been casually violated in 1940 to serve German strategic convenience.

Having joined the war, it was difficult to leave it. Defeated France agreed armistice terms in June 1940. Part was occupied, the remainder becoming a neutral state with its capital at Vichy. This, however, was not accepted either by the Free French under Charles de Gaulle, who were determined to fight on, or by Britain. British anxiety about the fate of the Vichy French fleet at Mers-el-Kebir in French North Africa, and its possible effect on the Mediterranean balance of power, led to a demand that it scuttle, join the British or sail to a harbour outside possible German control, and, when this was refused, it was attacked in July 1940. This set a pattern for hostilities between Britain and Vichy, including the British invasion of Syria and Lebanon in 1941 and of Madagascar in 1942. Both were motivated by fear – of German influence in Syria and of possible Japanese submarine bases in Madagascar – reflecting the way in which geostrategy could be a reason for action. Thus, the British also overthrew a pro-German government in Iraq in May 1941, and, that August, British and Soviet troops entered Persia (Iran) in order to gain control of supply routes.

The collapse of France and the Netherlands to German attack in 1940, and the weakening position of Britain, already vulnerable in the Pacific, created an apparent power vacuum in East and South-East Asia, encouraging Japanese ambitions southwards into Indo-China and the East Indies, while leading the Americans to feel that only they were in a position to resist Japan, which had been making conquests from China since 1931. Japanese aggression and expansion in Indo-China, where the colonial power was France, helped to trigger American commercial sanctions, specifically an embargo on oil exports that was tantamount to an ultimatum, because, without oil, the Japanese armed forces would grind to a halt; this provoked the Japanese to act against the USA. Unwilling to accept limitations on their expansion in the Far East, they were confident of securing a rapid military advantage and hopeful that the difficulties of driving them back would dissuade the Americans from trying, despite their greater strength to do so. As with Hitler and Britain and France, a conviction of the weakness of the opposing system led to a failure to judge its resolve.

Neither power wanted to fight the other, but the Japanese government and military, although divided, were determined to expand at the expense of others, particularly from 1940 in South-East Asia, which was to Japan 'the southern resources area', and the American government was resolved to prevent them. In October 1941, a hardline ministry under General Tojo gained power and, on 7 December, the Japanese launched a devastating attack on Pearl Harbor, the base of the American Pacific fleet, without any prior declaration of war.

In part angered by American co-operation with the British against German submarine operations in the Atlantic, Hitler then declared war on the USA, in accord, he said with German obligations under the Tripartite Treaty (with Italy and Japan), although, strictly, the terms of the treaty did not require it. This was a crucial step that prevented any chance of the USA fighting only Japan. It let Roosevelt off the hook, since he agreed with Winston Churchill (British Prime Minister and lion of empire 1940–5) that Hitler was a greater menace than the Japanese, but not all American opinion shared this view. Aside from his declaration of war on the USA, Hitler was also foolish in not having earlier encouraged the Japanese to invade the Soviet Union; instead the two powers had signed a neutrality agreement earlier in 1941, enabling the Soviets to concentrate their forces against Germany.

The initial Japanese ability to mount successful attacks and to gain great swathes of territory in the face of weak and poorly led opponents, and to establish an apparent stranglehold on the Far East, did not deter the Americans from the long-term effort of driving them back. The American government and American public opinion was not interested in the idea of a compromise peace with the power that had attacked Pearl Harbor. The lack of a realistic Japanese war plan in part arose from the confusion in Japanese policymaking, with differences between military and civilian politicians and between army and navy interacting with rifts over strategy.

German successes in 1939–41 led to the conquest of Poland, Denmark, Norway, the Netherlands, Luxemburg, Belgium, France, Yugoslavia, Greece and much of the western part of the Soviet Union, but the Germans were to be outfought by the Soviets. By June 1942, the Japanese had overrun the western Pacific and South-East Asia, and the Germans made fresh advances against the Soviets that year, but both powers were defeated in 1942, especially at Midway and Stalingrad, respectively, and the Allies moved over to the offensive. Their insistence on an unconditional surrender and the fanatical nature of Hitler's regime ensured it would be a fight to the finish.

The war, in part, took on the character of attrition, on land, at sea and in the air. The high tempo of campaigning used up resources, but the Allies were able to attack on a number of fronts at once. The Germans were pushed back by the Soviets and, after Anglo-American forces landed in France in 1944, also from the west; Germany was invaded; Hitler committed suicide in Berlin as the Soviets conquered it; and Germany surrendered unconditionally in May 1945. The Japanese were also pushed back in the Pacific and Burma, but the use of the atom bomb by the USA was seen as necessary in order to overcome their suicidal determination to fight on, and to force them to surrender unconditionally, which indeed they did in August 1945.

The war was followed by the occupation of the defeated powers and the reconstruction of their civil societies in accordance with the norms of the victorious. Germany and Austria were partitioned between American, British, French and Soviet occupation zones, while Japan was occupied by the Americans. There were also significant territorial changes, rather than a return to prewar boundaries, with Germany losing territory to Poland and the Soviet Union. Particularly in Eastern Europe, territorial changes were accompanied by major population moves, among the most important of the numerous involuntary migrations of the century. In 1945–6, nine million Germans fled Eastern Europe, particularly from large parts of what had been Germany.

EMPIRE AND THE WAR

The leading colonial powers, Britain and France, were among the victors in World War II, but their empires were largely to have disappeared within two decades, one of the most important shifts of power in global history. The war massively weakened the imperial powers. Two, Italy and Japan, lost their empires, but neither empire was treated as the German and Turkish empires had been at the close of World War I. During World War II, the British occupied both Italian Somaliland and Libya, and Churchill considered the annexation of the latter, but such views now seemed anachronistic. The dominant role in the victorious coalition had been taken by the USA and the USSR both of which, albeit from different perspectives, had anti-colonial ideologies and saw no reason to view the expansion of the European empires with any favour; in fact, they questioned their continued existence. In practice, both the USA and the USSR were imperial, if not colonial, powers and the war strengthened both their systems. Although the Philippines were, as promised, granted independence in 1946, American territorial power in the Pacific increased as a result of gains of Japanese territory, while the Soviet state not only maintained its grip on Siberia, Central Asia, the Caucasus and Mongolia, and made territorial gains on its western frontiers, but now also controlled most of Eastern Europe. In addition, in 1944, the ostensibly independent 'people's republic' of Tannu Tuva, formerly a vassal state of Mongolia, was incorporated into the USSR.

Italy and Japan had lost their empires because of defeat in the war, but other powers, on the winning side, found theirs gravely weakened by the strains of the conflict. In particular, the British, Dutch and French had suffered heavily at the hands of Japan in South-East Asia. The prestige of the British empire in the region was held to be fatally compromised by the humiliating surrender of Singapore in 1942 to the Japanese (a non-white Asian people).

> **THE LEADING COLONIAL POWERS, BRITAIN AND FRANCE, WERE AMONG THE VICTORS IN WORLD WAR II, BUT THEIR EMPIRES WERE LARGELY TO HAVE DISAPPEARED WITHIN TWO DECADES, ONE OF THE MOST IMPORTANT SHIFTS OF POWER IN GLOBAL HISTORY.**

However, alongside the view that Japanese success helped ensure the redundancy of European imperial strategies in Asia, and, crucially, destroyed their prestige, it is also possible to focus on the political and resource costs of the European wars of 1914–45. Britain's decision to abandon its colonial presence in India can be seen as stemming in part from the strains of conflict within the Western system, rather than as simply a response to the war with Japan or to growing indigenous pressure on Britain to 'quit India', as the World War II slogan put it. Shrewd observers at the end of the war might have seen that the end of overseas European empire was in sight, especially as the metropolitan powers were financially exhausted.

Nevertheless, there were still hopes among some in Europe of a recovery of imperial military greatness. Imperial authority was reimposed, and rebellions, for example against the French in Madagascar in 1947–8, were suppressed, or at least confronted. However, there was also a major retreat from empire. The British renounced control over India (1947), which became India and Pakistan, as well as over Burma, Ceylon (now Sri Lanka) and Palestine (1948), and opposition to the reimposition of French rule in Syria was successful in 1945, the country becoming independent the following year.

These bland details conceal major discontinuities. The division of the British empire in South Asia led to an upsurge in communal violence between Hindus and Muslims, with maybe one million killed and another fourteen million fleeing as refugees to the new states of India or Pakistan. The process of independence was determined by earlier identities not only in the shape of religion (Pakistan was essentially where Islam was dominant) but also because the rulers of princely states were allowed to decide on association with India or Pakistan or neither. In the event, the Indian government took over Hyderabad and Junagadh (ignoring the views of the rulers), while in Jammu and Kashmir, where the Hindu maharaja opted for India while the majority of the population were Muslims, the result was a longstanding conflict that still persists. British departure from Palestine was followed by conflict between Jews and Muslims, with the foundation of the state of Israel, largely by Jewish refugees from Europe, leading to another flood of refugees, in this case Arabs.

Returning to Indonesia after the Japanese withdrawal, the Dutch were unable to suppress nationalist resistance in 1947, although, with the support of local allies, they did limit the extent of Java and Sumatra controlled by the nationalists who had declared independence in 1945. American anti-colonial pressure, post-World War II weakness, guerrilla warfare and nationalist determination forced the Dutch to accept Indonesian independence in 1949, and the Indonesians then moved into Dutch Borneo, the Celebes, the Moluccas, the Lesser Sunda Islands and West Timor.

However, both Britain and France were determined to remain imperial powers and were ready to fight to that end. Independence for the Indian sub-continent was intended to provide the means for continued informal control there by Britain. Indeed, the government sent troops to maintain the British presence in the economically crucial colony of Malaya, in the face of a communist insurrection, the Malayan Emergency of 1948–60. Ernest Bevin, Foreign Secretary from 1945 until 1951, hoped to use imperial resources to make Britain a less unequal partner in the Anglo-American alliance. Nevertheless, India had been the most populous and important part of the empire, and the area that most engaged the British imagination. Once India had been granted independence, it was difficult to summon up much British popular interest in the retention of the remainder of the largest empire in the world.

CONCLUSIONS

The most populous areas under imperial control had gained independence in the late 1940s, while, in another major blow for Western interests, the Nationalists, despite American support, were defeated in the Chinese Civil War of 1945–9 by the communists. They proclaimed the People's Republic of China with Mao Zedong (1893–1976) both Chairman of the Chinese Communist Party and President of the Republic. In 1950, China signed a treaty of alliance with the Soviet Union. With India independent, China communist, America overwhelmingly dominant in the world economy as well as the leading global power, the states of Western Europe now with far less room for independent manoeuvre and fascism defeated, the world was set for the situation that was to prevail in the second half of the century.

nine

FALL OF EMPIRES: POLITICS AND WAR 1950—2000

INTRODUCTION

As the new century advances, it becomes increasingly difficult to determine how best to understand the politics of the second half of the twentieth century. For long, this period was understood in terms of the Cold War, the great ideological and 'super-power' stand-off between capitalism and communism, and their leaders, the USA and the Soviet Union, that lasted from the close of World War II in 1945 until the collapse of the Soviet Union in the early 1990s. After that, it was still possible to see the 1990s in terms of the winding down, or consequences, of the Cold War. Now, how-ever, it appears less convincing to structure the second half of the century in these terms and, instead, more necessary to search for new concepts and to reconsider the Cold War in this context.

The Cold War thesis subordinated events elsewhere in the world, especially in the developing world, to the confrontation. That was inappropriate, and it is more helpful to suggest that the developing world should not be seen in terms of such a subordination but, rather, in its own terms. Furthermore, the Cold War can be

THE COLD WAR CAN BE PRESENTED AS BUT A STAGE IN RELATIONS BETWEEN COUNTRIES, AS WELL AS A STAGE IN THE IDEOLOGICAL RIVALRIES OF THE CENTURY.

presented as but a stage in relations between countries, as well as a stage in the ideological rivalries of the century.

DECOLONIZATION

The independence of the developing world was enhanced by decolonization, however much Western influence remained strong, not only in economic and financial terms (see chapter 5), but also with reference to weapons supply. After the burst of decolonization in the late 1940s referred to in the previous chapter, there was, for the early and mid-1950s, a determined attempt to maintain imperial power. Although Britain and France had reduced their global commitments, they were ready to fight for what remained. The biggest effort was made by France. This involved bitter conflicts against nationalist independence movements in Indo-China in 1946–54 and in Algeria in 1954–62. In Indo-China, the Chinese-supplied Viet Minh succeeded in 1954 in defeating the French in position warfare at Dien Bien Phu. This was a forward base developed across Viet Minh supply lines by French parachutists in order to lure the Viet Minh into a major battle. Thanks to their mass infantry attacks, the Viet Minh suffered more casualties, but the isolated French stronghold, denied air support due to artillery bombardment of the airstrip, fell after a fifty-five-day siege.

Despite their superior weaponry, the poorly led French had finally proved unable to defeat their opponents in either guerrilla or conventional warfare, and they abandoned Indo-China in 1954. They were also unsuccessful in Algeria, despite committing considerable resources. French forces in Algeria rose from about 65,000 in late 1954 to 390,000 in 1956, after first reservists and then conscripts were sent. The dispatch of both these groups was unpopular, and greatly increased opposition to the conflict within France. In order to concentrate on Algeria, which had been declared an integral part of France in 1848, the French granted neighbouring Tunisia independence in 1956, although nationalist guerrilla activity there since 1952 had made only limited impact in the towns. The French protectorate in Morocco, where guerrilla activity had become widespread in 1955, also ended in 1956.

Algeria was dominated by a settler population (*colons*) of over a million, and the eight and a half million native Muslims had no real power and suffered discrimination. An insurrection by the *Front de Libération Nationale* (FLN) began in October 1954, but, at first, it was restricted to small-scale terror operations. These destabilized the French relationship with the indigenous Muslims: loyalists were killed, while the French found it difficult to identify their opponents and alienated Muslims by ruthless search-and-destroy operations; relations between *colons* and Muslims also deteriorated. In 1955, the scale of FLN operations increased, and the war hotted up with massacres, reprisals and a commitment by the French to a more rigorous approach. This also led to more effective French tactics. Static garrisons were complemented by pursuit groups, often moved by helicopter.

In some respects, the Algerian war prefigured that in Vietnam involving the Americans. The FLN was badly damaged in 1959, just as the Viet Cong was to be in 1968, but the continued existence of both created pressure for a political solution. This helped to set General de Gaulle, who had formed a government in 1958 and become President of France at the close of the year, against the *colons* and much of the military leadership in Algeria who were against negotiations with the FLN. In 1960, the *colons* tried to seize power in Algiers, but were faced down by de Gaulle. In early 1961, de Gaulle ordered a truce with the FLN, and an attempt by some of the army to seize power in Algeria was unsuccessful. The *Organisation Armée Secrète* then began a terror campaign against both the Gaullists and Muslims. The resulting three-part struggle of the government, the OAS and the FLN led to extensive slaughter in 1962 as independence neared. The agreement with the FLN promised security for the *colons*, but most chose to flee to France.

A summary of this conflict illustrates the general difficulty of mounting effective counter-insurgency operations. Tough anti-insurrectionary measures, including torture, which was seen as a justified response to FLN atrocities, gave the French control of Algiers in 1957. However, although undefeated in battle, the French were unable to end guerrilla action in what was a very costly struggle. And French moves were often counter-productive in winning the loyalty of the bulk of the population: 'hearts and minds', as it was later called in Vietnam. Aside from the difficulty of operating active counter-insurgency policies, there was also a need to tie up large numbers of troops in protecting settlers and in trying to close the frontiers to guerrilla reinforcements.

Although it is easy to see the failure of the French as a failure of colonialism, the FLN-ruled state also failed to preserve peace, proving unable to meet popular expectations and being perceived as corrupt and Westernized. Thus, in 1992, Algeria returned to civil conflict. The fundamentalist Islamic terrorists of the *Front Islamique du Salut* (FIS) destabilized the state by widespread, brutal terror, and the government adopted the earlier techniques of the French, including helicopter-borne pursuit groups, large-scale sweep-and-search operations and the use of terror as a reprisal.

The intractable nature of this conflict, which is still continuing, suggests that it is misleading to see Western military and political structures and methods as at fault in the failures of counter-insurgency operations in the 1950s and 1960s. It is also appropriate to note successes, as with the British suppression of the Mau-Mau uprising in Kenya in 1952–6. In this, the British benefited from a wide-ranging social reform policy, including land reform, in which the government distanced itself from the white colonists, and made successful use of loyal Africans, including former insurgents, and also of air-supported forest patrols and larger-scale sweep operations.

Nevertheless, support within Britain for imperialism had fallen. In 1956, the weakness of the imperial response and the limited domestic popularity of empire were exposed in the Suez crisis. Britain and France attacked Egypt, an intervention publicly justified as a way of safeguarding the Suez Canal, which had been nationalized by the aggressive Egyptian leader Gamal Abdel Nasser. His Arab nationalism was also seen as a threat to the French position in Algeria and to Britain's Arab allies. The invasion was poorly planned, but it was abandoned, in large part, because of American opposition. Concerned about the impact of the invasion on attitudes in the Third World, the Americans, who were ambivalent about many aspects of British policy, refused to extend any credits to support sterling, blocked Britain's access to the International Monetary Fund until it withdrew its troops from Suez, and refused to provide oil to compensate for interrupted supplies from the Middle East. American opposition underlined the vulnerability of the British economy, was crucial in weakening British resolve, and led to a humiliating withdrawal. It can be seen as the end of Britain's ability to act wholly independently; from then on, there was an implicit reliance on American acceptance, as with the British recapture of the Falkland Islands after the Argentinians seized them in 1982.

The Suez crisis and the overthrow of the pro-British Iraqi government in 1958 revealed the limitations of British strength. This encouraged a new attitude towards imperial rule in Britain, which still had the largest empire. There was rapid decolonization, especially in Africa, but also in the West Indies and Malaysia. Decolonization was hastened by a strong upsurge in colonial nationalist movements, particularly in Ghana in West Africa, which policy-makers did not know how to confront, as they sought to rest imperial rule on consent, not force. Decolonization proceeded on the simple assumption that Britain would withdraw from those areas that it could no longer control (or, equally importantly, from those areas where the cost of maintaining a presence was prohibitive). Colonies also appeared less necessary in defence terms, not least because Britain had in 1957 added the hydrogen bomb to the atom bomb. The American government encouraged decolonization, and also sought to manage it as a means of increasing informal American control. Within Europe, particularly in Britain, imperial roles seemed redundant, and were replaced by pressure for social welfare in order to secure a 'better' society.

Although criticized by some right-wing Conservatives, decolonization was not a central issue in British politics. In part, this was because the empire was seen as being transformed into the Commonwealth, rather than lost. The British view of empire was important. The logic of Britain's self-proclaimed imperial mission, bringing civilization to backward areas of the globe, allowed it to present the granting of self-government as the inevitable terminus of empire. The contraction of empire was also relatively painless, because interest in much of it was limited.

> **THE LOGIC OF BRITAIN'S SELF-PROCLAIMED IMPERIAL MISSION, BRINGING CIVILIZATION TO BACKWARD AREAS OF THE GLOBE, ALLOWED IT TO PRESENT THE GRANTING OF SELF-GOVERNMENT AS THE INEVITABLE TERMINUS OF EMPIRE.**

Independence was granted to Ghana and Malaya in 1957, Nigeria and Cyprus in 1960, Sierra Leone and Tanganyika in 1961, Jamaica and Uganda in 1962 and Kenya in 1963. The Labour government of Harold Wilson (Prime Minister 1964–70), decided to abandon Britain's military position 'east of Suez' and to focus defence priorities on Western Europe. British forces were withdrawn from Aden in 1967, the Persian Gulf in 1971 and Singapore in 1974 (they had been much scaled down there in 1971). This reflected both serious British economic problems and a political decision for a more modest imperial reach and a different international stance.

In 1960, France had granted independence to most of its African possessions, although it did not withdraw from its last African territory, Djibouti, until 1977, and was to maintain considerable political, economic and military influence in the continent. Defence and military co-operation agreements were the basis for a system of military advisers, and the French also secured their influence by military intervention.

Other empires also crumbled. Belgium abandoned the Belgian Congo in 1960. The major effort to retain a colonial empire after the French withdrew from Algeria was made by Portugal. Guerrilla movements in Portugal's colonies began in Angola in 1961, Guinea-Bissau in 1963 and Mozambique in 1964. The Portuguese, however, benefited from divisions among their opponents, especially between the MPLA and UNITA in Angola, from the support of the white-rule apartheid government of South

Africa, and from their weaponry, including tactical air support and helicopters. Napalm and aggressive herbicides were also used. The Portuguese were able to retain control of the towns, for example crushing a rising in Luanda, the leading city in Angola, in 1961; but found it impossible to suppress rural opposition. In addition, their opponents could operate from neighbouring states. Guerrillas moved from attacks on border villages to a more extensive guerrilla war that sought to win popular support and to develop liberated rural areas. Nevertheless, the Portuguese were still able to control many key rural areas, especially the central highlands of Angola. Until 1974, the 70,000-strong Portuguese army in Angola, supported by secret police, paramilitary forces, settler vigilantes and African informers, effectively restricted guerrilla operations there and, more generally, protected the 350,000 white settlers in the colony. However, a left-wing revolution in Portugal in April 1974, which owed much to military dissatisfaction with the war and to popular hostility to military service, led to the granting of independence to the colonies the following year. In 1975, the long-standing Spanish dictator, Franco, died, and, with him, the dictatorship came to an end. This was followed by withdrawal from the Spanish Sahara the following year.

Opposition to imperial rule in Africa looked back to earlier resistance to the imposition of imperial rule, but post-1945 mass nationalism was also affected by political movements current in the period, not least socialism. Indeed, it is possible to trace a development in postwar decolonization struggles, with a growing politicization in terms of more 'modern' political ideologies, as well as their location in the Cold War. This was particularly the case in Africa from the mid-1960s. Some earlier risings, such as the Mau-Mau and that in northern Angola among the Bakongo, showed many facets of old-style peasant uprisings or militant tribal identity. Although these elements still played a part, the risings from the mid-1960s were more explicitly located in a different ideological context, that of revolutionary socialism. There was direct reference to the Mao Zedong principles of revolutionary war, as well as training by foreign advisers, especially from the Soviet Union and China, and a provision of more advanced weapons, although many did not arrive in any quantity until the early 1970s. This provision was an important example of the interaction of different parts of the world. Anti-personnel and anti-vehicle mines restricted the mobility of counter-insurgency forces on land and Soviet SAM-7 missiles hit their low-flying aircraft and helicopters. This was an aspect of the rapid action/reaction cycle in which technology and industrial production responded to new challenges, in both war and peace.

The impact of these shifts could be seen in Portuguese Africa. In Angola, the MPLA's military wing, the EPLA, received weaponry and training from communist powers, including Cuba, and sought to follow Maoist principles, although the Portuguese were able to inflict heavy casualties on them. The sense of a wider struggle was captured in the name of two forward bases, Hanoi I and II: Hanoi was the capital of communist North Vietnam. Also in Angola, the FNLA received Chinese weaponry. In Mozambique, FRELIMO was steadily able to widen its sphere of operations. A wider economic strategy was seen in operations from 1968 against the Cabora Bassa dam project on the Zambezi, a project that linked South Africa to Portugal, and a reminder that the infrastructural and other changes through which humanity moulded the environment (see chapters 1 and 2) had specific political causes and consequences, as well as reflecting a more general ideology of improvement through human action.

Militarily, Soviet and Chinese rocket launchers, and, from 1974, SAM-7 anti-aircraft missiles shifted the balance of military advantage in Mozambique, and it was clear that Portugal could not win. In Guinea-Bissau, PAIGC had SAM-7 missiles from 1973, and Cuban instructors. The missiles challenged Portuguese air superiority and powerfully contributed to a sense that the Portuguese had lost the initiative. Although the Portuguese were reasonably successful in Angola, failure elsewhere sapped support for the war in the army and in Portugal.

In part, the struggles of decolonization can therefore be located in the Cold War. The same was also true of the struggle to overthrow the independent 'white'-ruled states in southern Africa: South Africa and Southern Rhodesia (now Zimbabwe). Independence groups drew support from communist powers, although the overthrow of white rule in South Africa and of the discriminatory apartheid system occurred after the end of the Cold War. It reflected, instead, the domestic instability that stemmed from opposition to apartheid, the economic burdens of sanctions imposed by the USA and the European Union, and the belief among important elements of the white population that it was necessary to achieve progress through reform, the last a situation analogous to that of the Soviet Union under Gorbachev. In 1980, black majority rule was established in Zimbabwe, and, in 1990, South African troops withdrew from South West Africa (now Namibia) and it became an independent state. In South Africa, banned opposition parties were legalized in 1990, a multi-racial Executive Council gained power in 1991, and in 1994, elections held under universal franchise led to victory by the African National Congress.

POST-COLONIAL GOVERNMENT AND WARFARE

However, across much of the world decolonization was not followed by a stable democracy, as in South Africa. For example, in Pakistan, the military, under General

Ayub Khan, seized power in 1958, creating a government only replaced by another coup in 1969. Defeat by India in 1971 led to the return to civilian rule, but, in 1977, another coup put General Zia ul-Haw in control. He retained it until killed in 1988 in an air crash, probably caused by a bomb. The army seized power again in 1999 under General Pervez Musharraf. This was not the sum total of military intervention in Pakistan, as army support for 'constitutional coups' was also crucial, for example in 1993.

In Africa, the list of coups included Egypt (1952 and 1954), Sudan (1958, 1985, 1989), Togo (1963), Zanzibar (1964), Congo (1965), Nigeria (1966), Ghana (1966, 1972, 1978, 1979), Sierra Leone (1967 and 1997), Mali (1968), Libya (1969), Uganda (1971, 1980, 1985, 1986), Madagascar (1972), Ethiopia (1974), the Central African Republic (1979 and 1981), Equatorial Guinea (1979), Liberia (1980), Upper Volta (1982), Nigeria (1985), Lesotho (1986), Chad (1991) and the Ivory Coast (1999). There were also a whole series of attempted coups, including Gabon (1964), Gambia (1981), Uganda (1982), Nigeria (1990), the Ivory Coast (2000) and the Central African Republic (2001).

Force was also used to maintain the cohesion of new states, suppressing regional separatism. For example, in Burma a series of challenges led to a serious civil war in 1948–55. In 1959, the Moroccan army crushed a revolt by the Berbers in the Rif mountains, and, in 1967–70, Nigeria defeated the attempt by the Ibo minority to create a state of Biafra. In Iraq, force was used in the 1990s to suppress both the Kurds and the Marsh Arabs. Southern secessionism in the Yemen was crushed in 1994, while, in 1998, the Tajik army suppressed a rebellion in the Khojand region of Tajikistan where many Uzbek-speakers lived.

In many states, force became the normal means of politics. For example, in Syria, where the Baath party seized power in a coup in 1963, the military was used to suppress revolts in the late 1970s and the early 1980s. Post-colonial states frequently lacked any practice of tolerance towards groups and regions that were outside the state hierarchy. In turn, the use of state power encouraged a violent response.

IN MANY STATES, FORCE BECAME THE NORMAL MEANS OF POLITICS.

In addition, as colonial rule receded, there was a series of conflicts between states. Whether peaceful or not, decolonization immediately led to new international frontiers (where hitherto borders had often separated territories of the same colonial power) and to disputes. It also ensured that earlier disputes that would have been limited by the strength and influence of the imperial powers, whether as participants or as arbiters, became more urgent. This led, for example, to war between Britain and Argentina over the Falkland Islands in 1982, with an Argentine invasion eventually totally defeated, while in 1974 a Turkish invasion led to the creation of the Turkish Republic of North Cyprus.

Although direct European political control in the world receded, other than in North Asia, where the Russians remained in control of Siberia, European notions of territoriality had been assumed and internalized by non-Europeans, and colonial divisions of peoples were maintained. For example, the Anglo-French Treaty of 1898, which divided Hausaland, was maintained as the boundary between Niger and Nigeria, and the impact of colonialism continued to be felt in local government, education and economic practice. The Hausa became defined by the impact of a frontier that was no longer alien. Demarcation involved the imperial power, or powers seeking to enforce their authority, in poorly mapped and difficult terrain, as with the Sudan–Uganda and Nigeria–Cameroon Boundary Commissions in 1912–13. Most of the frontier lines drawn paid no attention to local identities, interests and views, and this led to much subsequent criticism: the practices of European imperialism were blamed for post-colonial ethnic conflict in Africa. More generally, the different values that were frequently advanced in neighbouring states ensured that frontiers could also mark important psychological boundaries.

Many state boundaries are relatively recent: under 150 years old. Boundaries were generally more stable in the second half of the twentieth century than in the first half, because decolonization proved less disruptive of frontiers than colonization and conflict between the European powers had been. However, decolonization did lead to some major conflicts. In South Asia, the end of British rule led to wars between India and Pakistan (1965 and 1971). In Africa, in order to seize control of the Spanish Sahara in 1975, Morocco staged a 'Green March' that led eventually to large-scale settlement that was unsuccessfully resisted by the Polisario guerrillas in a war that continued until 1991. Over 100,000 Saharawis had fled Moroccan rule. Tanzania invaded Uganda in 1979, and, in 1997, Rwanda helped overthrow President Mobutu of Congo. Subsequently, a major war broke out there with Angola, Namibia, Rwanda, Uganda and Zimbabwe all sending troops.

In the Middle East, there was a series of wars between Israel and Arab neighbours (1948–9, 1956, 1967, 1973 and 1982). The Arabs proved unwilling to accept the culmination of the Zionist movement in the form of an independent Israel, and this ensured a high level of tension in the region. Israel was able to establish its independence in the face of attacks by neighbouring Arab states in 1948–9. In 1956, Israel attacked Egypt in concert with Britain and France, overrunning the Sinai Peninsula, but withdrew in the face of American and Soviet pressure. In 1967, rising regional tension led to a pre-emptive Israeli attack on Egypt and, as the war spread, to the conquest not only of the Sinai but also of the West Bank section of Jordan and the Golan Heights in Syria. Israel remained in occupation of these regions, ensuring that it now controlled a large Arab population, while over 600,000 Arab refugees were based in neighbouring Arab states, where they challenged the stability of Jordan and helped overthrow that of an already divided Lebanon, which moved into full-scale civil war from 1975. In the long term, the presence of a large Arab population within Israel and in Israeli-occupied territories was to challenge the stability of a state that (in very difficult circumstances) proved unable to move beyond a Zionist rationale and was also affected by growing Jewish fundamentalism.

Meanwhile, in 1973, in the Yom Kippur War, Egypt and Syria failed, in a surprise attack, to drive Israel from its conquests. The USA tried to ease regional pressures, which threatened the world economy because of the concentration there of oil production and reserves (see chapter 5), and helped arrange a peace settlement between Egypt and Israel (1979). However, Israel's determination to act as a regional power and its concern about instability on its borders led to its invasion of southern Lebanon in 1978; Syria had occupied much of the country in 1976. In 1982, the Israelis occupied southern Lebanon, advancing as far as Beirut, but it proved impossible to 'stabilize' the situation there in Israel's interests. The Israelis had to withdraw from the bulk of Lebanon (1985) and eventually to abandon the Security Zone established along the frontier with Israel. In 1987, the Intifada, a rebellion against Israeli rule in occupied Arab territories, began. It was to underline the weakness of imposed political settlements in the Middle East if the bulk of the population felt alienated. The creation in 1993 of a Palestinian autonomous territory under Yasser Arafat failed to prevent an increased escalation of conflict from the late 1990s.

It would be misleading, however, to suggest that force and dictatorship supplied the post-colonial history of the developing world. The largest state, India, maintained the democratic system established at independence, albeit not without difficulties. Moreover, authoritarian regimes, such as Malaysia under Mahathir Mohammad of the United Malay Organization, who ran the country from 1981, often did so as a hybrid political form that included aspects of democracy and the rule of law.

The Cold War played a major role in politics and conflict in the developing world, but assumed a more central role in the developed world. Its origins rested in the revival of ideological and geopolitical tensions in the closing stages of World War II. Wartime alliances frequently do not survive peace. This was particularly true of World War II because of the ideological division between the USSR and the Western powers. Arguably, the alliance did not survive the war itself: by 1944 differences over the fate of Eastern Europe were readily apparent, particularly over Poland, which Stalin was determined to dominate.

The subsequent Cold War was not a formal or frontal conflict, but a period of sustained hostility involving a protracted arms race, as well as numerous proxy conflicts in which the major powers intervened in other struggles. The latter sustained attitudes of animosity, exacerbated fears and contributed to a high level of military preparedness. Just as nineteenth-century theorists of international relations had focused on conflict, so their Cold War successors concentrated on confrontation rather than conciliation, affecting both the public, and political and military leaders.

A feeling of uncertainty on both sides, of the fragility of military strength, international links, political orders and ideological convictions, encouraged a sense of threat, and fuelled an arms race that was to be central to the Cold War. Indeed, in many respects, the arms race *was* the Cold War. Both sides claimed to be strong, but declared that they required an edge to be secure: this was the inherent instability of an arms race, where only the Mutually Assured Destruction (MAD) threatened by massive

IN MANY RESPECTS, THE ARMS RACE *WAS* THE COLD WAR.

nuclear stockpiles eventually brought a measure of stability. The USA and the Soviet Union competed to produce and deploy more and better weapons.

The Soviet Union initially lacked the atom bomb, but its army was well placed to overrun Western Europe and could only have been stopped by the West's desperate use of nuclear weapons. Ideologically and culturally, in 1945 each side felt threatened by the other. The American offer of Marshall Aid to help recovery after World War II was rejected by the Soviet Union as a form of economic imperialism, and this created a new boundary line between the areas that received such aid and those that did not. The Soviet abandonment of co-operation over occupied Germany and the imposition of one-party communist governments in Eastern Europe, which culminated with the communist coup in Prague in 1948, led to pressure for a Western response. Soviet actions appeared to vindicate Churchill's claim in March 1946 that an 'Iron Curtain' was descending from the Baltic to the Adriatic. Force played an important role in the imposition of communist control. Thus, King Michael of Romania was forced to abdicate after the palace in Bucharest was surrounded at the close of 1947 by troops of the Romanian division raised in the Soviet Union.

The war had been followed by the creation of occupation zones in Germany and Austria. The *de facto* partition of Germany between the Soviets and the Western Powers ensured that Germany played a central role in the Cold War. Before the death of Hitler there had already been fighting in Greece. German evacuation in 1944 led to an accentuation of conflict between left- and right-wing guerrilla groups, and then, in order to thwart a left-wing take-over, to military intervention by the British on behalf of the right. Having arrived in October, the British were fighting the communist National Popular Liberation Army (ELAS) on behalf of the returned exile government two months later. Attempts to reach a compromise failed, leading to a second stage of the war in 1946–9, which was eventually won by the right.

Growing tension represented a failure of the hopes that it would be possible to use the United Nations, the body that replaced the League of Nations, to ensure a new peaceful world order. In 1943, the USA, the Soviet Union, Britain and (Nationalist) China had agreed the Moscow Declaration on General Security, including the establishment of 'a general international organization, based on the principle of sovereign equality'. The resulting United Nations was established in 1945, but it proved the setting, not the solution, for growing East–West tensions.

After World War II, there was interest in the idea of a Western European Third Force independent of the USA and the USSR, and Britain and France signed the Treaty of Dunkirk in 1947, but, in response to fears about Soviet plans, an American alliance appeared essential. In February 1947, the British acknowledged that they could no longer provide the military and economic aid deemed necessary to keep Greece and Turkey out of communist hands. Instead, the British successfully sought American intervention. Similarly, in 1949, the British encouraged the Americans to become involved in resisting communist expansion in South-East Asia: the French were under pressure in Indo-China, the British in Malaya.

Concerned about communism, the Americans did not intend to repeat their interwar isolationism; they had not responded to the expansion of Nazi Germany. The American economy had expanded greatly, both in absolute and in relative terms, during the war and it had the manufacturing capacity, organizational capability and

financial resources to meet the costs of postwar military commitments. The Berlin Crisis of 1948, in which the Soviets blockaded West Berlin, led to the stationing of American B-29 strategic bombers in Britain. In the event of war, they were intended to bomb the Soviet Union. The threat of the use of the atom bomb helped bring a solution to the crisis.

In 1949, the foundation of the North Atlantic Treaty Organization (NATO) created a security framework for Western Europe. The USA abandoned its tradition of isolationism, played a crucial role in the formation of the new alliance and was anchored to the defence of Western Europe. An analysis of World War II that attributed the war and Hitler's initial successes to appeasement led to a determination to contain the Soviet Union. The establishment of NATO was followed by the creation of a military structure, including a central command, and, eventually, by German rearmament.

The Korean War (1950–3), in which the Western powers intervened under the authority of the United Nations to prevent communist North Korea from taking over South Korea, led to a major increase in Western military spending, most heavily in the USA, but also important among its allies. Thus, in Canada, which sent troops to Korea and played an active role in NATO, defence spending rose from $196 million in 1947 to $1.5 billion in 1951. Under American pressure, Britain embarked in 1950 on a costly rearmament programme that undid recent economic gains and strengthened the military commitment that was to be such a heavy postwar economic burden. Having driven the North Koreans from South Korea, the Allies invaded the North, only to be driven back when the Chinese intervened. The conflict settled down into an impasse with front lines half-way up the peninsula.

By the early 1950s, the requirement and strategy for atomic defence and war in Europe were in place: the American forces there had to be protected. A clear front line was also in place across Europe. NATO and the Soviet-led Warsaw Pact prepared and planned for conflict throughout the rest of the period. There were variations in the intensity of confrontation. The Soviets came close to attacking in the early 1950s, but Stalin's death in 1953 led to a lessening of hostility. Yet, even when international tensions eased, there remained an uncertainty and a sense that the other bloc was seeking to take advantage. The Americans failed to appreciate the depth of Soviet economic problems. *Détente* between East and West, when it occurred, was a matter not of the end of the Cold War, but of its conduct at a lower level of tension. Furthermore, the front line in Asia, particularly in South-East Asia and the Middle East, was less fixed, and this kept tension high.

Soviet willingness to use force to maintain its interests within its own bloc, most prominently by invading Hungary in 1956 and Czechoslovakia in 1968, and suppressing reformist governments and popular movements in both, also helped to maintain tension. These invasions underlined the ideological nature of the Cold War: it was more than a confrontation between major states with differing political systems. The character of these systems was a crucial issue. In the communist countries, terror and force were routinely used to maintain control and implement policies. Like other totalitarian regimes, Stalinism worked in part by creating an all-pervasive sense of surveillance and fear. It was a regime that was felt but could not be seen or located: prison camps existed, but few knew their location or extent. Terror worked on ignorance, on the ungraspable nature and undefined scope of the arbitrary power of the oppressor. For this reason, communist states controlled information and made major efforts to block radio transmissions from the West. Terror regimes were also created in states brought under Soviet control, for example in Hungary from 1947. Secret police forces, such as the KGB in the Soviet Union and the AVO in Hungary, routinely used torture. In Czechoslovakia, the suppression of the reform movement in 1968 was followed by the reimposition of a police state, while agriculture was collectivized.

STALINISM WAS A REGIME THAT WAS FELT BUT COULD NOT BE SEEN OR LOCATED: PRISON CAMPS EXISTED, BUT FEW KNEW THEIR LOCATION OR EXTENT.

There were major social inequalities in the West and some American client states, especially in Latin America, were brutal dictatorships, but the leading Western states – the USA, Japan and the states of Western Europe – were democracies in which the rule of law operated and in which government was generally (but not always) constrained by the political process.

Overhanging all else was the nuclear deterrent. America's nuclear monopoly had lasted only until 1949, when the Soviet Union completed its development of an effective bomb. This had required a formidable effort, as the Soviet Union was devastated by the impact of World War II, and it was pursued because Stalin believed that only a position of nuclear equivalence would permit it to protect and advance its interests. However, such a policy was ruinous financially, harmful to the economy, as it led to the distortion of research and investment choices, and militarily dangerous, as resources were used that might otherwise have developed conventional capability. Although the communist regimes that followed Stalin, after he died in 1953, introduced changes in some aspects of policy, they did not break free of his legacy of nuclear competition. Britain, France and China followed with their own atomic bombs in 1952, 1960 and 1964, respectively.

In 1957, the Soviet Union launched Sputnik I, the first satellite, into orbit. This revealed a capability for intercontinental rockets that brought the entire world within striking range, and thus made the USA vulnerable to Soviet attack. The strategic possibilities offered by nuclear-tipped long-range ballistic missiles made investment in expensive rocket technology seem an essential course of action since they could go so much faster and, unlike planes, could not be shot down.

In 1965, Robert McNamara, the American Secretary of Defence, felt able to state that the USA could rely on the threat of 'assured destruction' to deter a Soviet assault. That did not prevent further attempts by the nuclear powers to enhance their nuclear attack and defence capabilities. In 1970, the Americans deployed Minuteman III missiles equipped with MIRVs (multiple independently targeted re-entry vehicles), thus ensuring that the strike capacity of an individual rocket was greatly enhanced. As a consequence, warhead numbers, and thus the potential destructiveness of a nuclear exchange, rose greatly.

The Cold War led to a new cartography that focused on the confrontation between America and the communist world. This approach was expressed in terms of containment and confrontation, themes most vividly illustrated by different map perspectives. Confrontation was demonstrated by maps centred on the North Pole, a suitable image for a world in which inter-continental missiles offered a crucial projection of power. Such maps served to demonstrate the apparent threat to the USA posed by a Soviet Union that was closer over the North Pole than across the Atlantic.

The fact that atomic weaponry has not been used since 1945 is a product of a balance of deterrence, concern about domestic and foreign opinion, the realization of the environmental damage they would cause and the degree to which the range of rocket-delivery systems has left no areas immune from attack. The latter, in turn, increased tension about the military plans of often distant powers, while attention was also focused on the deployment of rockets. Particularly in the 1990s, concern arose over the possible behaviour of so-called 'rogue states', such as Iraq and North Korea, that might get their hands on nuclear or biological weaponry, and in the early 2000s there was concern likewise about terrorist networks.

In the early 1960s, anxieties about the nuclear balance encouraged John F. Kennedy (US President 1961–3) to aim for a strategic superiority, and Nikita Khrushchev (First Secretary of the Soviet Communist Party, 1953–64) to decide to deploy missiles in Cuba, thus bringing the world close to nuclear war. In 1962, the Americans considered an attack on Cuba, and imposed an air and naval quarantine to prevent the shipping of further supplies. Kennedy also threatened a full retaliatory nuclear strike. The Soviet Union agreed to remove the missiles, but the gap between decision, use and strike had been shown to be perilously small. The world had for a while teetered on the edge of a nuclear holocaust.

In Europe, on the front line of the Cold War, where the armed forces of the two competing blocs were concentrated, the military had both to prepare for war and to play a major role in deterring attack. This led to a confrontation that continued until the collapse of Soviet Europe and the unification of Germany in 1990.

Meanwhile, political structures had changed, but in a very uneven fashion. The states that had been defeated in the war (Germany and Japan especially; Italy and France to a lesser extent) experienced political and institutional change, while their badly damaged economies were rebuilt. In contrast, the victors (the Soviet Union, the USA and Britain) essentially maintained their political structures. Nationalization and the creation or development of a social welfare and 'dependency' culture, the 'welfare state', in Britain, the latter stages of New Deal liberalism in the United States and the bureaucratic and economic centralization that contributed to characterize the later years of Stalin's rule all brought major changes, but they did not equal those in Japan, Continental Europe and China. During the American occupation of Japan (1945–52), the political structure of the state was transformed, most obviously with a new constitution (1946) and land-reform (1946–50). In Eastern Europe, the destruction of earlier political structures during World War II, and the subsequent establishment of Soviet hegemony and communist rule, cleared the way for COMECON (the Communist Economic Co-operation Organization, 1949) and the Warsaw Pact (1955), bodies dominated by the Soviet Union. The political structures of Italy, West Germany and France were transformed between 1945 and 1958, and a supranational body, the European Economic Community (later the European Community and, subsequently, the European Union), which covered much of Western Europe, was created in 1958 as a result of the Treaty of Rome of 1957. Different political and economic models in the two halves of Europe were an important consequence of the Cold War.

By the mid-1980s, when pressure for change became dominant in Soviet governmental circles, the Cold War had been clearly lost by the Soviet Union. This was less clear in the mid-1970s, as the Western colonial empires finally crumbled and as the Vietnam conflict closed with the fall of Saigon, the capital of South Vietnam, to the communists in 1975. The Americans had intervened in South Vietnam in the early 1960s to thwart a communist rebellion by the Viet Cong supported by communist North Vietnam, and by January 1969 had 541,000 troops there. However, unable to defeat their opponents and faced by mounting domestic criticism, the Americans withdrew in 1973. American action in Vietnam helped maintain Cold War tensions in the 1960s and early 1970s. It also played a major role in destabilizing the rest of Indo-China as American-led and communist forces competed for control of Cambodia and Laos. The Soviet Union was not to have its Vietnam until 1979–89 when Soviet intervention failed to sustain client communist regimes in Afghanistan in the face of American-supported popular opposition that drew on Islamic fervour and tribalism.

In the mid-1970s, the economic strength of the West seemed compromised by the economic strains following the oil price hike after the 1973 Arab–Israel war (see chapter 5). Simultaneously, the West appeared to be suffering from poor leadership. The Watergate scandal in the USA had led not only to the fall of President Nixon in 1974, but also to a crisis of confidence in American leadership. Nixon's paranoid response to opposition was in truth more a personality problem than a sign of breakdown in the American political system, but that was unclear to many contemporaries. Of the other Western powers, Britain was faced by a political crisis in 1974 linked to a miners' strike, and then by a more general crisis in the mid-1970s, as high inflation and trade union power contributed to an acute sense of malaise and weakness, while the stability of France had been challenged by major popular demonstrations in Paris in 1968. Germany faced terrorism from the anarchist Baadar–Meinhof Group, as part of a widespread wave of terrorism throughout the West.

These problems for the West were not registered in a major world conflict, although the Cold War heated up in Angola in 1975 with the USA supplying anti-communist forces in the civil war there. Instead, the mid-1970s saw a number of treaties, especially the Helsinki Treaty of 1975, that, in recognizing the position and interests of the Eastern bloc, appeared to consolidate its position and stabilize the Cold War. This *détente* was not the irritable harmony of allies, but a truce between rivals, and, insofar as it suggested that the Cold War was less intense, it did not do so by marking any victory of the West. Instead, it seemed that both East and West still had all to play for in a world adapting to the end of the European colonial empires. In 1979, when the Soviet Union invaded Afghanistan, it seemed at the peak of its power.

IN 1979, WHEN THE SOVIET UNION INVADED AFGHANISTAN, IT SEEMED AT THE PEAK OF ITS POWER.

The West, however, adjusted to the economic challenges of the last four decades of the century with far less difficulty than did the communist states, and shaped the opportunities far more successfully. In the 1930s, the crisis of the capitalist model had helped produce a new authoritarianism in the shape of Nazi Germany and other states characterized by populism, corporatism and autarky. In contrast, in the 1970s, early 1980s and early 1990s, widespread fiscal problems and unemployment, linked to globalist pressures, led either to the panacea of social welfare or to democratic conservative governments (particularly in Britain under Margaret Thatcher, 1979–90, and the USA under Ronald Reagan, 1981–9 and George Bush 1989–93) that sought to 'roll back the state' and that pursued liberal economic policies, opening their market and freeing currency movements and credit from most restrictions. The economic crises did not lead to authoritarian regimes or to governmental direction of national resources. Economic difficulties led to a rise of far-right political parties, for example in Austria, France and West Germany, but neither they nor the radical left were able to seize power.

Furthermore, in geopolitical terms, the West greatly improved its position as a consequence of its exploitation of the split in the communist bloc between China and the Soviet Union, which had become overt in 1960. In 1972, President Nixon of the USA opened relations with China, which had overcome a recent period of severe instability. In 1968–9, in response to the growing volatility of the Cultural Revolution, the army restored order and enforced Mao Zedong's control, and this military role was only slackened in 1971. Although not without many difficulties, closer relations with China gave the USA a vital advantage in the Cold War. So also did the resilience of the American economy and the ability of the Reagan government in the 1980s to use the state's capacity to raise money in the bond market in order to mobilize American resources for a military build-up that the Soviets could not match. They lacked the money, and could not raise the credit.

THE FALL OF COMMUNISM

The collapse of communism led to very different outcomes. In Eastern Europe and the Soviet Union, Russian/Soviet control and the domestic monopoly wielded by the Communist Party ended together. In contrast, in the Far East, communism remained more resilient as a monopolistic political force. In China, the China Democracy Party was destroyed in the 1990s, and rebellions in Xinjiang were crushed in 1990 and 1997. Tibet was kept under control, but in China, and, to a lesser extent, Vietnam, there was a major opening to free-market economies. In contrast, North Korea witnessed no economic liberalization.

The shift in Eastern Europe and the Soviet Union was unexpected, as Mikhail Gorbachev, who became Soviet leader in 1985, sought to modernize communism by introducing reforms, rather than to overthrow it. The communist command economies were in serious problems by the mid-1980s, and earlier attempts to reform them proved flawed. *Détente* had led to Western loans, but these had not been translated into economic take-off, and had, instead, increased indebtedness. Economic problems limited the funds available for social investment and consumer spending, and this increasingly compromised popular support for the system. Alongside a rise in political opposition, especially the Solidarity movement in Poland, there was a widespread privatization of commitment on the individual and household level that left government and the Communist Party in a vacuum. Boris Yeltsin, President of the Russian Federation 1990–2000, remarked that trying to mix communism and a free market was like trying to mate a hedgehog with a snake.

> **BORIS YELTSIN REMARKED THAT TRYING TO MIX COMMUNISM AND A FREE MARKET WAS LIKE TRYING TO MATE A HEDGEHOG WITH A SNAKE.**

In the Soviet Union, economic reform led to political change, while Gorbachev's attempts to push through modernization in Eastern Europe left the governments weak in the face of a popular demand for reform. This led to the successive collapse of communist regimes in Eastern Europe in 1989, and to multi-party politics and free elections. In 1990, East was reunited with West Germany, while in 1991 the Soviet Union was dissolved as the former republics, such as Ukraine, gained independence. An attempted coup in August 1991 to end democracy in Russia was foiled by popular pressure and bold leadership by Yeltsin. Other long-established non-communist political orders also fell in this period. In 1993, Japan's Liberal Democrats lost overall power for the first time in nearly forty years. In 2000, the Institutional Revolutionary Party, which had ruled democratic Mexico for seven decades, was ousted after elections.

The Chinese government proved more adept at managing the strains of change, although it was helped by a rapid rate of economic growth, which was not seen in the Soviet Union. Those in China who pressed for more rapid change were crushed, with the brutal suppression of a pro-democracy movement in Beijing in 1989. There was also no recurrence of the fracturing of the military on regional grounds seen in the warlord era of the 1920s.

THE RESHAPING OF POLITICS IN THE 1990S

The change in Soviet power and politics had a major effect on international relations elsewhere. The Western powers, led by the USA, were able to intervene decisively against states that would otherwise have looked for Soviet support. Thus, in 1991, a

Western-led coalition drove Iraq from Kuwait, which it had invaded the previous year, while, in the former Yugoslavia, Western settlements were imposed in Bosnia in 1995 and in Kosovo in 1999 at the expense of the expansionism and ethnic aggression of a Serbian regime that unsuccessfully looked for Russian sponsorship.

These successes led in the early 1990s to talk of a 'new world order' and the 'end of history', claims that rested on the belief that the fall of the Soviet Union represented a triumph for American-led democratic capitalism, and that there would be no future clash of ideologies to destabilize the world. In some respects, this optimism represented a resurgence of the high hopes held with the foundation of the United Nations in 1945, and a conviction that global multilateralism could work.

The confidence of the early 1990s was quickly tarnished, in particular by the resurgence of ethnic and religious conflict in the former Yugoslavia, a federal republic that had fallen apart in 1991, rather as the Soviet Union had done. The Serbian resort to violent 'ethnic cleansing' destabilized the situation. Similar conflict was also seen across much of Africa, not least in Sudan, Congo and Angola.

As a result, politics across much of the world were reshaped in the 1990s. American hegemony was not challenged by an imploding Soviet Union – although the Americans were concerned about the growth of Chinese power – and Russian finances collapsed in 1998. However, across much of the world, identity and conflict were shaped and expressed in much more local terms of ethnicity, while the 'internationalism' that had greatest impact was that of religion, particularly Islam. In 2000, ethnicity played a major role in a host of conflicts including those in Congo and Angola, as well as the Sri Lankan war with the separatist Tamil Tigers, while both ethnicity and religion were involved in the bitter resistance in Chechnya in the Caucasus to Russian rule. Islamic assertiveness also played a major role that year in bloody riots in Kaduna in northern Nigeria, while the leader of the Moro Islamic Liberation Front on Mindanao in the Philippines called for a *jihad*.

In many circles, this led to a crisis in confidence at the end of the millennium. The gaining of freedom that had followed the fall of European empires and of communism in Europe had not fulfilled liberal hopes. Instead of the progressive future that had been envisaged had come a menacing situation that, to many, represented a reversion to a dark past. Massacres in both Rwanda and Yugoslavia in the 1990s provided a clear indication of the depths of political depravity, but as serious in the long term was the resort to authoritarian solutions in newly independent countries such as Belarus and Kazakhstan. Furthermore, both within states and at the international level, it was far from clear that politicians and political and economic institutions could confront problems successfully or indeed elicit consent. In addition, within both democracies and authoritarian regimes, there was a widespread failure to reconcile differences between ethnic and other groupings.

At the same time, the economic competition and other worldwide changes summarized by the term 'globalization' threatened (and was seen as a threat to) not only traditional societies, but also more recent notions and practices of social cohesion, both in Western-style democracies and in communitarian regimes, especially communist China. Precisely because of this range, the local impact of the pressures of globalization has to be described carefully. If, in many countries, hostility to globalization meant opposition to modernism and modernization, and thus could draw on powerful interests and deep fears, elsewhere the focus was rather on the alleged global standard bearers of globalization, the USA, multinational companies, trade pacts and foreign borrowing. In some countries, such as China, the political elite was able to advance modernization without too much difficulty, but elsewhere they were made vulnerable by their identification with globalization. International tensions also led to high rates of military expenditure in the developing world: India and Pakistan alone spent $9.9 and $3.3 billion respectively in 1999, and both became nuclear powers. In 2001, the ability of an Islamic terrorist organization to strike with brutal impact at New York and Washington focused and accentuated Western concerns about developments in the Islamic world and their own vulnerability.

CONCLUSIONS

From a Western perspective, it was easy to find many changes in the developing world troubling, not to say unwelcome. This negative response was, in turn, challenged, from a variety of perspectives, by national apologists who argued for cultural and socio-political relativism, and, linked to that, for the value of specific non-Western traditions. This approach was pushed particularly hard by East and South-East Asians arguing in favour of a degree of social discipline and governmental control unacceptable in the West, and also by Islamic thinkers. These approaches not only denied claims that there were inherent human rights by which governments could be judged, but also invite questions for historians. How, for example, should the Iranian revolution of 1979, which replaced the progressive and brutal authoritarianism of the Shah by an Islamic state led by the Ayatollah Khomeini,

FROM A WESTERN PERSPECTIVE, IT WAS EASY TO FIND MANY CHANGES IN THE DEVELOPING WORLD TROUBLING, NOT TO SAY UNWELCOME.

be viewed, both in the short term and in the longer perspective? To Westerners, and many Muslims, the idea of an Islamic state presided over by a learned clergyman, who kept faith and government as one, was wrong and retrograde. It was certainly an intolerant regime; but it is unclear how such developments should be considered.

Thus the century closed with a greater degree of interconnectedness than ever before, and with information, opinion, economic assets and military power movable to an hitherto unprecedented extent, but with the cohesion, co-operation and unity of purpose that had inspired many who had planned at the international level as a goal throughout the century still only a distant hope.

ten

CONCLUSIONS

It will be readily apparent that there is an important discontinuity in this book. The early chapters address important environmental issues, not least the impact of greatly increased human numbers and of their very much greater demands on the available resources. The last chapters deal with beliefs and politics. These bear very little relation to the issues raised earlier. This may appear the sign of a poorly structured book but, in fact, is a product of the 'mismatch' of the two spheres. On the whole, the world of politics has not addressed the problems of the world. Instead, there has been a focus on the pursuit of power and on its use for ends, and in a fashion, that have assumed that environmental considerations are not a problem and, indeed, that the world's resources can be readily commodified and consumed without difficulty. This indeed has been the dominant relationship between the environment and politics during the period.

ON THE WHOLE, THE WORLD OF POLITICS HAS NOT ADDRESSED THE PROBLEMS OF THE WORLD.

These attitudes and politics constituted an important part of the history of the century and, indeed, reflected a powerful continuity with earlier ages. The unintended consequence, however, was that the most important development in the history of the century was that of the impact of human beings on the environment. This was far from new, but the scale was unprecedented. Thus, in China, Mao Zedong rejected the traditional Chinese notion of 'Harmony between the Heavens and Humankind' and, instead, proclaimed 'Man Must Conquer Nature'. In 1958, Mao declared 'Make the high mountain bow its head; make the river yield the way', and soon after, in a critique of an essay by Stalin stating that men could not affect natural processes such as geology, he claimed, 'This argument is incorrect. Man's ability to know and change Nature is unlimited.' Indeed, for Mao, nature, like humankind, was there to be forcibly mobilized in pursuit of the idea, an idea pushed with scant regard for human cost, scientific knowledge, rational analysis or environmental damage. Although not generally so bluntly stated, these ideas were widespread.

Furthermore, across the world, environmental changes, such as the clearance of natural vegetation, increasingly had an impact that extended to the atmosphere and the climate. The result was not only that many became anxious about specific aspects of the world – alienated from noxious seas, poisoned rivers, and dirty air – but also that serious doubt arose about the capacity of human society to tackle problems and secure improvements. The end result of planned and unplanned expansion was seen to be not only particular drawbacks (for example dams lessening the ability of rivers to 'flush out' deltas and estuaries, and also to replenish them with soil), but, more generally, a pernicious assault on an interdependent global environment.

If this led to doubt about technology, science and change, it did not prevent a continued determination to employ all three in order to improve the human condition, although there was greater unwillingness from the late 1970s to pay taxes or sanction government borrowing for major governmental projects to transform the infrastructure of human life. Proposition 13 in a California state referendum of 1978 limited local taxes, setting off a taxpayers' revolt against big government that greatly affected American politics and public culture, and also influenced those in a number of other states. Nevertheless, the last decades of the century saw publicly funded research, particularly in the USA, Japan and Western Europe, into biotechnology, fuel-cell technology, information technology, artificial intelligence and the use of outer space, all designed to increase the capacity of human society to overcome problems.

Indeed, as in the nineteenth century, it became possible to create what had hitherto existed only in the world of fiction. The latter offered important clues not only to anxieties, if not paranoias, but also to the hopes of the age. The idea of creating new and artificial lifeforms became increasingly insistent, although, in addition to the humanoids of films such as *Metropolis* (1926) and *The Terminator* (1984) came troubling super-intelligent computers that seized control from humans, as in *2001: A Space Odyssey* (1968) and *The Forbin Project* (1970). Both categories owed something to the depiction of aliens from other planets that might contest the Earth as well as share space. In fact, the predictive power of the imagination proved very deficient as no aliens were encountered during the century despite the massive increase in the human ability to scrutinize other planets. Not only were no life-forms found, as had been anticipated by many, on the Moon or Mars, but the *Voyager* mission launched in 1977 to visit the outer planets sent back pictures that also recorded no signs of life. This is an important, and not a frivolous, point that is totally neglected by all general accounts of the century. The absence of an encounter with extra-terrestrial life-forms ensured that there was no fundamental questioning of the relative nature of human values.

Politics will not be separable from environmental issues in the future. Disputes over resources will become more acute. Although the most sensible ways to maintain and enhance resources require international co-operation, this has proved difficult, and it is likely that confrontation and conflict will arise from unilateral attempts to control resources, especially oil and water. Greater prosperity, combined with needs driven by population growth, will help increase Chinese and Indian dependence on imports, for example of oil, and thus their sensitivity to the availability and distribution of resources. There is no ideology or governing practice able to prevent such disputes, and prospects are bleak.

A different form of bleakness was offered in *En Attendant Godot* (*Waiting for Godot*, 1952), by the Irish master of the 'Theatre of the Absurd', Samuel Beckett (1906–89). The world he depicted was unknowable and closed to human effort – 'they give birth astride of a grave, the light glimmers an instant, and then it's night once more'. This was a tone very different to the Hollywood films of the period, although the devouring nature of American materialism and values had been captured by Arthur Miller in his bleakly powerful play *Death of a Salesman* (1949), which was set in a consumerist and changing world in which values and beauty could not be retained.

Yet, for many, the situation today is not only very different to that in 1900, but also better. The fall of most empires, the challenging of conservative social practices, particularly insofar as women are concerned, and the advance, in at least some countries, of political and religious freedoms, technology and medicine all offer a more positive view than that of environmental degradation or moral bleakness.

CHRONOLOGY

1900   World population about 1,600 million, 76 million in USA. *The Interpretation of Dreams* by Sigmund Freud.

1901   Okapi 'discovered'. Marconi transmits radio signals across Atlantic. Commonwealth of Australia formed.

1902   Boer War ends.

1903   Manned heavier-than-air flight first officially achieved.

1904   Russo-Japanese War begins.

1905   Confucian educational and examination system abolished in China. Revolution in Russia. Russo-Japanese War ends with Russian defeat. Expressionist movement founded.

1906   Men gain vote in Persia.

1907   New Zealand gains dominion status.

1908   Model T. Ford car in USA.

1909   First flight across English Channel.

1910   Marquis wheat introduced on the Canadian Prairies. Nine million telephones in USA. Civil War begins in Mexico.

1911   Revolution in China. Vitamins discovered by Casimir Funk.

1912   Komodo dragon first sighted by Westerners. Republic in China.

1913   *Rite of Spring*, controversial avant-garde music by Igor Stravinsky.

1914   World War I begins. Panama Canal opened. Stainless steel manufactured in Germany. Conveyor-belt production line developed by Henry Ford. Pasteurization becomes compulsory in Toronto.

1915   British fail at Gallipoli to overthrow Turkish defence.

1916   Einstein publishes general theory of relativity. Battles of Verdun and the Somme.

1917   Revolution in Russia. USA enters World War I. *Parade Amoureuse*, painting by Francis Picabia.

1918   World War I ends. Spanish flu epidemic.

1919   First aeroplane crosses Atlantic non-stop. Walter Gropius establishes Bauhaus school of architecture. Versailles Peace Conference.

1920   USA population 106 million. Women gain vote in USA.

1921   First Indian Parliament meets.

1922   *The Waste Land*, poem by T.S. Eliot. *Ulysses*, novel by James Joyce. Insulin used in treatment of diabetes. Fascist government under Benito Mussolini founded in Italy.

1923   *Rhapsody in Blue*, symphonic jazz work by George Gershwin. Discovery of galaxies other than Milky Way. Turkish republic established.

1924   US Immigration Act. Turkish men gain vote and religious schools put under secular authority.

1925   Conviction in Tennessee for teaching evolution. Japanese men gain vote. *Battleship Potemkin*, film by Sergei Eisenstein.

1926   Opening of Gezira irrigation scheme in Sudan. Heart pacemakers invented. *Metropolis*, film by Fritz Lang.

1927   World's population about 2,000 million. Canberra becomes seat of Australian government. *To the Lighthouse*, novel by Virginia Woolf.

1928   Alexander Fleming discovers penicillin. Mickey Mouse devised by Walt Disney. Latin alphabet introduced. *Opus Dei* launched.

1929   Wall Street Crash. Discovery that universe expanding.

1930   Hawley Smoot Act in USA raises tariffs and hits trade.

1931   Nylon invented. Japanese invade Manchuria.

1932   *Brave New World*, futuristic novel by Aldous Huxley. Thailand becomes constitutional monarchy.

1933   Adolf Hitler comes to power in Germany. Franklin D. Roosevelt begins New Deal in USA. Film *King Kong*.

1934   Turkish women gain vote. 'Dust Bowl' in US Midwest.

1935   Fluorescent lighting introduced. Italy invades Ethiopia.

1936   *General Theory of Employment, Interest and Money* by Keynes. Germany introduces Four-Year Plan and occupies Rhineland. Berlin Olympics.

1937   Japanese attack China, capturing Beijing and Nanjing.

1938   Discovery of 'fossil fish'. Germans seize Austria. Munich crisis.

1939   World War II begins when Germany attacks Poland.

1940   US population 132 million. Germany conquers France. Plutonium discovered.

1941   Japanese attack Pearl Harbor. USA enters war. *Citizen Kane*, film by Orson Welles.

1942 German and Japanese advances stopped with defeats at Stalingrad, El Alamein and Midway.

1943 Major Allied gains at expense of Germany and Japan.

1944 Bretton Woods Agreement. Germans driven from France. Americans make major gains from Japanese in Pacific.

1945 Use of atom bombs ends war in Pacific; Germany already defeated. United Nations launched.

1946 *The Common Sense Book of Baby and Child Care* by Benjamin Spock. Japanese women gain vote.

1947 India's population about 300 million. General Agreement on Tariffs and Trade signed. Independence of India and Pakistan.

1948 World Health Organization established. First all-electronic computer to function goes into action. United Nations' Universal Declaration of Human Rights. Declaration of state of Israel.

1949 Maiden flight of the first jet-propelled airliner. *Death of a Salesman*, play by Arthur Miller. Soviet Union explodes atom bomb. NATO established. Communists take control of China. *Nineteen Eighty-Four*, novel by George Orwell.

1950 First kidney transplant. Agrarian Reform Law in China. Chinese conquest of Tibet. Korean War begins.

1951 First commercial computer built.

1952 *Waiting for Godot*, play by Samuel Beckett. USA explodes hydrogen bomb. Republican coup in Egypt.

1953 China's population 582 million. Discovery of correct atomic structure of DNA. Korean War ends.

1954 *Lord of the Flies*, novel by William Golding.

1955   Disney theme park opens in California. Racial segregation in public schools banned in USA. *Rebel Without a Cause*, film starring James Dean.

1956   Sudan becomes independent. Polio vaccine administered (developed by Jonas Salk). Europe linked to USA by underwater telephone cable. FORTRAN computer programming language. First trial of contraceptive pill. Suez crisis.

1957   *West Side Story*, musical by Bernstein. First space sputnik, Sputnik I, launched. Treaty of Rome establishing the EEC.

1958   USS *Nautilus* travels under North Pole.

1959   Great Leap Forward Policy begins in China. Singapore becomes independent.

1960   World's population 3,000 million, 179 million in USA. Methicillin, the first semi-synthetic penicillin. Laser invented. Belgian Congo becomes independent.

1961   Egypt nationalizes private industries. Soviet astronaut Yuri Gagarin becomes first man to orbit Earth.

1962   *Capitalism and Freedom* by economist Milton Friedman. Rachel Carson's *Silent Spring* warns about environmental damage. Trans-Canada Highway opened. Cuban missile crisis.

1963   Quasars discovered by American astronomer Haarten Schmidt. Organization of African Unity founded.

1964   High-speed 'bullet' trains in Japan. China explodes nuclear bomb.

1965   Unmanned probe reaches Venus.

1966   Cultural Revolution launched in China.

1967   First human heart transplant. Arusha Declaration by Julius Nyerere: socialist theory of development for Africa. *One Hundred Years of Solitude*, novel by Gabriel García Márquez. The Beatles' *Sgt Pepper's Lonely Hearts Club Band* released.

1968   *The First Circle*, novel by Alexander Solzhenitsyn depicting the Soviet police state. *2001: A Space Odyssey*, film. Tet offensive in South Vietnam. Richard Nixon wins presidential election in USA.

1969   Moon landing. Computer 'mouse' invented.

1970   *Sexual Politics* by Kate Millett.

1971   First heart–lung transplant. Convertibility of dollar into gold suspended. First microprocessor chip created. Pocket calculator invented.

1972   Idi Amin expels Asians from Uganda.

1973   American Supreme Court asserts right to abortion. Oil price hike after Yom Kippur war in Middle East. Coup ends monarchy in Afghanistan. US withdrawal from Vietnam.

1974   *Yuyo Maru No. 10* oil tanker sinks off Japan. Haile Selassie, Emperor of Ethiopia, falls, as does Richard Nixon.

1975   *Viking* probes launched to land instruments on Mars. Vietnam War ends. Francesco Franco, dictator of Spain, dies.

1976   Mao Zedong dies.

1977   Coup in Pakistan.

1978   Announcement by World Health Organization that smallpox eradicated.

1979   'One-child family' policy introduced in China. Islamic revolution in Iran.

1980   End of white minority regime in Rhodesia. Ronald Reagan wins American presidential election.

1981   AIDS first recognized as an infection. First orbital flight by American space shuttle. Microsoft MS-DOS operating system launched.

1982   Mexico defaults on its international debt. Falklands War. Israel invades Lebanon.

1983   'Star Wars' defence system begun in USA. Disney theme park opens in Tokyo.

1984   China creates Special Economic Zones. Indian army forcibly reimposes control over Golden Temple in Amritsar against opposition by Sikh terrorists. *The Terminator*, film depicts threatening cyborg (part-human, part-machine).

1985   Mexico City hit by severe earthquakes.

1986   Moratorium on commercial whaling. 195 million televisions in USA; 10.5 million in India. Accident at Chernobyl nuclear reactor in Ukraine.

1987   *Glasnost* and *Perestroika* launched by Soviet leader Mikhail Gorbachev.

1988   Intermediate-range Nuclear Forces treaty signed by USA and Soviet Union.

1989   *Exxon Valdez* oil tanker sinks off Alaska. Communist governments collapse in Eastern Europe. Chinese suppress pro-democracy demonstration in Beijing.

1990   Iraq invades Kuwait. West and East Germany reunited. Nelson Mandela released from prison.

1991   American-led coalition drives Iraqis from Kuwait. Warsaw Pact dissolved. Soviet Union ceases to exist.

1992   Earth summit at Rio de Janeiro agrees the Framework Convention on Climate Change. Disney theme park opens in Paris. Communist government in Afghanistan overthrown.

1993   *A Suitable Boy*, novel by Vikram Seth, indicates success of cultural hybridization, as had *Satanic Verses* (1988), novel by Salman Rushdie. Single market established by European Community.

1994   Worldwide Web created. Channel Tunnel opened. North American Free Trade Agreement came into effect.

1995   Aum doomsday cult attacks Tokyo metro. Conflict in Bosnia ends with American air attacks on Serbs. World Trade Organization formed (replacing GATT).

1996   Fundamentalist Taleban capture much of Afghanistan.

1997   Vast forest fires in Indonesia hit air quality. Kyoto Protocol on greenhouse gases. Hong Kong reunited with China. Serious banking crisis in Japan. First cloned animal. Deep Blue computer defeats Garry Kasparov, world chess champion.

1998   About 130 million people in world with Internet access. Civil war begins in Sierra Leone.

1999   World population 6,000 million. Life expectancy rises to 70 in China. Railway reaches Kashgar. Kosovo conflict.

2000   USA population 274 million. Attempt to dollarize Ecuador's currency. Zambia denationalizes industry.

2001   China's population 1.26 billion, India's 1.03 billion. Euro launched as currency throughout most of European Union. Suicide attacks in New York and Washington precipitate widespread economic and political crisis.

FURTHER READING

American Association for the Advancement of Science, *Atlas and Population and Environment* (Berkeley, 2000).

Anthony Badger, *The New Deal* (London 1989).

S.J. Ball, *The Cold War. An International History* (London, 1998).

Judith Banister, *China's Changing Population* (Stanford, 1989).

J.F.W. Beckett, *Modern Insurgencies and Counter-Insurgencies* (London, 2000).

Jeremy Black, *Warfare in the Western World 1882–1975* (London, 2000).

Brian W. Blouet, *Geopolitics and Globalization in the Twentieth Century* (London, 2000).

Ahron Breyman, *Israel's Wars, 1947–93* (London, 2000).

Alden Brinkley, *Voices of Protest: Huey Long, Father Coghlin and the Great Depression* (New York, 1982).

Cambridge University Press, *New Cambridge Modern History Atlas* (Cambridge, 2000).

Patricia Clavin, *The Great Depression in Europe, 1909-1939* (London, 2000).

Wanda Corn, *The Great American Thing. Modern Art and National Identity, 1915–1935* (Berkely, 1999).

T.R.H. Davenport and C. Saunders, *South Africa. A Modern History* (5th Edition, London, 2000).

Lowell Dittmer, *China's Continuous Revolution: The Post-liberation Epoch, 1949–1981* (Berkley, 1987).

Paul Dresch, *A History of Modern Yemen* (Cambridge, 2000).

Bill Freund, *The Making of Contemporary Africa* (2nd Edition, 1998).

David Garrow, *We Shall Overcome: the Civil Rights Movement in the United States in the 1950s and 1960s* (Brooklyn, 1989).

Todd Gitlin, *The Sixties: Years of Hope, Days of Rage* (New York, 1987).

Neil Gregor (ed.), *Nazism* (Oxford, 2000).

Donald Kerr (ed.), *Historical Atlas of Canada III. Addressing the Twentieth Century* (Toronto, 1990).

Patrick McCarthy (ed.). *Italy since 1945* (Oxford, 2000).

B.D. and T.R. Metcalf. *A Concise History of India* (Cambridge, 2001).

Barry Naughton, *Growing out of the Plan: Chinese Economic Reform, 1978-1993* (Cambridge, 1995).

Suzanne Pepper, *Radicalism and Education Reform in 20th-Century China: The Search for an Ideal Development Model* (Cambridge, 1996).

Chris Read, *The Making and Breaking of the Soviet System* (London, 2001).

Joseph Schwartzberg, *Historical Atlas of South Asia* (2nd Edition, Oxford, 1992).

Charles Tripp, *A History of Iraq* (Cambridge, 2000).

James White, *Lenin* (London, 2001).

Garry Wills, *Reagan's America: Innocents at Home* (Garden City and New York, 1987).

Margery Wolf, *Revolution Postponed: Women in Contemporary China* (Stanford, 1985)

Juaqi Yan and Gia Gao, *Turbulent Decade: A History of the Cultural Revolution* (Hornblack, 1996).

Benjamin Yang, *Deng: A Political Biography* (New York, 1998).

INDEX